From City Space to Cyberspace

Cities and Cultures

Cities and Cultures is an interdisciplinary book series addressing the inter-relations between cities and the cultures they produce. The series takes a special interest in the impact of globalization on urban space and cultural production, but remains concerned with all forms of cultural expression and transformation associated with modern and contemporary cities.

Series Editor:
Christoph Lindner, University College London

Advisory Board:
Ackbar Abbas, University of California, Irvine
Myria Georgiou, London School of Economics and Political Science
Derek Gregory, University of British Columbia
Mona Harb, American University of Beirut
Stephanie Hemelryk Donald, University of Lincoln
Shirley Jordan, Newcastle University
Nicole Kalms, Monash University
Geoffrey Kantaris, University of Cambridge
Brandi Thompson Summers, University of California, Berkeley
Ginette Verstraete, VU University Amsterdam
Richard J. Williams, University of Edinburgh

From City Space to Cyberspace

Art, Squatting, and Internet Culture
in the Netherlands

Amanda Wasielewski

Amsterdam University Press

The publication of this book was made possible by the Social Science Research Council's International Dissertation Research Fellowship, with funds provided by the Andrew W. Mellon Foundation.

Cover illustration: Caption/credit: Jan Marinus Verburg, poster for *Beeldstroom* exhibition at Aorta, July-August 1982, 62 × 44.5 cm. Internationaal Instituut voor Sociale Geschiedenis (IISG)/Staatsarchief, Amsterdam.

Cover design: Coördesign, Leiden
Lay-out: Crius Group, Hulshout

ISBN	978 94 6372 545 3
e-ISBN	978 90 4855 372 3
DOI	10.5117/9789463725453
NUR	670

Printed and bound by CPI Group (UK) Ltd, Croydon, CR0 4YY

Table of Contents

List of Illustrations

Acknowledgements

The completion of this research was facilitated by the Social Sciences Research Council, IDRF. During the duration of my funding I was based at University of Amsterdam/ASCA, to which I owe my thanks for a fruitful affiliation.

Many people have helped me improve and enrich the contents of this book. I am first and foremost grateful to my doctoral advisor, David Joselit, for his insightful and highly constructive feedback. David's support was a grounding force throughout the writing of this book. Many thanks as well to two other key readers of the text, Marta Gutman and Marga van Mechelen. In particular, Marga's guidance and support was invaluable in navigating the field of media art in the Netherlands. I am ever so grateful for her generosity and warmth. Thanks as well to peer reviewers, Michael Goddard and Sven Lütticken.

Additionally, some of the people whose work is profiled in this book were kind enough to allow me to interview them. Thank you to Michiel van den Bergh, Maja van den Broecke, David Garcia, Menno Grootveld, Geert Lovink, Raúl Marroquin, and Willem Velthoven. Special thanks to Rogier van der Ploeg who not only gave me access to episodes of PKP-TV during the course of our interview but also went out of his way to help me track down many of the details I was looking for surrounding PKP's broadcasts. I would also like to thank Arie Altena for helping me access and navigate the V2_ archive in Rotterdam and to Sanneke Huisman for providing me with access to the LIMA video archive as well as the research that had been conducted around Talking Back to the Media.

There are also several colleagues, friends, and family members that I would like to acknowledge. My deepest thanks to Agri Ismail for his unwavering belief in me. Thank you to Jasmijn Visser for insightful conversations and proofing my translations. Thank you to Janna Schoenberger for your guidance. And finally thank you to Katie Sullivan and Michael, Nancy, Mike, and Melissa Wasielewski for your support.

Introduction

The narrative of the birth of internet culture often focuses on the achievements of American entrepreneurs in Silicon Valley, but there is an alternative history of European internet pioneers who developed their own model of network culture in the early 1990s. Drawing from their experiences in the leftist and anarchist movements of the '80s, they built do-it-yourself (DIY) networks that give us a glimpse into what network culture could have been if it were in the hands of squatters, hackers, punks, artists, and activists. In the Dutch scene the early internet was intimately tied to the aesthetics and politics of squatting. Untethered from profit motives, these artists and activists aimed to create a decentralized tool that would democratize culture and promote open and free exchange of information.

The first publicly accessible Dutch internet service providers—XS4ALL and De Digitale Stad (The Digital City)—were developed in 1993. Hack-tic, the group of anarchist hackers who facilitated the projects, expressed their idealism by naming their service XS4ALL ("access for all"), and, working together with artists and cultural producers, they created the groundbreaking public internet portal De Digitale Stad (launched January 1994). The aim of this book is to construct a pre-history of internet art and theory in the Netherlands leading up until this groundbreaking moment. It explores what happened in the 1980s that allowed an alternative model of the internet to develop, looking at both traditionally-defined artistic practices and political/spatial practices over the course of the decade.

There is an artistic strategy—or de Certeauian "tactic"—that unites practices as disparate as urban squatting, painting, television, and exhibition/event curation. Rather than a medium born when the first web browsers were developed in the early '90s, this book argues that the practices which have subsequently been labelled "internet art",[1] particularly European browser-based work, were part of a longer aesthetic development that began

All translations are my own unless otherwise stated.

1   See Tilman Baumgärtel, *Net.art: Materialien zur Netzkunst* (Nürnberg: Verlag für Moderne Kunst, 1999); Tilman Baumgärtel, *Net.art 2.0: New Materials Towards Net Art* (Nürnberg: Verlag für Moderne Kunst, 2001); Rachel Greene, *Internet Art* (New York: Thames & Hudson, 2004); Josephine Bosma, *Nettitudes: Let's Talk Net Art* (Amsterdam: Institute of Network Cultures, 2011).

Wasielewski, A., *From City Space to Cyberspace: Art, Squatting, and Internet Culture in the Netherlands*. Amsterdam: Amsterdam University Press, 2021
DOI 10.5117/9789463725453_INTRO

before the World Wide Web was invented. The constellation of practices profiled in the following pages are anchored theoretically to the concept of *kraken* ("squatting" in Dutch), which has the same roots as the English verb "to crack" and is literally translated as "to crack open."[2]

Linguistically speaking, squatting is a more active gesture in Dutch: the act of breaking open as well as occupying. The idea is that the tactic of "cracking open," developed successfully in urban space, could also be used as a technique in media and art to crack open a new space within the established order and create what Hakim Bey has termed "temporary autonomous zones."[3] The fact that the word *kraken* is also deployed in the context of computer hacking, like the English words crack and hack, speaks to the elasticity of *kraken* as a practice. The DIY forms that are created through the use of this tactic are temporary platforms, spaces of autonomy wedged within the cracks of existing infrastructures rather than outside of them. The internet platforms that were created in the early '90s in the Netherlands were therefore the manifestation of a constellation of practices that arose before the internet was invented.

2   Eric Duivenvoorden, *Een voet tussen de deur: geschiedenis van de kraakbeweging (1964-1999)* (Amsterdam: De Arbeiderspers, 2000), pp. 24, 28. The earlier Dutch term for squatting was *clandestien bezetten* (clandestine occupation). The verb *kraken* is borrowed from the coded slang of traveling people and thieves, which is called *Bargoens* or *dieventaal*. The term *kraker* (squatter) came into use in 1969 in conjunction with the emerging activism around squatting. The term *huispiraat* (house pirate) was also proposed but not taken up.

3   Hakim Bey, *TAZ.: The Temporary Autonomous Zone, Ontological Anarchy, Poetic Terrorism* (Brooklyn: Autonomedia, 2003). Hakim Bey is a controversial figure in leftwing anarchism whose thinking evolved from LSD and occult-fueled countercultural spheres in the late 1960s to hardline anarchism in the 1980s. Much of his writing has a poetic, speculative and eclectic tone and, so, is neither empirically nor argumentatively constructed and should not be treated as standard academic theory or philosophy. He borrows liberally (and fetishistically) from a variety of non-western cultures and traditions. His most controversial writings contain arguments for pedophilia via anarchist thought. As Bey's concepts frame a significant portion of this book, primarily the "temporary autonomous zone," I would like to clarify the reasons for my use of his writing in this context. My reasons are twofold: firstly, that it is an expression of '80s anarchist thought *from the time period* under discussion and thus encapsulates many of the concerns that fringe leftwing/anarchist thinkers had at the time, and, secondly, that, although it has its faults and inconsistencies, it is nevertheless a useful starting point and apt theoretical model for thinking about radical urban spatial practice and art in Amsterdam during the '80s. The idea of the temporary autonomous zone represents an alternative method of resistance and a counterpoint to the (futile, as Bey says) leftwing revolutionary goals for permanent change or totalizing political reversal. It allows for micro-revolts *within* the fabric of the hegemonic order rather than from an untenable *outside*. Even so, I would like to clearly state, as the extensive use of this material might be misconstrued as a form of endorsement, that citing Bey's or any other theorists' work does not constitute personal support for any of their views.

The choice to focus on the Netherlands, rather than the histories of squatting and media art in other European countries, grew out of the observation that there is a special confluence between urban spatial practie and media practice there, which was supported by the legal and social structures in place in the country. Indeed, the Dutch landscape has been molded by human intervention for centuries. Life in the swampy lowlands has long been a do-it-yourself endeavor. As Hub Zwart writes:

> The reclamation, by means of dikes and ditches, of formerly remote, impassable, soggy and swampy areas, where the imprint of human presence had been absent or slight, irrevocably altered the physical appearance of the Netherlands. The landscape was thoroughly humanised. [...] a geometrisation of the landscape took place at an increasing pace and the natural matrix was increasingly fragmented until only a few marginal leftovers remained. Gradually, through diligent manual labour by generations of anonymous farmers, a diffuse, ambiguous, soggy and brackish landscape, in which clear boundaries between land and water (as well as between fresh and saline water) were absent, was replaced by a discrete, highly compartmentalised landscape. For indeed, whereas vague and gradual transitions are characteristic of natural landscapes, human influences tend to produce abrupt boundaries.[4]

These abrupt boundaries are a distinguishing feature of the modern built environment from the nation-state down to the city itself.

In *The Production of Space*, Henri Lefebvre describes this phenomenon using different terms. He designates this as a transition from "absolute space" to "abstract space" and explicitly ties absolute space to nature. In his conception, the dissolution of absolute space as well as the "cryptic" space of the medieval period begins in the sixteenth century when the "town overtook the country."[5] Despite the suspect periodization and primitivist perspective found in Lefevbre's text, the changes in how boundaries have been defined historically supports his argument. Describing abstract space, Lefebvre writes:

> Internal and invisible boundaries began to divide a space that nevertheless remained in thrall to a global strategy and a single power. These

---

4   Hub Zwart, "Aquaphobia, Tulipmania, Biophilia: A Moral Geography of the Dutch Landscape," *Environmental Values* 12, no. 1 (2003): p. 110.
5   Henri Lefebvre, *The Production of Space*, trans. Donald Nicholson-Smith (Malden, MA: Blackwell, 1991), pp. 267–9.

boundaries did not merely separate levels—local, regional, national and worldwide. They also separated zones where people were supposed to reduce to their "simplest expression," to their "lowest common denominator" [...] As a matter of fact "boundaries" is too weak a word here, and it obscures the essential point; it would be more accurate to speak of fracture lines.[6]

The abstract nature of these boundaries, paradoxically, creates a rigidness in the landscape of human geography. This rigidness— as much as it might be virtual or invisible—means that gray zones are increasingly hard to find. In order to subvert established boundaries, activists in the Netherlands needed to create their own "fracture lines" or cracks in the fabric of abstract space.

Addressing this quandary, Hakim Bey (né Peter Lamborn Wilson) theorized the temporary autonomous zone (TAZ) as a means by which radical anarchists might circumvent the rigidness of contemporary political structures. He defines the TAZ as a temporary free anarchist enclave within the totalizing matrix of the built environment. Bey despairs at the Left's continued struggle for revolution, which he defines as permanent change (or, in his words, change that has "duration"). He writes, "What of the anarchist dream, the Stateless state, the Commune, the autonomous zone with duration, a free society, a free culture? [...] I have not given up hope or even expectation of change—but I distrust the word *Revolution*."[7] The TAZ, then, fills this void left by a seemingly unachievable permanent revolution in that it allows for change from within via acute actions and temporary sites of difference and freedom.

Referencing Jean Baudrillard's theory of "simulation," in which Baudrillard proposes that late capitalism is characterized by the irrelevance of originality as the "simulacrum," or copy, precedes the absent original, Bey writes:

> Because the State is concerned primarily with Simulation rather than substance, the TAZ can "occupy" these areas clandestinely and carry on its festal purposes for quite a while in relative peace. [...] In sum, realism demands not only that we give up *waiting* for "the Revolution" but also that we give up *wanting* it.[8]

6   Ibid., pp. 316–7.
7   Bey, *TAZ*, p. 98.
8   Bey, *TAZ*, p. 99; Jean Baudrillard, *Simulacra and Simulation*, trans. Sheila Faria Glaser (Ann Arbor: University of Michigan Press, 2014).

This release from dreaming of or desiring permanent revolution has a corollary in the punk movement's slogan "no future," which expresses not only the pessimism of the era or a lack of political idealism but also a feeling of liberation from the constant, futile struggle of revolution. "No future" resonates with the postmodern moment, signaling not an end but an endless present. Revolution demands a vision of the future and, in the late '70s and '80s in Europe, youth movements increasingly focused on in-the-moment rebellion and deviance rather than forward-looking idealism.

In a revolution-free, endless present, there is no "outside" that will replace society. Instead, there are only ruptures, fissures, and cracks that disrupt its stability. What Bey is describing, then, in his conception of the TAZ are "cracks" formed within the established order or dominant systems of control. A crack cannot exist apart from the substance it cracks into and is thus a negative space, carving out its form and creating a void. At the same time, however, it is a space of creation; it creates something new on the surface and also opens up space within a smooth and continuous field.

Looking at squatting in Amsterdam with this model in mind, it is evident that squatters in the late '70s and '80s effectively established TAZs—or cracks—in the city structure that pushed for radical change from within. These fissures in the fabric of the city space open up new boundaries *within* the city rather than apart from it, which were porous and destabilizing to the system as a whole in part due to their internally autonomous manifestation. In light of the instability they cause, they had to either be temporary—as one is closed, another might spring open somewhere else—or, in the most extreme cases, precipitate total destruction. Cracks are agents of chaos, on one hand, but also catalysts for reparation, regeneration, renewal, change, or reconstruction.

Art historian Hal Foster, who helped define postmodernism in contemporary art in the early '80s, often returns to the concept of "fissures" as spaces of potential for a re-defined *avant-garde*. His writing on the subject resonates with the definition of "cracks" outlined above. According to Foster:

> ...the avant-garde that interests me here is neither *avant* nor rear [...] it is immanent in a caustic way. Far from heroic, it does not pretend that it can break absolutely with the old order or found a new one; instead it seeks to trace fractures that already exist within the given order, to pressure them further, even to activate them somehow.[9]

9   Hal Foster, *Bad New Days: Art, Criticism, Emergency* (London: Verso, 2015), p. 4.

For the "no future" generation, the space for something new was not in a utopian future or a romantic vision of revolution but, instead, in the cracks or the margins. As the former-squatter/critical theory collective BILWET writes, "We always said, in the '60s and '70s people thought revolution was possible, that society could be fundamentally reformed. That's bullshit. All you can do is what you do yourself, with each other."[10] Quoting Eric Santner, Foster writes that "fissures or caesuras in the space of meaning" become places where "power can be resisted or at least withstood and perhaps reimagined."[11] Whereas Foster discusses fissures and cracks in a theoretical sense, squatting takes the construct into a more concrete, pragmatic space. In other words, for squatters, the use of cracks as sites of resistance is realized in a very literal, very intimate way.

A TAZ or a crack is constituted by exploding the givenness of the existing frame of the city and cracking into it from within its boundaries. In the modern era, cracking/*kraken* can be seen not only as a Lefebvrian urban "spatial practice" but also as a far more broadly applicable de Certeauian "tactic."[12] Within the field of modern artistic practice, avant-garde artists have largely concerned themselves with investigating the boundaries of art. As artists became ever more focused on investigating what *framed* art—what institutions, what rules, what qualities, what materials, what space, etc.—they were essentially working on deconstructing its borders from within. Over and over again, modern artistic movements have investigated the role of art in society and whether any new definition of art was sustainable or merely temporary. Attendant to this inquiry, modern artists concerned themselves with the question of art's autonomy to mass media, popular culture, and everyday life. The great project of modern art has been in exploring these boundaries, which, in turn, has led to works which open up, destabilize, or redefine the limits of art practice.

In art, cracks often find expression and form through play or playfulness. One of the ways that we make sense of our surroundings is through play: the ability to rehearse or perform various aspects of human life within a microcosm of the surrounding environment. The most rigidly defined of these microcosms of play are called games. Both the game and the frame are bounded systems that are not apart from the whole but rather inside it, representing it, performing variations on it.

10   ADILKNO, *Cracking the Movement: Squatting Beyond the Media* (Brooklyn: Autonomedia, 1994), p. 101.
11   Foster, *Bad New Days*, pp. 106–7.
12   Lefebvre, *The Production of Space*, p. 38.

The activities of the squatters' movement in Amsterdam between 1979 and 1983 had, simultaneously, the qualities and ambitions of a game and that of a work of art. Under both interrelated models, the formation of TAZs or cracks allows new boundaries to be constructed, as long as their temporary nature is embraced. Within the squatter network and the acts of protest that were staged during these years, the practice of squatting coalesced into a brief political movement and then dissipated quickly into factionalism. The key quality of this era of squatting was its *temporary* nature and the use of media as a tool to bind resistance efforts. Although squatting continued in Amsterdam for many years afterward, this temporary autonomous zone in the cracks of the city spurred the government to respond positively to the demands of the squatters and also execute protective actions, policing its existing boundaries and re-establishing a sense of 'order'. Despite its brief appearance, the squatters' movement in Amsterdam altered the shape of the city long after its demise and inspired radical media and networking experiments in the years to come.

The four chapters of this book are arranged thematically and follow an overlapping chronological trajectory. In the first chapter, "Cracking the City," the practice of squatting in urban space serves as a metaphor and framing device for the artistic and aesthetic practices explored subsequently. The argument is that an attitude rather than a political position developed within the practice of squatting that spreads to artistic practices and, ultimately, the use of emerging network technology. The first section of the chapter looks at how the Dutch countercultural movement Provo put urban activism and art on the map in the Netherlands. The next two sections concern the dialectical relationship between Dutch artist/ utopian architect/member of the Situationist International (SI) Constant Nieuwenhuys ('Constant') and SI founder Guy Debord. They outline how the squatters' movement was both an expression of Constant's *New Babylon* and a Debordian game of war, and detail how the practice of squatting in the late '70s and early '80s foregrounded emerging media and performance art in urban space.

Chapter 2, "Cracking Painting," looks more closely at artist-squatters, particularly the group of neo-expressionist painters known as De Nieuwe Wilden (The New Wild Ones). Although art schools around the country became important meeting places for artists during the late '70s and early '80s, rebellious young artists often dropped out or broke off from the more traditional curricula offered at these institutions in favor of pursuing collective DIY projects, such as starting their own bands and developing their own music/art venues in squatted spaces. Media and squatter venues like

Mazzo, W139, Aorta, and V2_ focused on media art, performances, and anarchic exhibitions. Reacting against 1970s conceptual and minimalist art, the Nieuwe Wilden painters were interested in creating an "image flow"—cracking into and occupying the "dead" field of painting. These artists used painting as a platform for a frantic outpouring of imagery, where they processed pop culture and television through a filter of raw, unpolished materials.

During this time, artists in the Netherlands benefited from generous state subsidies and social benefits as well "free" housing via the widespread practice of squatting, which gave them the time and financial resources to develop DIY art spaces and new media experiments outside of traditional art institutions. Many also benefited from the BKR (Beeldende Kunstenaars Regeling, Fine Artists Regulation), a government program established after World War II that gave artists welfare payments in exchange for artwork. This program was in crisis in the early '80s, denounced for its uncritical accumulation of "bad art." The excess/over-production of imagery created by the Nieuwe Wilden painters is therefore mirrored in the government's accumulation of a literal mountain of artworks that was relegated to vast warehouses and eventually given away or disposed of in the '90s.

In addition to painting and making music, some of the Nieuwe Wilden painters discussed in chapter 2 were also pioneers of pirate television in Amsterdam. Chapter 3, "Cracking the Ether," analyzes the earliest artist-led pirate TV project, PKP-TV, as an example of how squatter tactics were applied to the media. This illegal channel, which was created by the artists Maarten Ploeg (né van der Ploeg), Peter Klashorst, and Rogier van der Ploeg, made it its mission to crack open the closed medium of television. PKP and pirate cable TV in the Netherlands are situated within a longer history of both alternative TV projects internationally—such as the Videofreex and TVTV—as well as video and film-based artworks shown on television both in the Netherlands and abroad. The argument is that artist-led pirate television in the Netherlands, like squatters in urban space, cracked open the media space of television and created temporary autonomous platforms.

Attendant to this, chapter 3 looks at how pirate TV had an impact beyond television: its destabilizing influence gave voice to a short-lived political movement, De Reagering. Led by Mike von Bibikov, this absurdist performance distilled the ennui of the "no future" generation and operated under the slogan, "We have agreed that we do not agree, and we have decided not to decide." Rabotnik TV, the successor of PKP, played a central role in De Reagering, as it provided the platform on which this type of work could stage greater societal disruptions. The belief that pirate TV, particularly Rabotnik, was inciting squatter riots led to the government of Amsterdam shutting down all pirate broadcasters in the city in 1982.[13]

The final chapter of the book, "Passageways," investigates the transitional period during which these early '80s practices fed into the emerging field of new media art in the Netherlands, led by artists like David Garcia and organizations like V2_ and Mediamatic. Urban space served as a bridge and a metaphor to understanding how the practices of "cracking open" existing structures and creating platforms within them could be continued through the use of new media and new technological tools, primarily computer networks. The rhetoric of interactivity was initially developed around television rather than computing, starting with the 1985 media art festival Talking Back to the Media. This festival used the city of Amsterdam as a platform to "talk back" to mainstream popular culture and media, showing artworks in alternative gallery spaces and squats as well as on television and radio. Former squatter venue V2_ also transitioned during this time into an institute for "unstable media," within which the potential for freedom and autonomy in media space was explored. Additionally, Mediamatic, which was started by a group of artists organizing video art screenings in squatted spaces in the early 1980s, transitioned into a media art magazine and a platform for new media theory during this time. By the end of the decade and in the first few years of the '90s, a series of "networked events"— events that utilized nascent internet technology—were staged, establishing a link between former squatters (and their tactics) and the radical leftwing media art platforms, practices, and theory of the '90s.

On one side of the passageway described in chapter 4 is the city and, on the other, is the digital city. The conclusion of this book addresses the creation of the internet portal De Digitale Stad in early 1994, arguing that it is the culmination of the tactical media practices and platform-building outlined in the previous chapters. From the city to the *digital* city, the period covered in this book bridges the fuzzy divide between old and new media. More pressingly, however, this book aims to investigate the specific origins of new media art, how it has been defined and developed, and what histories influence not only the works themselves but the discourse

13   Grootveld, interview by author; "Kabelnet in Amsterdam afgesloten voor piraten," *NRC Handelsblad*, October 23, 1982; "Elektronisch systeem weert signaal van radio-piraat op kabel," *De Volkskrant*, October 16, 1982; "Burgemeester Polak Weert Televiziezender Kraak Beweging A'dam," *Nederlands Dagblad*, October 20, 1982.

they participate in. Paradoxically, what we call internet art was not born purely as a product of computer networking but rather as part of a longer history of media tactics that began with squatters and the ideal of urban automony.

1.   Cracking the City

Abstract

This chapter investigates the history of squatting in the Netherlands in order to understand how it evolved from a pragmatic solution for a shortage of housing to an organized social movement. It begins with a discussion of how the counterculture movement in the Netherlands—Provo—established a tradition of activism and ludic protest that promoted social liberalism, anarchy, progressive welfare programs, and public housing. These values were inherited by the next generation of activists in the squatters' movement of the late '70s and '80s, who developed and molded them to conform to the less optimistic atmosphere and circumstances of their time.

Keywords: squatting, Provo, public housing, Netherlands, Stads Kunst Guerrilla, Constant Nieuwenhuys

The last bit of Earth unclaimed by any nation-state was eaten up in 1899. Ours is the first century without terra incognita, *without a frontier. [...] And—the map is closed, but the autonomous zone is open.*[1]
                                                                                    – Hakim Bey

The Dutch consider themselves a pragmatic people, a mindset that has often led to radical or unorthodox solutions to social and political problems. Squatting in the Netherlands, which was legal between 1914 and 2010, was one such unorthodox solution. In 1914 the Dutch High Court ruled that citizens had the right to squat vacant or abandoned properties as long as certain conditions were met. Even as the sociopolitical circumstances around squatting changed dramatically over the course of the century, legal

1   Hakim Bey, *T.A.Z.: The Temporary Autonomous Zone, Ontological Anarchy, Poetic Terrorism* (Brooklyn: Autonomedia, 2003), p. 100.

Wasielewski, A., *From City Space to Cyberspace: Art, Squatting, and Internet Culture in the Netherlands*. Amsterdam: Amsterdam University Press, 2021
DOI 10.5117/9789463725453_CH01

rights remained in place.[2] It was, for the most part, seen as a practical solution to a quotidian problem: the shortage of access to affordable, adequate housing.[3] While squatting in other parts of Europe coalesced alongside radical political theory and rhetoric, the Dutch—at first—approached the idea of squatting not so much as a deviant act but as a simple equation: if there was a surplus of empty properties and a surplus of people in need of housing, it was only logical that those in need of housing would take over the empty properties. By the time a more militant political movement began to form around squatting in the mid-1970s, the practice was already well established.[4]

The chaos created by the German occupation during the Second World War solidified the legitimacy of squatting in Amsterdam. Over 100,000 Dutch Jewish citizens never returned to the city, which left many of the houses in the formerly thriving Jewish quarter of Amsterdam— particularly the areas from Nieuwmarkt in the center to Waterlooplein, the Plantagebuurt, and Weesperplein to the south and east—empty. During the famine and shortages of the freezing cold Hunger Winter of 1944 and 1945, supply lines to the country were curtailed as the citizens waited for liberation by the allied forces, and wood from many of these vacant buildings was used for fuel, leaving them in a derelict state. After the liberation in 1945, many of the structures were again occupied, though the disarray at the end of the war left their ownership in dispute.

Hoping to rectify this situation, a law was passed in 1947 that allowed any occupants of these buildings to remain there, regardless of their legal rights to the properties.[5] This unforeseen neighborhood clearance—the deportation, murder, and exile of the Jewish people who lived there—and

2   Virginie Mamadouh, *De Stad in Eigen Hand: Provo's, Kabouters En Krakers Als Stedelijke Sociale Beweging* (Amsterdam: SUA, 1992), p. 169, 261 nn. 138–139; Eric Duivenvoorden, *Een voet tussen de deur: geschiedenis van de kraakbeweging (1964-1999)* (Amsterdam: De Arbeiderspers, 2000), p. 307. The Dutch government made squatting totally illegal in 2010. Before that time, squatting was not a punishable offense in itself, as outlined in the text below. Squatters were, however, charged with other punishable offenses such as trespassing, criminal damage/vandalism, and lack of residential permit/legal housing provision.

3   Mamadouh, *De stad in eigen hand*, pp. 175, 179–81; BILWET, *Bewegingsleer: kraken aan gene zijde van de media* (Amsterdam: Ravijn, 1990) / ADILKNO, *Cracking the Movement: Squatting Beyond the Media* (Brooklyn: Autonomedia, 1994); Geert Lovink, interview by author; David Garcia, interview by author.

4   Mamadouh, *De stad in eigen hand*, p. 131.

5   Mamadouh, *De stad in eigen hand*, p.133; Caroline Nevejan and Alexander Badenoch, "How Amsterdam Invented the Internet: European Networks of Significance 1980-1995," in *Hacking Europe: From Computer Cultures to Demoscenes*, ed. Gerard Alberts and Ruth Oldenziel (London: Springer, 2014), p. 193.

the general upheaval of the postwar era set the stage for *tabula rasa* urban planning initiatives, wherein the government sought to tear down the abandoned or decrepit housing stock in the city center to make way for new hotels, office complexes, highways, and metro stations in these areas in the following decades.[6] The plans for Amsterdam were by no means unique; they reflected widespread global urban planning trends during the era.[7] Squatters and residents vociferously protested these changes and, in so doing, preserved numerous historic buildings from demolition.

With the resolution—through defeat or completion—of many of these government urban renewal initiatives by the late 1970s, squatters increasingly saw their chief adversaries as real estate speculators rather than city planners.[8] The often-corrupt absentee landlords who owned vacant properties around the city regularly employed gangs of thugs to harass squatters who had, in fact, occupied the properties in accordance with the law. It was during this time that squatting in Amsterdam became more than just a question of practicality. The conflict between private property and squatting rights was essentially a conflict between competing conceptions of the city: whether the city is a cooperative entity that belongs to the people or whether it is a collection of commodities and assets that belong to private individuals. The logical solution for squatters was to begin "habiting" urban space (rather than existing in pre-prescribed "habitats").[9] In other words, they needed to develop their own sense of what Henri Lefebvre called the "right to the city."[10] The squatters set about using (and

6   Kees Schuyt and Ed Taverne, *1950: Prosperity and Welfare* (Assen: Royal Van Gorcum, 2004), p. 163. These planning initiatives were mostly geared toward the creation of business districts and propelled by Dutch entrepreneurs.

7   Christopher Klemek, *The Transatlantic Collapse of Urban Renewal: Postwar Urbanism from New York to Berlin* (Chicago: University of Chicago Press, 2012).

8   There were some city-led projects—particularly those that reflected the city's interest in developing tourist facilities and offices in the city center—that pitted the municipal government and the squatters against each other (for example, the Wijers/Holiday Inn issue in 1984, see chapter 1, note 97). The ongoing campaign against the Stopera (city hall/opera complex) development at Waterlooplein and the objections to the city hosting the 1992 Olympics (which they bid for beginning in 1985) were also issues in which the squatters faced off against the municipal government. Additionally, the squatters still saw the police and the city government as "enemies" due to the increasingly violent tactics used during evictions. See Mamadouh, *De stad in eigen hand*, p. 197; ADILKNO, *Cracking the Movement*, p. 90.

9   Henri Lefebvre, *The Urban Revolution*, trans. Robert Bononno (Minneapolis: Minnesota Press, 2003), pp. 81–82.

10   Henri Lefebvre, "The Right to the City," in *Writings of Cities*, trans. Eleonore Kofman and Elizabeth Lebas (Cambridge, MA: Blackwell, 1996), p. 158. Lefebvre's concept the "right to the city" has subsequently been interpreted in a number of ways that are often not clearly

re-using) the city instead of allowing it to become a ghost town of dormant assets. To use Lefebvre's terminology, they playfully and creatively staked out a claim to urban life.[11] In so doing, the squatters first had to rethink the configuration of space, draw up new boundaries and invent new structures in the cracks of the existing city's limits. The city space had long since been (almost) entirely parceled out, carved up, and delineated, with boundaries designed to protect the ownership rights of individuals. This foreclosed any possibility of new, communal spaces *outside* the tightly controlled system of private property and forced squatters to find solutions *within* the existing system.

As noted in the introduction to this book, the Netherlands has a long political and spatial history of working to extract maximum utility from the built environment. The historic self-sufficiency of the Dutch and their capacity to shape the landscape could be characterized as revolutionary pragmatism, and it has, over the course of Dutch history, produced radical forms of tolerance, governance, and individual freedom. During the centuries-long development of the nation, the common thread has been practicality, or even utility. This pragmatic attitude fostered both early forms of capitalism and private enterprise as well as distinct forms of cooperation and coexistence. And so, a paradoxical balance is created between unanimity and autonomy, between individualism and community.

This chapter sets up a theoretical and historical framework for chapters 2 to 4. The city and the practice of squatting act as entrypoints to and metaphors for a host of practices in media, art, and technology that developed in or were inspired by the squatters' movement. While squatting and urban activism are by no means unique to the Netherlands during this period, my focus on the specificity of this locality yields a more nuanced understanding of the particular character and attitude within Dutch media art in the ensuing years.

defined. Lefebvre defines it as a revolutionary demand by the people for "a transformed and renewed right to urban life." He describes the flight of populations out of the "deteriorated and unrenovated city" (i.e., increasing depopulation of urban centers and suburbanization). For interpretations see Peter Marcuse, "From Critical Urban Theory to the Right to the City," *City* 13, no. 2–3 (June 1, 2009): pp. 185–97; David Harvey, *Rebel Cities: From the Right to the City to the Urban Revolution* (London: Verso, 2012); David Adler et al., *The Right to the City: A Verso Report*, ed. Verso Books (London: Verso, 2017). For a critique of the amorphous use of the concept to apply to urban activism subsequently, see Mark Purcell, "Excavating Lefebvre: The Right to the City and Its Urban Politics of the Inhabitant," *GeoJournal* 58, no. 2 (October 1, 2002): pp. 99–108.

11   Lefebvre, "The Right to the City," 147; Lefebvre, *The Urban Revolution*, 18.

Provocation

On the 26th and 27th of November 1962, the Netherlands was captivated by its first nationwide telethon. The program *Open Het Dorp* was a continuous 24-hour television and radio broadcast, organized to raise funds for a new community for the physically disabled outside of Arnhem called Het Dorp (The Village). People tuned in across the country, staying up through the night to watch the broadcast and pledge donations.[12] A day later, on the 28th of November, the former Queen of the Netherlands died. Queen Wilhelmina's funeral on the 8th of December was the first royal funeral to be broadcast on television. The spectacular endurance test of the telethon, hosted by presenter Mies Bouwman during its entire length, and the media pageantry that accompanied the passing of the monarch a week later served as inspiration for the first self-described "happening" in the Netherlands.[13] On December 9, 1962, artists and poets gathered in the studio of the painter Rik van Bentum to stage *Open het graf* (*Open the Grave*), the title of which referenced both media spectacles.[14] The event consisted of beat-style poetry readings and a variety of performances around the theme of "necrophilia" and was organized by Dutch poet and performance artist Simon Vinkenoog together with Americans Melvin Clay and Frank Stern.[15]

This first happening was a key moment in the years before Provo, a youth movement of artists, poets, and anarchist activists that sought to provoke the authorities and institutions in the Netherlands between 1965 and 1967. Provo laid the foundations for Amsterdam's persistent reputation for youth culture, liberalized drug policy, individual freedom, and tolerance. The symbol that was later adopted as the logo of the movement, known

12   Harry Dietz and Wim Coster, *Het Dorp van binnen en buiten, 1962-1997: ontstaan en ontwikkeling van een woonvorm voor mensen met een lichamelijke handicap in maatschappelijk perspectief* (Arnhem: Stichting Het Dorp, 1997), p. 26.

13   Eric Duivenvoorden, *Magiër van een nieuwe tijd: het leven van Robert Jasper Grootveld.* (Amsterdam: Arbeiderspers, 2009), pp. 226–27. Artist Wolf Vostell organized the first happening a few months before on October 5, 1962 in Monet gallery on the Rokin in Amsterdam and outside the Stedelijk Museum.

14   Duivenvoorden, *Magiër*, p. 228.The organizers did not plan to reference Wilhelmina's funeral (i.e., *her* grave) ahead of time, but they were nevertheless pleased with the coincidence of the two events. In a personal communication, art historian Marga van Mechelen stated that the grave in the title was a reference to Marilyn Monroe's death in that year.

15   Wim A. L. Beeren, *Actie, werkelijkheid en fictie in de kunst van de jaren '60 in Nederland* ('s-Gravenhage: Staatsuitgeverij, 1979), p. 55. James Kennedy suggests that the theme may also have been inspired by Allan Kaprow's *A Service for the Dead* (1962) in "Building New Babylon: Cultural Change in the Netherlands during the 1960s" (Ph.D., The University of Iowa, 1995), p. 241 n. 95.

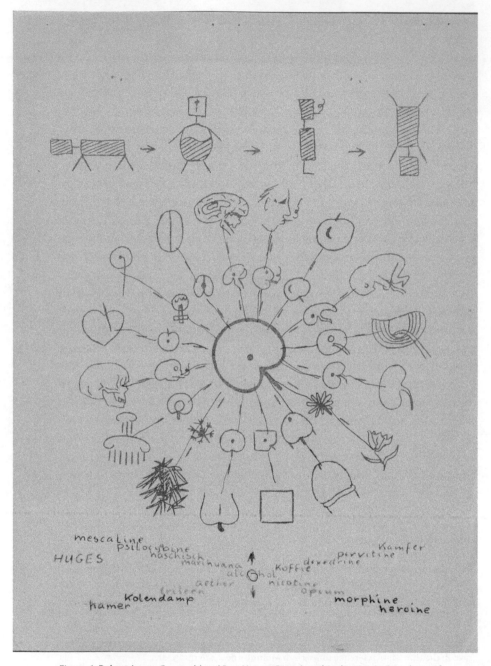

Figure 1: Robert Jasper Grootveld and Bart Huges, Gnot-Appeltje drawing in *Open het graf* publication, 1962, pen drawing, 57.4cm × 40,3 cm. Rijksmuseum, Amsterdam.

as the Gnot-appeltje (Gnot apple) [Fig.1], was created for *Open het graf* by performance artist/"magician" Robert Jasper Grootveld and medical student Bart Huges. It was in part a representation of the circumambulatory canal rings of the old city of Amsterdam, dubbed the "Magisch Centrum" ("the magic center") by Grootveld, and a boundary within which a new idea of Dutch society was forming with new rules of play. At the center of the drawing is the Gnot-*appeltje*; Gnot was a portmanteau of *God* and *genot* (pleasure) that Grootveld used as a ritualistic incantation. It resembled "*een appeltje met stip*" ("an apple with a stem").[16] Branching out around the Gnot-*appeltje* are a variety of doodles that are shown evolving into the central symbol, including a fetus, a brain, a marijuana plant, a penis, an anus excreting, a flower, a man smoking, and, of course, the city of Amsterdam. The city's central canal rings form the outer shell of the apple, its stem the Amstel River, and the hole at the center would later come to represent the position of the Lieverdje, a small statue of a boy in the square at the Spui that had been financed by a cigarette manufacturer and thus became the site of Grootveld's anti-smoking performances in the '60s.[17]

Dutch artists, like artists internationally in the early '60s, were simultaneously fascinated and revolted by the rise of advertising and the role of the media in promoting consumption. For Grootveld, who was addicted to cigarettes, tobacco advertising was the epitome of unhealthy consumerism and corporate greed, and his first anti-smoking action in 1961 was to deface these ads with the letter K for *kanker* (cancer).[18] This anti-consumerist attitude was carried through Grootveld's activities within the Provo movement. According to Niek Pas, "In the eyes of the Provos, the individual was at risk of becoming a faceless plaything in an increasingly massified, bureaucratic, and consumerist society."[19] As Pas argues, Provo expertly utilized the mass media, including television, to promote their activities as well as to critique their increasingly mediated society.[20]

As a young man in the 1950s, Grootveld found his way into the bohemian milieu of writers and poets who gathered around the subcultural hotspot of Leidseplein in Amsterdam. During that time, he invented and enacted a variety of roles for spontaneous performances in public space, which were

16   Niek Pas, *Imaazje! De verbeelding van Provo, 1965-1967* (Amsterdam: Wereldbibliotheek, 2003), p. 89.
17   Ibid., p. 95.
18   Ibid., p. 91.
19   Niek Pas, *Provo!: mediafenomeen 1965-1967* (Amsterdam: Wereldbibliotheek, 2015), p. 9.
20   Ibid.

reported on by the local press.[21] He often dressed as a shaman-like figure or as the blackface character Zwarte Piet from the Dutch Sinterklaas (Saint Nicholas) holiday. After a hospital stay in 1961, during which he was not allowed to smoke, Grootveld realized the extent to which he was addicted to cigarettes and began an obsessive solo campaign to deface the many billboards and outdoor advertisements for cigarettes around Amsterdam. Grootveld's target was not primarily the cigarettes—paradoxically, he continued to smoke his entire life—but, rather, the advertising that he blamed for his addiction, saying, "advertisement, that was my enemy."[22]

This interest in advertising was inspired by his experiences traveling around the world while working as a crew member on a ship. He recalled encountering medicine men in Africa, whose magic spells created trance-like states, which, according to Grootveld, were similar to the state of addiction in Western culture. Advertising was hypnotizing the public, casting magic spells and creating a dependence on consumption that forced people to relinquish control and responsibility for their actions. Grootveld said:

> I was fascinated by the phenomenon of advertising: the repetition of the image, always that image, the repetition of the advertising slogan. [...] In Africa, I understood what a disastrous influence hypnosis and magic can have. [...] I saw the public influencers [including the creators of advertising] as medicine men.[23]

This initial revelation about the Western medicine man of the advertising world ushered in his next step towards becoming a "magician" himself.

After being prosecuted and imprisoned for thirty days for the vandalism of the advertisements, Grootveld decided to change his tactic.[24] When he was released, Grootveld was able to find a venue for his elaborate performances, obtained with the help of an eccentric restauranteur Nicolaas Kroese. Kroese was impressed by Grootveld's mystical anti-smoking rituals and offered him an old carpentry workshop at Korte Leidsedwarsstraat 31 with the hope that he would spread cancer awareness through his performances there.[25] Grootveld set to work creating the K-Kerk (K-Church) and, with the help of friends, publicized his rituals there.

21   Grootveld also more privately staged photograph of himself in these roles, including a series of photographs of himself dressed in feminine attire.
22   Qtd. Duivenvoorden, *Magiër*, p. 179.
23   Ibid., p. 182.
24   Ibid., p. 187.
25   Ibid., pp. 192–93.

The K-Kerk opened on March 17, 1962, and Grootveld performed nearly every day for a month with a crowd of around 25–30 people. He conducted his ritual at an altar of burning cigarette butts, accompanied by African music and surrounded by cigarette advertisements. The church was prepared with a thick layer of cigarette smoke and the participants in the ritual were required to smoke as an "offering." The second part of the ritual consisted of "mass hysteria" where the participants would perform the "*Hoest* Song" ("cough song"), repeatedly making a cough-like sound: "uche, uche, uche." Then, in order to "defeat" the addiction, the participants evoked the spirit of "publicity" with the "Publicity Song" where the (English) words "publicity, publicity, publicity... mooooore publicity..." would be chanted in a wave of sound. And, finally, the participants would "laugh the advertisements away" to symbolize they were not addicted.[26]

In May 1964 Grootveld began performing at the Spui in Amsterdam next to the Lieverdje statue. The fact that a cigarette manufacturer donated the money for the statue fit well with Grootveld's anti-smoking mythology and it was, therefore, an ideal location. The statue's subject, a mischievous young boy, had further symbolic potency for Grootveld: childhood and its magical aspects were a recurrent theme for him. Various fringe religious groups in Amsterdam were attracted to Grootveld's performances to pray for his soul, which did not bother Grootveld in the least.[27] Grootveld was, it seems, happier to classify himself as a priest than an artist, which may explain why he has not been integrated into histories of European performance art of the 1950s and '60s. He first became involved with exhibitions, performances, and happenings—sometimes in galleries, sometimes not—through friends he had met while hanging around Leidseplein, listening to jazz, and smoking marijuana. According to Grootveld, his happenings superseded mere art. "I am not an artist," he said, "what I do is real."[28]

In late 1964 Grootveld also began incorporating the word "*imaazje*" in his performances at the Lieverdje—a take on (and pronounced similarly to) the French word *image.* As noted, Grootveld was concerned with the repetition of images in advertising from the very start of his anti-smoking activities in 1961, and his rituals were a way to strip away the layers of artifice that surrounded modern media images. For an artist who was, above all, concerned with exorcizing the manipulation of advertising

26   Ibid., p.197.
27   Ibid., p. 284.
28   Qtd. ibid., p. 287.

culture, it was essential for him to go beyond the image and create a kind of alternate reality through ritualistic performance. By staging rituals, Grootveld attempted to open up doorways to an alternate reality rather than create images or representations of the current reality of consumption. He thrived in the dope-fueled youth culture of Amsterdam, among fringe religious groups and in the public realm rather than within art galleries or institutions. His life and work were part of series of free-floating associations, without much in the way of planning or foresight. Despite his ambivalent politics, however, he is mainly remembered for his connection to the Provo youth movement. His association with Provo gave the movement an aesthetic and artistic component and gave Grootveld a political affiliation.

In 1965 a group of young anarchists began attending Grootveld's weekly performances at the Lieverdje and, in the summer of that year, handed out the first issue of their anarchist magazine *Provo* at the event. *Provo* maintained the stance that the role of anarchist youth culture was to provoke the mainstream. Roel van Duijn, the political and ideological heart of the publication, was attracted to Grootveld's provocative energy and originality. Thus began the collaboration between leftwing radicals and the magician of Amsterdam.

The term *provo* was coined in the doctoral dissertation of sociologist and criminologist Wouter Buikhuisen, whose work analyzed the deviant behavior of the *nozems*, the Dutch subcultural equivalent of teddy boys in the UK and greasers in the US in the 1950s. Buikhuisen's dissertation characterized the behavior of working class youths as a negative and disruptive force in Dutch society; he created the term *provo* from the Dutch verb *provoceren* (to provoke) to describe youths who engaged in provocative and anti-social behavior.[29] The media were quick to pick up Buikhuisen's term, and, following the media's lead, the nascent anarchist movement led by Roel van Duijn soon ironically adopted the term as their own.[30] Van Duijn was joined by Rob Stolk, Hans Metz, Hans Tuynman, Olaf Stoop, Luud Schimmelpennink, and others in producing the magazine from their headquarters at Karthuizerstraat 14 in the Jordaan neighborhood of Amsterdam, and they soon began to frequent Grootveld's performances at the Lieverdje.[31]

29   Wouter Buikhuisen, "Achtergronden van de nozemgedrag" (Utrecht, Utrecht University, 1965).
30   Pas, *Provo!*, pp. 40–43.
31   Aad de Jongh, *Provo: een jaar Provo-activiteiten* (Rotterdam: Kerco, 1966), pp. 12–13.

As a student of art history as well as philosophy and politics, Van Duijn connected his anarchist political ideology to the Dada movement.[32] Although Grootveld was not a well-educated intellectual like Van Duijn, his Dada-like activities and attitude appealed to Van Duijn. The first issue of *Provo* was published on July 12, 1965, and began with a manifesto heralding a movement that would be open to everyone and against everything, stating:

> PROVO is a monthly for anarchists, provo's, beatniks, *pleiners*, scissor-grinders, jailbirds [...] PROVO is against capitalism, communism, fascism, bureaucracy, militarism, snobbery, professionalism, dogmatism, and authoritarianism. [...] PROVO realizes that it will ultimately lose, but it does not want to pass up the chance to provoke this society at least one more heartfelt time.[33]

The message of Provo was noteworthy in its cynicism and irony, eschewing the typical utopianism of leftwing movements in favor of resignation and pre-emptive defeat. In this way, Provo captured the youthful ennui that sociologists like Buikhuisen found so troubling. It was proto-punk in its lack of hope for the future, a sentiment that is captured in Buikhuisen's analysis; he cites the hardships and upheaval of the Second World War and the ensuing threat of nuclear annihilation as factors that "make the future hopeless and lead to a provisional way of living, to living in the *now*, in *this moment*."[34]

Due to the effects of the war on the young people of the Netherlands, Provo was already more pessimistic than some of their counter-cultural counterparts in the United States who celebrated the "summer of love". When punk arrived in the Netherlands in the late 1970s, it could not avoid the long shadow of Provo. In the early '80s, former Provo members such as Grootveld could still be found hanging around bars and clubs at the Spui and the Leidseplein. As a result, they mingled with the younger generation of anarchists and punks, and these veteran provocateurs served as inspiration for protest activities in Amsterdam in the early '80s.

Provo's embrace of the media reflects the ambiguous political position they took: they organized provocative gestures of resistance but forswore the possibility these gestures would effect lasting revolutionary change. According to Pas:

32 Pas, *Provo!*, pp. 25, 32.
33 Jongh, *Provo*, p. 168.
34 Buikhuisen, "Achtergronden van de nozemgedrag," 16–17.

...the Provos were also children of their time: they tried out the latest printing techniques, embraced the upcoming computer age, and played avidly on the latest achievements of mass communication, such as television and illustrated press.[35]

The Provo movement was more concerned with the artificiality of a new consumer world that created a populace that was "drugged" and "dehumanized" rather than a denouncement of new media communication and consumerist objects in and of themselves.[36] Like Grootveld conducting his anti-smoking rituals while continuing to smoke himself, Provo was both critical of and unable to resist the world of advertising, media promotion, and image consumption.

Despite the cynicism of their manifesto, Provo did in fact alter the shape of Dutch culture and society in meaningful ways. The activities of Provo fostered Amsterdam's reputation for openness, tolerance, decriminalization of drugs and sex, and vibrant youth culture; it is a reputation that, whether justified or not, lives on today. According to Marga van Mechelen:

> The happenings by both Grootveld and Provo were very much media events. The Provo strategies, with provocations as their aim and not just as effect, were contemporary strategies par excellence, inevitably acted out in front of the eye of the camera. Whoever controlled the channels to mass media had the power in their hands.[37]

And, indeed, Provo was hugely media savvy in the way they publicized their activities.[38]

The most dramatic media spectacle staged by Provo revolved around the royal wedding of Dutch Crown Princess Beatrix in 1966. The announcement in 1965 that the princess would marry a former member of the German army and the Hitler Youth, Claus von Amsberg (né Klaus), was extremely controversial for the Dutch people, as the indignities of the German occupation were still fresh in many people's minds. The wedding thus became a flashpoint of protest for Provo. On the day of the wedding March 10, 1966, members of Provo set off smoke bombs as the royal carriage made its way

35   Pas, *Provo!*, p. 9.
36   Ibid., pp. 38–39.
37   Marga van Mechelen, *De Appel: Performances, Installations, Video, Projects, 1975-1983* (Amsterdam: De Appel, 2006), p. 24.
38   Pas, *Provo!*

through Amsterdam. These protests made the front page of international newspapers the following morning.

Although the protests during the royal wedding proved to be their most far-reaching media spectacle, Provo is also remembered for their less spectacular but far more prescient proposals for improvements in everyday life. Beginning in the summer of 1965, they began to introduce their "white plans," a series of plans that proposed an alternative vision for urbanism in opposition to the typical highway-and-high-rise development models of the 1960s. They articulated these visions in playful ways, imagining an environmentally-friendly city space, with a focus on social and economic justice.

The first white plan, the White Bicycle Plan, was introduced on July 28, 1965. It was inspired by Grootveld's slogan, *"Fiets is iets, maar bijna niets!"* ("A bike is something but almost nothing") and conceptualized by Luud Schimmelpennink. For the unveiling of the project, the Provos met at the Lieverdje to paint a bike white and introduce the plan, which called for everyone to follow their lead and paint their bikes white and leave them around the city so that anyone could pick up a bike and ride for free.[39] It was the first proposal for a city-wide bicycle sharing program.

The next white plan that the Provos proposed was the White Chimney Plan, which sought to cut down pollution in the city through a tax and which, again, proposed using white paint as a marker, this time for the offending chimneys.[40] Subsequently, in 1966, there was a flood of white plan ideas, as Provo invited anyone to offer up further suggestions.[41] The White Chicken Plan[42] sought to remake the police through disarming the force and allowing police chiefs to be democratically elected, the White Wives Plan[43] advocated for women's reproductive rights and access to contraception, the White Children Plan proposed a communal childcare initiative, and others addressed a variety of social issues.

These plans, for the most part, were designed as and functioned as publicity stunts or gimmicks rather than realistic proposals.[44] Provo, by their

39   Luud Schimmelpennink, "Provo Fietsenplan," *Provo*, no. 2 (August 17, 1965): pp. 1–5; Pas, *Provo!*, p. 83.

40   Luud Schimmelpennink, "Provo's Witte Schoorstenen Plan," *Provo*, no. 6 (January 24, 1966): pp. 1–6.

41   Pas, *Imaazje!*, p. 118.

42   Auke Boersma, "Witte Kippenplan," *Provo*, no. 9 (May 12, 1966): pp. 12–13. The Dutch word *kip* means chicken and is slang for the police in Amsterdam.

43   Pas, *Imaazje!*, pp. 191, 229.

44   Pas, *Imaazje!*, p. 118.

own declaration, seemed to be mainly interested in publicity and media attention and, perhaps not unlike other youth subcultures before them, a fashionable alternative lifestyle.[45] Provo Auke Boersma said:

> The punchline of the white plans was that they were not white plans but rather mind-openers. [...] There were few people that understood that [...] They were plans that puzzled people so much that they had to think about it. They were, thus, really fantastical plans.[46]

This utopian urbanism was, at least in part, inspired by the Dutch Situationist Constant, who wrote for *Provo* and whose influence on both Provo and the squatters' movement is discussed at greater length in the next section.

In April 1966 Provo publicized a new White Housing Plan, which directly addressed the housing shortage in Amsterdam, and was equal parts utopian fantasy, pragmatism, activism, and aesthetic concept. This plan politicized the housing shortage in an unprecedented way and, thus, has the most bearing on the discussion of squatting in the following sections. Although squatting in the Netherlands was legally codified by the High Court in 1914 as a pragmatic stopgap to address lack of adequate housing, the political consciousness behind it was new. The White Housing Plan not only addressed Amsterdam's lack of housing and proposed a ban on speculation but also advocated the squatting of empty or disused buildings in response.

In sync with the other white plans that called for various parts of the urban fabric to be marked with white paint to signal their connection to Provo's radical new models of urban life, the White Housing Plan called for the doors of vacant dwellings to be painted white, giving potential squatters a cohesive political identity for the first time. The Provo slogan *"redt een pandje bezet een pandje"* ("save a property, occupy a property") broadened the implication of squatting from a way to solve individual housing needs to a political activity to save the fabric of the city from largescale urban redevelopment projects. In the Nieuwmarkt neighborhood, for example, developers planned to demolish large parts of the historic center of the city in order to build a highway and metro station. In 1975 the protest actions of the emerging squatters' movement, which had evolved out of Provo, forced the government to abandon the plans to build the highway, but the metro construction was completed as planned.[47]

45   H.J.A. Hofland, "Van Zazou Tot Provo," *De Gids* 129, no. 1 (1966): p. 5.
46   Qtd in Pas, *Imaazje!*, pp. 118–19.
47   Mamadouh, *De stad in eigen hand*, p. 142.

White bikes, white doors, and white chimneys were one way that Provo began marking space. Grootveld added ritualistic and mystical symbols to the equation, combining primitivism and pop art. From the very first performances, he was an expert at attracting the attention of the media and utilizing it to promote his ideas. The symbols that emerged from his work were both brands/trademarks/logos and new occult symbols. The Gnot-*appeltje* appeared not only across Provo publications and Grootveld's performances but also as anonymous graffiti across the city. This embrace of this "branding" of Amsterdam reflects the ambiguous stance that Provo took between critique of consumer capitalism and media savviness. They were children of a new media age, raised alongside the rise of television and advertising and comfortable harnessing it for their own personal and political ends.

Homo Ludens

...where others saw only hardening concrete, as a band of self-consciously modern revolutionaries the situationists thought they glimpsed a crack. They had come together [...] in the belief that they could find that crack, map it, pry it open until the old world disappeared into its hole.[48]

– Greil Marcus

The legal history of squatting in the Netherlands is unique, and the practice was viewed favorably by the public throughout much of its early history. The 1914 High Court decision that allowed squatting specified that, if a vacant property had been unused for at least a year, it could be legally squatted. All a squatter needed to stake their claim was a table, a chair, and a bed to prove their occupancy.[49] This mandate, which was still in effect in the decades that followed, developed into a quirky and somewhat absurd part of the game of squatting. From the mid-1970s onward, breaking into vacant properties in Amsterdam increasingly required covert action, speed, and precision. Despite this need for stealth, squatters still abided by the rules of the game, which dictated that they bring along these specific items of bulky furniture in order to secure the premises.

48   Greil Marcus, *Lipstick Traces: A Secret History of the Twentieth Century* (Cambridge, MA: Belknap Press of Harvard University Press, 1989), p. 122.

49   Duivenvoorden, *Een voet tussen de deur*, p. 14; Lynn Owens, *Cracking Under Pressure: Narrating the Decline of the Amsterdam Squatters' Movement* (Amsterdam: Amsterdam University Press, 2009), p. 20.

By the 1980s the practice had grown significantly riskier, although the laws around squatting had not changed. At the time of the ruling in 1914, the court's decision to legally sanction squatting meant that building owners were forced to offer rental contracts to the squatters, which they often did in short order once a property was squatted.[50] In the 1980s, on the other hand, offering rental contracts to squatters was either not an option or not desireable for owners, as many of the squatted properties were commercial buildings in valuable and prestigious areas of the center of the city. As a result, building owners regularly hired gangs of thugs to rough up or illegally evict squatters occupying their buildings. Increasingly, heavily armed Dutch riot police were also involved in squat evictions, and building owners were more regularly fighting for and being granted evictions by the courts.[51]

Not unlike other countries in Europe after World War II, the need for housing in the Netherlands was great. In addition to the effects of the war, lifestyle and space requirements were also changing drastically during this time, as people wanted more space for individual family members and modern facilities in their apartments such as private bathrooms.[52] By the early 1960s activism around housing and urban renewal projects began to take shape. As described in first section of this chapter, the Provo movement agitated against demolition and urban renewal in their White Housing Plan of 1966 by calling for people to save the existing vacant housing stock by squatting it. After this point, the practice of squatting became more explicitly political.[53]

Provo leader Roel van Duijn realized early on that assimilating the absurd, ludic, or utopian aesthetic work of artists could complement the political side of the movement as well as provide precisely the kind of "provocation" that

50 Duivenvoorden, *Een voet tussen de deur*, p. 14; Owens, *Cracking Under Pressure*, p. 46. In the later period, from 1980 onward, squatter groups did sometimes attempt to gain rental contracts or buy properties. It was more common, however, for disputed squats to go through a process of legalization, often with the help of the city government, particularly since squats were increasingly former government buildings or large commercial buildings rather than buildings designed as apartments and dwellings. See Mamadouh, *De stad in eigen hand,* pp. 185–86

51 Owens, *Cracking Under Pressure,* p. 50.

52 Duivenvoorden, *Een voet tussen de deur,* pp. 13–15.

53 The Provo movement put squatting on the table as a political issue. Subsequent activism around housing in Amsterdam, in which many ex-Provos were involved, shifted the focus of squatting from individual housing needs to issues around urban renewal. Additionally, there were squatting actions in the Bijlmermeer (particularly the Gliphoeve area) tied to Surinamese immigrant families who had left Suriname in the wake of the country's independence movement. These actions were, for the most part, politically separate from inner-city squatter activism. See Mamadouh, *De stad in eigen hand,* pp. 123, 143.

the name implied. One of the ways aesthetics were assimilated into Provo was via Robert Jasper Grootveld's performances. In addition to Grootveld, the leaders of Provo also harnessed the work of Dutch artist/architect Constant for their nascent political movement.[54] As an older artist with a history of participating in avant-garde art movements—notably CoBrA and the Situationist International (SI)—Constant was a good match for Provo. His project *New Babylon*, a utopian architectural plan that envisioned a future where automation would facilitate a global city space of freedom and play, helped bolster Provo's ideas both intellectually and in terms of public optics.[55]

Like Grootveld, Constant's affiliation with Provo added an element of dreamy idealism and lighthearted playfulness to an anarchist movement whose primary aim was at first provocation and, later, practical change through established political channels. Social geographer Virginie Mamadouh argues that the status of *New Babylon* as a "respectable artwork" gave legitimacy to Provo.[56] She quotes Roel van Duijn from 1967, who says:

The White Bicycle, Chimney, Chicken, Housing, and Wives Plan were necessary to make Amsterdam the first sector of New Babylon. The Magic Centrum can, then, become a Ludic Centrum, that is not made un-playable [*onspeelbaar*] by cars, banks, and depopulation, but that is creatively stimulated through happenings.[57]

The Provo leaders thus positioned their ludic plans and happenings as practical first steps towards creating *New Babylon* and overlaid their political ideology on Constant's vision of a nomadic civilization.[58]

---

54 There is some debate over how to label Constant's role in Provo. See Martin van Schaik, "Psychogeogram: An Artist's Utopia," in *Exit Utopia: Architectural Provocations 1956-76*, ed. Martin van Schaik and Otakar Máčel (Munich: Prestel, 2005), p. 220-21; Pas, *Imaazje!*, p. 138; Pas, *Provo!*, p. 99; Janna Schoenberger, "Ludic Conceptualism: Art and Play in the Netherlands from 1959 to 1975" (New York, Graduate Center, CUNY, 2017), pp. 72–73; Mark Wigley, *Constant's New Babylon: The Hyper-Architecture of Desire* (Rotterdam: Witte de With, 1998), pp. 57, 70; Hugo Brems, *Altijd weer vogels die nesten beginnen: geschiedenis van de Nederlandse literatuur 1945-2005* (Amsterdam: Bert Bakker, 2013); Kennedy, "Building New Babylon," p. 3 n.11; Mamadouh, *De stad in eigen hand*, pp. 77–78.

55 Constant was one of the founders of CoBrA (short for Copenhagen-Brussels-Amsterdam), active between 1948 and 1951. He was also a founding member of the Situationist International in 1957, which he left in 1960 after disagreements with Guy Debord.

56 Mamadouh, *De stad in eigen hand*, p. 73.

57 Mamadouh, *De stad in eigen hand*, pp. 78, 242–43 n. 142.

58 Constant showed his support for the Provo movement mostly from the sidelines, with the exception of being listed on the ballot in the 1966 municipal elections under the Provo party. See ibid, p. 72.

Figure 2: Constant, *New Babylon – Holland*, 1963, ink on street map, 59 × 59.9 cm. Kunstmuseum, The Hague.

The premise of *New Babylon* was that in fifty to one hundred years a new society, new architecture, and new way of life would be realized that emphasized play and freedom rather than labor and strife, thanks to auto-mation. This new architecture would be superimposed on top of existing cities and geographies, which would be replaced by meandering field of interconnected sectors. To illustrate this, Constant constructed maps of major urban areas with his new sectors charted on top of them. In his map of Holland [Fig.2], the sectors form a spindly web—a network—over the region (and the city of Amsterdam). Gone is the traditional urban hierarchy of center and periphery and in its place is a horizontal series of nodes.

Within the sectors of *New Babylon*, there would be no work, no conflict, and no inequality. Automation of everyday tasks would allow people the complete freedom to spend the day wandering where they pleased and occupied with free play. According to Constant, there would be no more routines and even diurnal rhythms would be done away with. He states:

...in the enormous sectors of New Babylon I have eliminated daylight altogether, because people are breaking free more and more anyhow, especially from the rhythms of nature. Man wants to follow his own rhythm. Because usefulness has less of a grip on life, the whole rhythm of day and night will disappear.[59]

The residents of *New Babylon* would essentially be wandering around in a timeless, interior space.[60]

This section explores the history and content of *New Babylon* in order to position the project as a theoretical and historical lens for the playful, fun, and radical occupation of urban space during the squatters' movement in Amsterdam. The ludic spirit of *New Babylon* can also be found in much of the media activism and artwork attendant to squatting. Although the raw/ DIY materiality of squatting in Amsterdam during that time contrasted with Constant's technocratic vision, the squatters' network could be seen as a kind of virtual *New Babylon*, formed from interconnected fissures on the surface of the old city. Much like the residents of *New Babylon*, labelled *Homo ludens* (the human that plays), the squatters occupied their network of cracks in the fabric of the city in a playful and mobile way.

Constant began working on *New Babylon* in the mid-'50s but only received widespread public attention for the project a decade later in 1965, when it was featured in an exhibition at the Gemeentemuseum in The Hague.[61] He continued working on the project for another decade until 1974, when he staged a final show of his collection of drawings, maps, and maquettes of *New Babylon*, again, at the Gemeentemuseum. By 1974, in the context of the economic, social, and political strife of the early '70s and as the idealism of the counterculture turned to frustration, *New Babylon*'s 1960s brand of utopianism and optimism was decidedly out of fashion, leading some scholars to speculate that Constant had given up hope that the project would truly be realized.[62] But just as *New Babylon* was ending, the squatters' movement in Amsterdam was emerging, creating a punk, DIY version of Constant's ludic, mobile urbanism in the cracks of the existing city.

During his CoBrA period, Constant had explored the liberating potential of play by creating paintings inspired by the "freedom" he saw in children's

59   Rem Koolhaas and Betty van Garrel, "The City of the Future," in *Exit Utopia: Architectural Provocations 1956-76*, ed. Martin van Schaik and Otakar Máčel (Munich: Prestel, 2005), p. 11.
60   Schaik, "Psychogeogram," p. 112.
61   Schoenberger, "Ludic Conceptualism," pp. 70–71.
62   Laura Stamps, "Constants New Babylon: Pushing the Zeitgeist to its limits," in *Constant New Babylon: aan ons de vrijheid*, ed. Laura Stamps (Veurne: Hannibal, 2016), p. 23.

drawings and the artwork of "primitive" cultures.[63] During his time with the SI, a movement that eschewed the production of physical art objects, he began thinking about nomadism and the ways in which one might create new pathways for freedom in urban space. He was particularly inspired by his interactions with Roma people in Alba during the First World Congress of Free Artists in 1956, a meeting of European avant-garde groups that would lead to the formation of the Situationist International. By the time Constant joined the Situationists in 1957, he had begun working on spatial constructions, including his *Ontwerp voor een zigeunerkamp* (*Plan for a Gypsy Camp*) (1956), that could be seen as precursors to *New Babylon* in that it depicted a utopian structure with moveable/adaptable parts.

After officially joining the SI, Constant began a lively intellectual correspondence with Guy Debord and adopted much of the terminology and rhetoric of the SI for his project. Despite this influence, *New Babylon* cannot be considered a purely Situationist work.[64] Its core concept, namely the optimism around automation and leisure time, diverged significantly from the dominant thread of Situationist theory, which denounced post-war society's fascination with new consumer convenience gadgets and leisure activities. *New Babylon* was therefore a synthesis: an architectural proposal, an artwork, and a work of utopian theory, inflected by Constant's work in CoBrA and the SI while remaining a separate endeavor.

One of the early influences on both *New Babylon* and the SI was Johan Huizinga's book *Homo Ludens* (1938), which was immensely popular in Europe after the war and was translated to all the major European languages in the '40s and early '50s. Huizinga, a scholar who began his career studying Indian drama and later expanded to a diverse range of cultural-historical topics, argues that the "play-element" is an essential facet of culture and civilization and, so, human beings should be classified as *Homo ludens* rather than *Homo faber* (the human that makes).[65] Inspired by Huizinga's conception of humanity, Constant designed *New Babylon* as the theoretical social and geographic construction that would be inhabited by *Homo ludens*.

63   Nieuwenhuys, "Manifest," pp. 2–13; Schaik, "Psychogeogram," pp. 36–38.

64   In 1980 Constant said that Situationism had "originally baptized" the first maquettes of New Babylon. "New Babylon na tien jaren," p. 216.

65   Johan Huizinga, *Homo Ludens: proeve eener bepaling van het spel-element der cultuur* (Amsterdam: Amsterdam University Press, 2010), p. 8; Schaik, "Psychogeogram," p. 106; Stamps, "Constant's New Babylon," pp. 12–13. The term *Homo faber* as a substitute for *Homo sapiens* was re-popularized in 1907 by Henri Bergson book *L'Évolution créatrice* (*Creative Evolution*). The term has also been associated with Marxism and Marxist thinkers.

The progressive idea underpinning *New Babylon,* that total automation will lead to total individual liberation, has been proposed many times since the early days of the Industrial Revolution.[66] History has shown, however, that—from the industrial factories that tied workers to alienating labor in the nineteenth century to the twenty-first century algorithms that increasingly influence and direct individuals' choices today—automation limits freedom just as often as it facilitates it.[67]

If play is assumed to be a source of liberation, the liberation it affords seems to appear *temporarily.* Sooner or later, the game must end and its players once again enter the "real" world. If we consider play in its raw form as a means of representation, a continuous state of play would mean that the map becomes the territory. Where there is no boundary or borders defined in space or time, there is no workable definition of what constitutes play versus non-play (or, reality). But *temporarily* staged, play can create cracks and new possibilities. Although *New Babylon* is governed by constant movement, it is characterized by a permanent state of play.[68] The squatters of Amsterdam seemed to realize that the game of squatting, and its attendant freedom, must be temporary. As the squatter/media activist group BILWET writes:

> They proclaimed that the moment that squatting began was its essence. Actually squatting couldn't go on at all, because it if did it could only turn into living. To preclude this, it had to repeatedly start over. The term 'squatting' had to remain vacant, and the restorers called that vacancy 'politics'.[69]

In other words, to maintain the radicality of squatting, it had to be temporary.

66 Constant believed that automation was not in itself the reason for lack of creativity or imagination in everyday life but that it was not being used properly. See J.L. Lochner, *New Babylon* (The Hague: Haags Gemeentemuseum, 1974), p. 8. Constant's emphasis on play and playfulness as the essential expression of human freedom also has its roots in Romanticism. For example, poet Friedrich Schiller connected art and play explicitly, theorizing that there is a "play drive" inherent in humanity, which navigates between the faculties of sensation and reason. See Friedrich Schiller, *On the Aesthetic Education of Man*, trans. Reginald Snell (Mineola, NY: Dover Publ., 2004); Sven Lütticken, "Playtimes," *New Left Review*, II, no. 66 (2010): p. 127. For more on this topic, see Amanda Wasielewski, *Made in Brooklyn Artists, Hipsters, Makers, and Gentrification.* (Winchester, UK: Zero Books, 2018) pp. 51–77.

67 See Joshua B. Freeman, *Behemoth: A History of the Factory and the Making of the Modern World* (New York: W.W. Norton, 2018).

68 Constant's emphasis on constant motion and rootlessness has led to some readings of *New Babylon* as a totalitarian dystopia. See John Heintz, "New Babylon – A Persistent Provocation," in *Exit Utopia: Architectural Provocations 1956-76*, ed. Martin van Schaik and Otakar Máčel (Munich: Prestel, 2005), p. 214.

69 ADILKNO, *Cracking the Movement*, p. 112.

After the White Housing Plan and the dissolution of Provo, political thought around squatting continued to develop. In 1969 a group of ex-Provos led by Roel van Duijn formed a new movement: the Kabouter movement, which was more explicitly focused on environmentalism, conservation of existing buildings, and urban solutions to maintain the small-scale structure of Amsterdam than their Provo predecessors. They used the word *kabouter*, which means garden gnome in Dutch, to draw association to small-scale care for the land. Constant greeted this new movement with disapproval, as it was more aligned with emerging back-to-the-land movements than the futuristic techno-urban utopianism of the early '60s.[70]

The following year, Roel van Duijn and Ben Dankbaar established the Volksuniversiteit voor Sabotage (People's University for Sabotage). At their first meeting on 27 January 1970, two sociology students Ruud Vermeer and Wouter de Graaf proposed that they start an alternative state within a state, which they named the Oranje Vrijstaat (the Orange Free State). Officially established on February 5, 1970, the Oranje Vrijstaat soon began agitating around pressing urban issues.[71] They used loaded terminology in their activism, referring to vacant buildings as "freed" rather than "occupied."[72]

Activists in the early '70s prioritized making connections with their neighbors, advocating against urban renewal projects, and supporting local residents who protested against redevelopment. The primary goal of the Kabouters or the Oranje Vrijstaat was no longer to provoke a complacent older generation who conformed to an outmoded social order, but to effect real change in the city. Due to this practical turn in their activities, they garnered a reasonable amount of sympathy and support from the general public. Thanks to the Kabouters, the housing needs of young people and young families became part of the public conversation. There were two city council debates on the topic on April 15, 1970 and June 23, 1971.[73] From this point onwards, squatting was instrumentalized as a tool for political protest, not just as a solution to housing needs, and thus squatting became a protest action that was no longer intended to be permanent or primarily practical.[74]

In the mid-1970s the practice of squatting in Amsterdam began to coalesce into an organized political movement rather than the clandestine activity of individuals. According to Mamadouh, this formalization occurred after

70   Schaik, "Psychogeogram," p. 223.
71   Duivenvoorden, *Een voet tussen de deur*, p. 49.
72   Mamadouh, *De stad in eigen hand*, p. 89.
73   Ibid., p. 108.
74   Ibid., 109.

1975 when the *Handleiding kraken* (*Squatting Handbook*) first published the contact addresses of established squatters, which allowed aspiring squatters to seek out community and advice. Although the Woningburo de Kraker (The Squatter Housing Agency, a Kabouter-affiliated activist group) had begun producing handbooks in 1969, it took another half a decade before squatters began to form networks on a city-wide level.[75] The greater solidarity between squatters not only within the city of Amsterdam but across the country was precipitated by their resistance to an anti-squat law, which was first proposed in 1973 and would have made squatting criminally punishable. The Tweede Kamer of the Dutch parliament passed the law in 1976, but vociferous protest over the next two years persuaded the Eerste Kamer to reject a hearing on it in February 1978, thereby killing the proposal.[76]

At the end of 1976, squatters across Amsterdam were organizing *kraak-spreekuren* (squatting office hours), which were designed to offer information and advice to other squatters. They also began to open squatter cafés, the first of which, De Vergulde Koevoet (The Gilded Crowbar) on the Harlem-merplein, opened at the end of 1976.[77] Around the same time, squatters were busy forming various action groups and squatter organizations. In November 1975, the first issue of the first citywide newspaper for squatters, the *Kraakkrant* (Squat Newspaper), was published.[78]

When the city government finally took action to evict the squatters in Nieuwmarkt neighborhood in early March 1975, the first large-scale violent conflicts between squatters and police erupted. The city of Amsterdam's plan to demolish the neighborhood in order to build a large highway and a new metro station was initiated in 1965, but it had been delayed since that time largely due to the activism of the Provos, Kabouters, and their associates. The redevelopment plan spurred the formation of the activist group Woningburo De Kraker in 1968 and, by 1970, more and more young

75 Duivenvoorden, *Een voet tussen de deur*, pp. 13, 15, 32–34, 63, 78; Joost Seelen, *De stad was van ons*, 1996; Owens, *Cracking Under Pressure*, p. 63; Mamadouh, *De stad in eigen hand*, p. 142. Duivenvoorden begins his history of the squatters' movement in 1969, dating the first "sign" of the movement to 1964 and the definitive moment of formation to the Nieuwmarkt activism in 1975. The documentary *De stad was van ons* (1996) begins with the 1978 eviction of the squat at Jacob van Lennepstraat 207–211. Owens also favors 1978 (and the Jacob van Lennepstraat eviction) as the date that catalyzed squatters into forming a social movement. Placed within the longer history of squatting, Mamadouh dates the movement to 1976–1984.

76 Duivenvoorden, *Een voet tussen de deur*, pp. 73–75, 132; Owens, *Cracking Under Pressure*, pp. 50–51.

77 The *koevoet* (literally cow foot, in English crowbar) was the tool the squatters used to crack into empty buildings and was often used as a symbol for Dutch squatters.

78 Mamadouh, *De stad in eigen hand,* p. 143.

people had squatted the neighborhood.[79] Independent media played an important organizational role in activism against the city's plans for Nieuwmarkt; former Provo member Rob Stolk ran a press in the neighborhood that published no less than four newspapers catering specifically to the local area and the campaign to preserve it.[80] The first squatter pirate radio broadcaster, Sirene, was also established, and called itself "the activist broadcaster of the Niewumarkt neighborhood, the *luchtwapen* [i.e. German *luftwaffe*] of Amsterdam."[81]

From March 24 to April 8, 1975, riots broke out in protest to the imminent evictions of long-established squats.[82] These events largely changed city officials' attitude toward the squatters. According to Mamadouh, "Until that time squatters were tolerated as long as they were not visible: they could not publicize their illegal living situation and they had to, above all, disappear as soon as the city wanted to demolish the buildings in question."[83] The relative success of the Nieuwmarkt actions, however, only further solidified the political power of squatting.[84]

Constant's *New Babylon* was created in the context of an outpouring of utopian architectural plans that arose in the 1960s. Similar to plans by Yona Friedman and Archigram, *New Babylon* favored mobility and large-scale networking. Access to new communication technology, computers, and video certainly played a role in this.[85] Mark Wigley draws a connection between the network of sectors of *New Babylon* and communication networks, writing:

> This 'world wide web,' as Constant called it, is a physical image of interconnectivity in a flat world [...] the ability of the new technology of radio to transcend all physical borders and wrap the planet in a single web had produced intense debate [...] about a new kind of interconnectivity. The first images of a world wide web—as in Telefunken's 1913 map showing the new global network that could be formed by linking all major radio networks together—were captivating documents [...] Constant became

79   Ibid., p. 113.
80   Ibid., p. 114.
81   Ibid., p. 118.
82   Ibid., p. 137.
83   Ibid., p. 131.
84   While the new metro station was built, the planned highway was cancelled. Although the buildings along Sint Antoniesbreestraat were demolished, they were replaced largely by social housing rather than offices or hotels (to appease the activists). The historic seventeenth-century mansion of a Portuguese trader, Huis De Pinto, was also preserved from demolition, which was seen as a major victory for the activists.
85   Schaik, "Psychogeogram," p. 227.

part of a generation of post-Second World War designers who offered a palpable image of society as a self-organizing communication system by echoing these invisible systems.[86]

The Situationists were also involved in theorizing a connected city, a virtual network created through the use of new technology. They regularly used walkie-talkies to create the experience of a kind of primitive augmented reality in the city space during their *dérives*.

According to Debord, the *dérive* is, "a technique of rapid passage through varied ambiences. *Dérives* involve playful-constructive behavior and aware-ness of psychogeographical effects, and are thus quite different from the classical notions of journey or stroll."[87] Indeed, the famous psychogeographic maps of Paris produced by the SI, including the *Naked City* (1957), with their red arrows connecting fragments of the city, become less abstract when read through the lens of mobile communication methods. By using mobile radio transmitters and walkie-talkies to keep in contact while on their *dérives*, they were performing the connections between the map fragments in a virtual way, literally connecting the spatially disconnected pieces of the city.[88]

For the squatters, too, communication was the binding mechanism for their conception of the city, not only via print media like newspapers and zines (aided, of course, by increasingly affordable DIY printing techniques) but also through pirate radio and television, discussed in more detail in chapter 3.[89] Even if the squats themselves were not adjacent (or even in the same neighborhood), communication created a sense of a close-knit network. The most important squatter pirate radio station, the Vrije Keiser, was mobile from late 1980 onward, broadcasting from different neighborhoods. This activity created an unofficial network communication map between disparate sites in the city.

While the previously mentioned organizational strategies for the emerging squatters' movement were already underway by 1978, another episode of police violence during the eviction of a squat at Nicolaas Beetsstraat/Jacob

86   Mark Wigley, "Extreme Hospitality," in *Constant New Babylon: aan ons de vrijheid*, ed. Laura Stamps (Veurne: Hannibal, 2016), pp. 39–40.

87   Ken Knabb, *Situationist International Anthology: Revised and Expanded Edition* (Berkeley: Bureau of Public Secrets, 2006), p. 62.

88   Kristin Ross and Henri Lefebvre, "Lefebvre on the Situationists: An Interview," *October* 79 (1997): p. 73.

89   The relationship between the Situationists and the birth of the punk movement in the UK has been widely established. See Marcus, *Lipstick Traces*.

van Lennepstraat 207–211 in that year spurred squatters to step up their defensive tactics.[90] Subsequent attempts by police to evict long-standing squats in Amsterdam between 1979 and 1980 forced the squatters to establish a stronger and more militant network, which meant that they increasingly fought for and maintained not only their own living quarters but other squatted spaces within the city, rotating amongst them. Both the squatters and the Mobiele Eenheid (ME), the Dutch riot police, quickly escalated the level of violence during this period. In response to the increasingly fraught evictions happening around the city, the leaders of the nascent movement designated one squat in particular, nicknamed the Groote Keijser (also spelled Keyser) and located in six properties at Keizersgracht 242–252, as the symbolic heart of the resistance.

The collection of historic seventeenth and eighteenth-century buildings that made up the Groote Keijser was an impressive asset for the movement, located at the heart of Amsterdam on one of the central canal rings. The properties had mostly been used, in the past, as offices and factories rather than living quarters, and the enormous size of the squat reflected that. Both by virtue of the architecture and its location, the property was among the most prestigious in the city. According to Duivenvoorden:

> The [Groote Keijser] properties offered an excellent opportunity to bring everything that the squatters' movement was fighting against into the spotlight simultaneously: the shortage of housing, real estate speculation, the gangs of thugs that landlords hired to forcibly remove squatters, and the failure of government policy.[91]

Nevertheless, the role of the Keijser as a symbol of the squatters' movement rang false to many squatters. As BILWET wrote:

> The Keyser was big and empty, and everyone fit inside it. [...] But why should a house whose front-door key had been handed around by tourists just last summer, one where Israelis had barbecued on the floor, start to function as a symbol of the people's will? There was nothing particularly special about it.[92]

90   Seelen, *De stad was van ons*; Duivenvoorden, *Een voet tussen de deur*, pp. 141–42; Owens, *Cracking Under Pressure*, pp. 63–65. One of the squatters made a film of the eviction that was subsequently screened throughout the movement, stimulating a discussion around the use of violence and the response to violence from the ME.

91   Duivenvoorden, *Een voet tussen de deur*, p. 155.

92   ADILKNO, *Cracking the Movement*, p. 47.

The idea of permanence, after all, went against the mutating, temporary, nomadic ethos of the movement.

The complex was first squatted on November 1, 1978 and existed as an informal (i.e., not well organized and, compared to other squats, unfortified) flophouse for local squatters and tourists during its first year of occupation.[93] In November 1979, a judge determined that the squatters on the property could be evicted as of December 14 of that year. The resistance to the pending eviction attracted squatter activists from around the city to the Groote Keijser, during which time it largely stopped functioning as a practical living space. The majority of the fifty people living in the complex at the time left the premises; ten decided to stay and fight.[94] These squatter-activists set to work heavily fortifying the building and took turns keeping watch. As ever, communication was paramount: they set up a pirate radio station that they called de Vrije Keijser (the Free Keijser), which first broadcast on January 13, 1980 and quickly became the voice of the squatters' movement.[95] Such was the level of commitment from the increasingly militant activists that some of them even claimed they were ready to die defending the Groote Keijser.[96]

As it emerged in the late '70s, the squatters' movement largely took the shape of a virtual network, made up of a loose confederation of people who came together in shifting, temporary configurations at different locations across the city. Although local nodes and communities of squatters existed in each neighborhood, they were increasingly linked. Their activities were facilitated not only by traditional meeting points in physical space, such as squatter cafés and *kraakspreekuren,* but by a diversified communication network that consisted of pirate radio and TV broadcasting, telephone trees (used to raise the alarm on a pending eviction), leaflets/pamphlets, and print media. Rather than floating above the city space in a network of superstructures, as in Constant's *New Babylon,* the squatter network floated on the airwaves and embedded in the cracks of the city. Once a property was squatted, an adjacent property might be infiltrated by cracking through the interior walls, alleyways, or roofs, leading to new configurations in space and the establishment of large multi-building mega-squats like the Groote Keijser, the Handelsblad complex, and the Wijers complex.[97]

93 Duivenvoorden, *Een voet tussen de deur,* p. 153; Mamadouh, *De stad in eigen hand,* p. 144.
94 Duivenvoorden, *Een voet tussen de deur,* p. 153.
95 Ibid., p. 156.
96 ADILKNO, *Cracking the Movement,* p. 114; Mamadouh, *De stad in eigen hand,* p. 144.
97 A detailed discussion of all three of these mega-squats is outside the scope of this chapter. In addition to this brief discussion of the Groote Keijser, this book looks at the Handelsblad complex as well, which is the building most associated with artists and artistic practice during

No space was ever stable or permanent. As BILWET write, "Because the rigid functionality of the house blueprint had been abandoned, a state of continual rebuilding could be established."[98] Like *Homo ludens* in *New Babylon*, where everyone is an artist and a player (although play and art are never defined as such), squatters arranged and re-arranged their spaces to suit their own desires. According to BILWET, "Squatters were artists because they moved into the empty space to play in it, and on no account to 'furnish' it."[99] Over the course of the decade, squatters in Amsterdam broadened their playground, not only to squats around the city and the country but also to various forms of print and electronic media.[100]

The squatter publication *Bluf!* was born out of a meeting on September 5, 1981, during which squatters discussed the "media need" in the movement.[101] On January 22, 1982, the first issue came out, and the publication ran until 1988 with a rotating editorial board.[102] Unlike other squatter publications, *Bluf!* reported on a much wider range of global activist issues beyond squatting in Amsterdam or the Netherlands, indicating an interest in moving away from the local/pragmatic stance toward a more international and intellectual/ideological position. The paper was led by Eveline Lubbers (who went simply by "Evel"), Geert Lovink ("Geert"), Jo van der Spek ("Jojo"), Kees Bierkart ("Kees"), and a variety of other activists over the years.[103] In a text

the era. The Wijers complex, the largest squat in Amsterdam at the time, located not far from the Handelsblad complex on the Nieuwezijds Voorburgwal, will not be thoroughly discussed, but it is noteworthy to mention in conjunction with these other two mega-squats due to the sheer number of different activities taking place within it, making it a veritable city within a city. In addition to dozens of diverse activities taking place in Wijers, both artist and architecture collectives also made the complex their base. For more detailed analysis of the Wijers, see Mamadouh, *De stad in eigen hand*, pp. 206–16; Duivenvoorden, *Een voet tussen de deur*, pp. 253–57; Owens, *Cracking Under Pressure*, pp. 133–68.

98   ADILKNO, *Cracking the Movement*, p. 44.

99   Ibid., p. 42.

100 Duivenvoorden, *Een voet tussen de deur*, p. 219; Owens, *Cracking Under Pressure*, p. 100.

101 Evel and Geert, "Bluf! Aan de Gang! Skriptie over de Kraakbeweging & Bluf," February 22, 1984, Instituut voor Sociale Geschiedenis – Staatsarchief, pp. 65–66.

102 Ibid., p. 69.

103 Caroline Nevejan, whose work in organizing conferences around emerging internet culture is discussed in more detail in chapter 4, was an active part of *Bluf!* from the beginning. Normally, squatters went by either nicknames or only first names within the movement, to avoid being targeted or identified by the police. Some later revealed the nature of their work in the '80s and are now professionally identified by their full names. There are still some former squatters who will not give their full name in print. See also, Bas Blokker, "'Ik Voer Actie Tot de Dood,'" *NRC-Handelsblad*, June 20, 2016.

about *Bluf!* written by Lubbers and Lovink in 1984, they state, "...from the first moment, the idea has been that the weekly would be an activist paper [...] [that] the paper must be for more people than just the squatters."[104] Commenting on the development of *Bluf!* in the context of other squatter media, BILWET writes:

> The inside [squatter] media were there to inform the outside world, but especially each other, what all had happened. [...] it was these papers and radio stations that were responsible for the larger whole you felt part of. [...] While a general movement paper like *Bluf!* considered itself a "megaphone to the media," when warning of a riot, for example, other scenes opposed it for exactly this reason, as a 'springboard for careerists.'[105]

The ideas fostered in *Bluf!* were part of a new front in the movement that was increasingly interested in the power of media, not only in the local sense but also in the sense that media could forge connections nationally or internationally. The editors published articles not only on local squatters' issues but also broader leftwing activist and social justice topics of the day.

By 1984 many of the original editors of *Bluf!* were moving on to other projects, leaving the day-to-day operation of the paper to a new group of people. In 1983 Lovink became involved with the aforementioned theory group BILWET (aka ADILKNO, "Stichting tot Bevordering van Illegale Wetenschap"/"Foundation for the Advancement of Illegal Knowledge"), whose other members included Arjen Mulder, BasJan van Stam, Lex Wouterloot, and Patrice Riemens. The formation of BILWET was a continuation of not only the internationalizing of the Dutch squatters' movement but also a desire to infuse the movement with some degree of intellectualism and theory, which had long been taboo for the pragmatically-minded squatters.[106] According to Lovink:

> Adilkno's media theory has to be read within developments in Amsterdam since the 1980s. This self-willed free state, international home and operations base of hippies, queers, the unemployed, artists and tourists, sat in the shadow of great upheavals on the European continent. [...] The anti-intellectual attitude of the punks' and squatters' movement, which have

---

104 Evel and Geert, "Bluf!," p. 49.
105 ADILKNO, *Cracking the Movement*, p. 95.
106 Ibid., p. 37.

been important breeding grounds for many media initiatives, embroiders on the general attitude that people should not chatter, but get to work.[107]

The synthesis of pirate and autonomous media and the volatile political issues around squatting created, within BILWET, the roots of contemporary new media theory in the Netherlands. This culminated in the internet art and theory of the early to mid-1990s, which can be traced directly back to these media "experiments" of the early and mid-'80s. The following chapters will look at art, pirate broadcast, alternative media, new media exhibitions/events, and—eventually—early versions of the internet and online mailing lists, which were influenced by and initiated by many of the same key players who were involved in the squatters' movement and the network of squats and squatter media in the Netherlands in the 1980s.

The relationships that BILWET cultivated with German squatters and theorists continued to be important in the decade that followed. Germany and the Netherlands led the way in new media studies at the dawn of the internet age due to the heavy cross-pollination of political and media theory between the two countries during the 1980s. In 1983 Lovink finished his master's degree in political science and sociology and decided to move to Berlin. He says, "And then, a big shift happened, also intellectually [...] I started to move away more and more from the day-to-day politics of the social movements. And I started to become more of a theorist in the making."[108] BILWET nurtured not only the existing activist and squatting connections in the Netherlands and Germany but also aided in the development of new media and media art theory that was emerging in the mid- to late '80s.

In 1990 BILWET published *Bewegingsleer: kraken aan gene zijde van de media* [*Cracking the Movement: Squatting Beyond the Media* (1994)], a hybrid text that both narrates the movement, mainly through quotations, and briefly theorizes on the makings of a movement and the clash of mainstream media and alternative "antimedia scenes" or "extra-media" activities. Writing at the dawn of the internet era, they comment on how hacking and disruption of the mainstream media creates the potential for both DIY media and also *liberation* from media. They write:

> The strategy is to fight the enemy with its own methods. [...] The antimedia scenes' lightning strikes cause puzzling breaks in the data circuits. They

107 Geert Lovink, *Dark Fiber: Tracking Critical Internet Culture* (Cambridge: MIT Press, 2002), pp. 276–7.
108 Lovink, interview by author.

briefly create media-free zones where meetings arise between people who suddenly can't get a picture and come to ask what's going on. The antimedia arsenal is unlimited: short-circuiting telephone exchanges, bringing satellites off course, burning down cable boxes [...] communicating with the hammer: 'Talking back to the media."[109]

Indeed, the *Talking Back to the Media* exhibition and festival in 1985 in Amsterdam, which is discussed in chapter 4, paved the way for this transition in thinking.

While hacking and destroying established media has its place, BILWET also write about the preference for "sovereign media," i.e., autonomous media like that which was developed in the squatters' movement. They write:

The sovereign media do not compete with reality, but aim to make it the exception. These are not conquered media, but handmade hybrids from age-old to hypermodern. They appear irregularly in print, on the air, in data networks. The program producers do not show themselves; we see only their masks in formats familiar to us. [...] The sovereign media dare reality to prove it exists by denying it. [...] While the media compress the world and history to screen size, the sovereign media move in the opposite direction. They suck us into a universe to sail the sea of noise and update the oceanic feeling. For a moment, only media exist. In this transit space, too, the thing is not to hang around too long, lest you end up in art or politics, for the sovereign media's denial of reality borders on that.[110]

This drive to "not hang around too long" is the ideal state of the temporary autonomous zone or the crack; the power of the resistance comes from its temporary nature.

As noted, BILWET classifies squatters as artists who make and re-make the spaces around them, echoing *New Babylon*. In the preface to the English edition of the book, Steven Englander writes:

ADILKNO considers squatters to be artists: they appropriate empty space in order to play in it, to live 'artfully,' but without the pretensions of the self-conscious creative personality. Their playground materializes through the occupation of vacancy by all sorts of interesting and useable junk discarded by mainstream society. In the *bricolage* constructed,

109 ADILKNO, *Cracking the Movement*, pp. 234–35.
110 Ibid., p. 236.

waste and refuse is [sic] assigned a new value, one in accordance with the transformation and transience appropriate to an often nomadic lifestyle that rejects permanence and stability as ideals, and as instruments to achieve a prosaic functionalism.[111]

And so, squatters, through media tools and in physical space, were bringing an alternate version of *New Babylon* into focus.

The squatters' movement and its use of media laid the foundations for an emerging theory of "tactical media," a term that was coined at the Next Five Minutes conference in 1993 and largely inspired by the theory of Michel de Certeau.[112] Developed by artist David Garcia (a co-organizer of *Talking Back to the Media*) and Lovink, the emergence of tactical media, which will be covered in greater depth in chapter 4, was still around a decade away, but its roots were already present. Garcia and Lovink define tactical media as:

> what happens when the cheap 'do it yourself' media, made possible by the revolution in consumer electronics and expanded forms of distribution (from public access cable to the internet) are exploited by groups and individuals who feel aggrieved by or excluded from the wider culture. Tactical media do not just report events, as they are never impartial they always participate and it is this that more than anything separates them from mainstream media. [...] Tactical media are media of crisis, criticism and opposition.[113]

Tactical media was more than media activism. Although it developed in tandem with internet art in the '90s, it was a continuation of the politically engaged artistic practices that emerged in Amsterdam during and directly after the squatters' movement in the 1980s. As such, it was defined by its temporariness. Geert Lovink writes that tactical media is "short-term concept, born out of disgust for ideology. [...] By definition, tactical media is nonsustainable, always on the verge of disappearance."[114] Although the term itself came about in the '90s, the practices underpinning it were present in urban space, through squatting, pirate media, and, even, in painting and street art.

111   Ibid., p. 8.
112   Michel de Certeau, *The Practice of Everyday Life* (Berkeley: University of California Press, 1984).
113   David Garcia and Geert Lovink, "The ABC of Tactical Media," <nettime> mailing list, May 16, 1997, http://www.nettime.org/Lists-Archives/nettime-l-9705/msg00096.html.
114   Geert Lovink, *Zero Comments: Blogging and Critical Internet Culture* (New York: Routledge, 2008), p. 187.

Homo Bellicus

> *Without anyone studying for it, the squatters discovered the three*
> *central principles of fortification formulated by Marshal Vauban*
> *at the end of the 17th century and put them into practice.*[115]
> – BILWET on the fortification of the Groote Keijser

The notion that squatters created a virtual *New Babylon* in the late '70s and early '80s in Amsterdam is not without its caveats, particularly with regard to the underlying motivations for the activities undertaken. While Constant imagined that freedom would be achieved through automation and endless leisure time, it was actually boredom rather than leisure that fueled the squatters' autonomy and eventual creative endeavors. Throughout his life, Constant refused to adequately address the essential dialectic at the center of his project, namely, the possibility that automation and lack of employment would create an overwhelming and perhaps oppressive idleness. This idleness could, given the right conditions, produce an outpouring of latent creativity, but the negative and destructive feelings around boredom would first have to be overcome.

Unlike Constant, his counterparts involved in French Lettrism and Situationism were deeply suspicious of automation and the promises offered by modern household gadgets.[116] Their writing on boredom, consumption, and modern convenience remain relevant to the creative activities of squatters in the '70s and '80s. For example, Ivan Chtcheglov's text, "Formulary for a New Urbanism" (1953) famously begins, "We are bored in the city," before offering a critique of the way automation has created a population "hypnotized by production and conveniences."[117] As Tom McDonough writes, boredom is "both the site of our greatest alienation and the site of that alienation's potential overcoming since, as Blanchot insists, boredom at least makes that alienation visible, perceptible: 'Boredom is the everyday become manifest: as a consequence of having lost its essential—constitutive—trait of being *unperceived.*'"[118] This section looks at the ways in which some of the squatters in Amsterdam in the late '70s and early '80s harnessed the creative potential of boredom for war games rather than peaceful play. Instead of *"Homo*

---

115 ADILKNO, *Cracking the Movement*, p. 49.
116 Lochner, *New Babylon*, p. 11.
117 Constant, in fact, expressed skepticism of Chtcheglov's text in his essay *Sur nos moyens et nos perspectives"* from *Internationale Situationniste* 2, December 1958. See Schaik, "Psychogeogram," p. 51; Knabb, *Situationist International Anthology*, pp. 1–2.
118 Tom McDonough, ed., *Boredom* (London: Whitechapel Gallery, 2017), p. 16.

ludens" occupying Constant's *New Babylon*, they were increasingly turning the city into a chess board and fighting for territory. While many squatters continued to playfully move through squatted fracture lines in Amsterdam, as detailed in the following chapters of this book, the squatters profiled in this section began to stake out territory in the city and arm themselves against the authorities.

Play, as Johan Huizinga defines it in *Homo Ludens*, opposes the everyday and thus opposes boredom and leisure. "Play is not 'normal' or 'real' life," he writes, "It steps out of it into a temporary sphere of activity with its own purpose."[119] Play has clear boundaries—what Huizinga terms the "magic circle"—and clear rules that may or may not diverge from the rules of the "real" world.[120] As such, play has the capacity to create temporary autonomous zones with their own governing rules. They are not only representations of but also demonstrations of what the outside world could be.[121]

Following avant-garde artists before him, notably Piet Mondrian and others associated with De Stijl, Constant believed that the realization of *New Babylon* would break down the distinction between art and life and create a society where, by dissolving the boundaries between normal life and play, the category of "art" would no longer be necessary.[122] Likewise, the Lettrists/Situationists rejected Huizinga's distinction between play and "normal life" and advocated for a revolution of playful existence in everyday life.[123] If art, in a defined form, ceases to exist once the creative acts that produce it are no longer framed or otherwise separated from normal life, play, should, by the same logic, also cease to exist once it has been merged with daily life. Both play and art require borders or boundaries if they are to be acknowledged and defined as such. It could be said that their power derives from this tension. Thus, *New Babylon*'s proposed continuous state of play, transforming everyone into an "artist," would eradicate the need for art *and* play. This is the essence of Constant's utopian vision: a total transformation of human life that removes the categories of art and play and makes both of these things, simply, everyday life.

119 Huizinga, *Homo Ludens*, p. 20.
120 Ibid., pp. 26, 28.
121 Ibid., p. 13-14, 30; Although the English translation of *Homo Ludens* from 1949 (which was translated from German) uses the word "representation" as one of two essential functions of play, Huizinga uses the Dutch word *vertoning*, which means to show, exhibit, or demonstrate.
122 Willemijn Stokvis, "Constants New Babylon en De Stijl," in *Constant New Babylon: aan ons de vrijheid*, ed. Laura Stamps (Veurne: Hannibal, 2016), pp. 28–37.
123 Lochner, *New Babylon*, p. 10.

Like the perambulatory "man of play" in Constant's *New Babylon* or Situationists on *dérives*, squatters and other travelling people have long been drifting through their own network of "sectors." The practice of squatting in the late '70s and '80s in Amsterdam incorporated essential elements of Huizinga's ludic man and Constant's *New Babylon* (which was likely received second- or third-hand via their Provo predecessors), but they were generally far less optimistic than their '60s counterparts. Their creativity was born more from the boredom of unemployment and lack of opportunity than from idealistic utopianism.[124] The boundaries between art and life, squatters and ordinary people, remained firmly intact, no matter how porous those borders were or how much they shifted through the urban space. The squatters' movement was, then, not a peaceful and permanent utopia but rather a temporary or brief appearance of playful, artistic, and (in the end) warlike resistance. Their temporary autonomous game created temporary autonomous zones, which forged new avenues for freedom and individual expression.

In the 1950s Guy Debord began developing a board game—a Game of War—which was patented in 1965 and published over thirty years later in 1987.[125] Although it was designed around an older, Napoleonic structure of warfare, Debord placed instantaneous communication at the center of the in-game conflict, nodding to the contemporary moment. The game is, in a way, the pessimistic double of Constant's *New Babylon*. Instead of an open-ended playground and labyrinth free from conflict, as Constant imagined it, Debord's game celebrates the art of war and struggle within a logically-arranged gridded structure. Both are built from complex interrelated networks, layered on top of each other, but one draws inspiration from an obsolete past while the other looks to an impossible future. While *New Babylon* fastidiously elides geographical concerns and the particularity of place, the *Jeu de la guerre* attempts to account for as many specific factors as possible.

In his explanatory text on the game, Debord writes that a true cybernetic synthesis of geography, communication, climate, psychology/morale, and the physical properties of military equipment was not possible within the

---

124 Constant, in fact, separated the "play" of New Babylon from the "boredom" of leisure in the contemporary city. See Constant, "Een nieuwe stad voor een nieuwe leven, 1959," in *Constant New Babylon: aan ons de vrijheid*, ed. Laura Stamps (Veurne: Hannibal, 2016), p. 206.

125 In 1987, after working on the game for several decades, Debord published both a limited edition and mass-market version of the game and an explanatory book, *Le jeu de la guerre*, together with Alice Becker-Ho. See McKenzie Wark, "The Game of War: Debord as Strategist," *Cabinet*, no. 29 (Spring 2008): p. 73; Sven Lütticken, "Guy Debord and the Cultural Revolution," *Grey Room*, no. 52 (Summer 2013): p. 120; Len Bracken, *Guy Debord: Revolutionary* (Venice, CA: Feral House, 1997) p. 214; Lütticken, "Playtimes," p. 139.

confines of a board game such as his, but he has at least considered these issues and has attempted to capture as many contributing vectors as possible.[126] In *New Babylon*, Constant envisioned humans as *Homo ludens* who had shed their animal nature, living in a world with no connection to the cycles of day/night, seasons, or the natural world. Instead of a timeless utopia of the present free from diurnal attachments and routine, Debord's game reflects the interplay of instantaneous communication with the constraints of geographic and material time.[127] Preserving lines of communication not only determines victory or defeat but the ability of the physical means of war to move and operate on the board.

Harkening back to the use of radios and walkie-talkies by the Situationists, the game creates pathways and connections through communication networks that are constantly changing and mutating. Debord writes, "This is a war of movement [...] where the territory has no interest in itself, but only by tactical or strategic positions that are necessary to an army or harmful to its enemy."[128] Immaterial communication networks are the key to forming temporary sites of resistance to the established order in physical space, a way to create new connections where both the physical architecture/ geography as well as the legal restraints limit new creation. In essence, Debord's game centers around claiming temporary autonomous zones, i.e., continually mutating strategic positions rather than revolution "with duration". Debord's game is therefore a useful framework within which to view the militaristic wing of squatters' movement in Amsterdam in the late '70s and early '80s, which contrasts the idealism of the previous generation of squatter activists. Instead of *Homo ludens*, the city was quickly occupied by *Homo bellicus* (human of war).

As detailed in the second section of this chapter, the Groote Keijser squat at Keizersgracht 242–252 became a lasting symbol of the squatters' movement and also marked a moment when squatters became more militant.[129] Despite the protestations of the *Homo ludens*-type squatters, like those in BILWET, that a squat as informal and open as the Keijser should not become a permanent fixture or a lasting symbol of the movement as a whole, the fortification of the Groote Keijser remade squatters as *Homo bellicus*, who drew their first battle lines there.

---

126 Guy Debord, "The Game of War," in *Guy Debord: Revolutionary*, trans. Len Bracken (Venice, CA: Feral House, 1997), pp. 248–49.
127 Ibid., p. 248.
128 Ibid., p. 247.
129 See Amanda Wasielewski, "From Rogue Sign to Squatter Symbol," *City* 23, no. 2 (March 4, 2019): 256–67.

Ultimately, the Groote Keijser was not evicted, as the city feared the levels of violence that might ensue if they tried to breach the heavily forti-fied structure. Instead, riots broke out across town around the eviction of another squat at Vondelstraat 72, on the corner of Vondelstraat and Eerste Constantijn Huygensstraat, between February 29 and March 3, 1980. A notorious property speculator owned the squat in question and the eviction came suddenly in the middle of the night. When the squatters attempted to re-squat the building on February 29, fights broke out with the police and the ME. The squatters set up barricades in the middle of the Eerste Constantijn Huygenstraat so that the tram lines were forced to halt their services through the area.

Unwilling to move from their barricades, the squatters put forth several demands: that the former residents would be allowed to remain in the property in question, that the police withdraw entirely from the scene, and that a recently arrested squatting activist, Nanda, be released from jail.[130] The mayor and police responded to the activists on the barricades by distributing leaflets out of a helicopter warning them that the police had been given discretion to shoot with live ammunition, if worst came to worst, and that people should remain in their homes. Twelve hundred ME personnel were brought in, including officers with machine guns, armored vehicles, water cannons, and tanks, which were used to roll over and demol-ish the barricades.[131] They were faced by ten thousand demonstrators who, in particular, took issue with the huge show of militaristic force in clearing the barricades from the Vondelstraat. Despite the upheaval and chaos of the conflict, the authorities agreed to all of the squatters' demands.[132]

The battle was over, but the war was just beginning. Major riots continued through 1980 over a variety of squats in Amsterdam and city residents grew used to the sound of the ME's sirens blaring through the city and the constant upheaval around street protests and riots. At the end of the year, the city announced the purchase of the Groote Keijser complex in order to turn the building into legitimate government-funded housing. The squatters reached a consensus that the radio station located in the building, which had become such an important source of information during that year, must somehow be preserved. The last broadcast of the Vrije Keijser from the Groote Keijser

130 Mamadouh, *De stad in eigen hand*, p. 145; Duivenvoorden, *Een voet tussen de deur*, p. 161; Owens, *Cracking Under Pressure*, p. 43.
131 H.J.A. Hofland, Ronald Hoeben, and Steye Raviez, *De Stadsoorlog: Amsterdam '80* (Alphen aan den Rijn: AW Sijthoff, 1981), p. 11; Mamadouh, *De stad in eigen hand*, p. 145.
132 Owens, *Cracking Under Pressure*, p. 43.

location was on October 26, 1980, after which it went mobile, broadcasting from a new neighborhood every day under the slogan, "Let a thousand antennas bloom."[133] Despite the relatively peaceful resolution of the Groote Keijser stand-off, the ludic playground was increasingly looking like a game of war, with each side moving their pieces strategically across the board.

The squatters' movement in Amsterdam had reached an impasse in the early 1980s. After the formation of HAT (*Huisvesting voor Alleenstanden en Tweepersoonshuishoudens*, Housing for Single and Two-Person Households) in 1975, the government was actually addressing the key demands the squatters had put forth since the late 1960s (i.e., that there was not enough housing for young people and young couples). Even if the progress was slow, HAT had finally begun investigating and purchasing squatted buildings to convert into legitimate housing for singles and couples in the early 1980s. The goal of *living*, which was at least partially being addressed, was then subsequently pushed aside in favor of continuing the struggle under altered terms. This is perhaps unsurprising as, by the early 1980s, many squatters had grown used to a high level of autonomy. The network of squats in the city afforded young people the ability to make and re-make their world as they desired, and they therefore found themselves suddenly unwilling to give up this freedom for a government-subsidized apartment.

Although mainstream squatter activism still revolved around a desire for concrete housing solutions, the more radical elements of the movement increasingly sought to maintain the status quo or even prolong the conflict, refusing any concessions or provisions made by the municipal or national governments (of which there were many). *Homo ludens* increasingly became *Homo bellicus* (the human of war) in the playing field of Amsterdam. Riding high on the successes (and spectacle) of the Vondelstraat riots a month earlier, squatters declared April 1980 "squatting month" and, on April 2nd, squatted forty-seven luxury apartments on the Prins Hendrikkade in the center of the city.[134]

Simultaneously, a group calling themselves De Autonomen (the Autonomists) began spreading flyers around Amsterdam to advertise a massive protest around the coronation of Queen Beatrix, planned for Queen's Day on April 30, 1980. Clearly inspired by the smoke bombs and protests that had occurred during Beatrix's wedding in 1966, the group used the slogan "Geen Woning Geen Kroning" (No Housing No Coronation), arguing that too much money was being spent on the coronation ceremonies instead of addressing

133 ADILKNO, *Cracking the Movement*, pp. 79–80.
134 Mamadouh, *De stad in eigen hand*, p. 146.

30 APRIL AKTIEDAG !

PRESTIGE OBJECTEN

METRO ; 2 MILJARD
(20000 WONINGEN)

STADHUIS _ OPERA
360 MILJOEN UIT
HUISVESTINGSPOT
(3600 WONINGEN)

KRONING ?
56 MILJOEN
(560 HUIZEN)

BEHARTIGT DE OVERHEID
HET VOLKSBELANG ? NEE!

Al tientallen jaren
wordt er door de
politiek verantwoorde-
lijken gekozen voor
prestige objecten:
Metro, Stadhuis, Opera
en nu dan weer die
kroning.
Alleen grote onder-
nemingen verdienen aan
dit soort zaken.

PRESTIGE OBJECTEN

PALEIS HUIS ten BOSCH
VERBOUWING 80MILJ.
(800WONINGEN)

DURE OBJECTEN IN
HET HELE LAND
VELE MILJOENEN
VELE WONINGEN

ONTRUIMING VAN DE
VONDELSTRAAT
10 MILJOEN
(100 HUIZEN)

DIT SCHREEUWT OM AKTIE (EN NU NIET LUDIEK)
LAAT DEZE BELACHELIJKE MILJOENEN ~
DANS NIET ONGESTOORD DOORGAAN
KOM NAAR AMSTERDAM
maar denk eraan : HELM HOOFDZAAK !!

Figure 3: *30 april aktiedag!*, 1980, poster, 61.5 × 43 cm. Internationaal Instituut voor Sociale Geschiedenis (IISG), Amsterdam.

housing needs in the city. The posters showed pictures of the future queen inside graphics of bombs [Fig.3] or alongside pictures of a demolished building. In their most direct appeals to nostalgia, the Autonomen also used an image from 1966 royal wedding protests for one of their posters.

Although representatives of the most militant wing of the squatters' movement, including Theo van der Giessen and Henk van der Kleij, were part of the Autonomen, many squatters saw the group as wholly separate from the squatters' movement and did not want to be associated with them.[135] In fact, Duivenvoorden reports that many squatters had no idea who this group was or where it had come from when posters started appearing around town.[136] As advertised on the flyers, the protests were supposed to start at 1:30pm on the day of the coronation at the symbol of leftist revolt, *De Dokwerker* (the Dock Worker), a sculpture near the Waterlooplein to commemorate dock workers and other working class Amsterdammers who resisted the Nazi occupation and persecution of the Jewish population by going on strike in February 1941.[137] As it turned out, protest actions were already well underway by the early afternoon.[138] Over the course of the day, battles between the police and rioters extended across Amsterdam, and the aftermath cast the whole movement in an unfavorable light.[139]

Even if sympathy for the squatters was on shaky ground after the coronation riots, the squatters' movement continued to grow over the course of the next year, as the frequency of evictions increased and the government/HAT tried desperately to appease the more reasonable elements of the movement with concrete housing plans. The battle over a squat in the museum district of Amsterdam from 1981 to 1982, however, marked a definitive turning point in public opinion against the more militant wing of the movement, which had largely hijacked the image of squatting as a whole. On April 4, 1981, a mansion located at Jan Luijkenstraat 3 and nicknamed the Lucky Luijk was squatted. The property was subsequently purchased by a well-known real estate speculation firm, Lüske and Bootsma, who set about arranging the eviction of the squatters so that they could sell the renovated property at a profit. Frustrated by lack of progress through legal means, the firm hired a gang of thugs to illegally evict the squat on October 12, 1981, as the police stood by.

135 Owens, *Cracking Under Pressure*, p. 83.
136 Duivenvoorden, *Een voet tussen de deur*, p. 170; Eric Duivenvoorden, *Het Kroningsoproer: 30 april 1980, reconstructie van een historisch keerpunt* (Amsterdam: De Arbeiderspers, 2005), p. 57.
137 Mamadouh, *De stad in eigen hand*, p. 146; Owens, *Cracking Under Pressure*, pp. 81–82.
138 Duivenvoorden, *Kroningsoproer*, pp. 96–101.
139 For more on the events of the day see Duivenvoorden, *Kroningsoproer*.

Figure 4: Tram on fire at the intersection of Van Baerlestraat / Willemsparkweg in Amsterdam following riots at the Lucky Luijk. Photo ANP, Amsterdam.

Outraged that firms such as Lüske and Bootsma were allowed to employ methods of illegal eviction with impunity, the squatters decided to try to re-squat the property on October 20, 1981, which surprised the new renter of the property, the hired thugs, and the police alike. In preparation for the re-squat, the leaders of the action decided to organize their followers into a quasi-paramilitary unit, which alienated many of their fellow squatters.[140] They reportedly staged training exercises in the countryside, drew up detailed strategic plans for how they would storm the building, and equipped themselves with bullet-proof vests, helmets, shields, and fire bombs.[141]

As was *de rigueur* by that point in time, the Lucky Luijk squatters demanded that the building be used as social housing. A group of squatters representing the building had even signed a statement saying that they would leave if that demand was met. After the municipal government offered to purchase the building and convert it into social housing—albeit for families rather than single people—the squatters occupying the building refused to stand by their earlier statement. According to Mamadouh:

140 Mamadouh, *De stad in eigen hand*, p. 149; Owens, *Cracking Under Pressure*, pp. 100–115.
141 Owens, *Cracking Under Pressure*, pp. 104, 108.

The squatters made it known that they would not leave the property and rejected their previous statement because they would have signed it under pressure. This move was widely reported in the media as a sign that squatters were unreasonable and untrustworthy...[142]

After much deliberation, the final eviction of the squat on October 11, 1982 resulted in another riot. A number 10 tram, set ablaze on the corner of Van Baerlestraat and Willemsparkweg, just outside the Stedelijk Museum [Fig.4], has become the lasting image of not only the riot but the beginning of the end for the movement. Although the media and the residents of Amsterdam largely assumed the tram was deliberately torched, the squatters maintained that the tram had driven through a flaming barricade and accidentally caught on fire.[143] The destruction during these actions further eroded any sympathy normal citizens had for squatters in the city.

According to Linus Owens, "Squatters viewed these challenges as robbing them of their power to define boundaries. They were no longer the ones contesting and redrawing the lines, their opponents were."[144] At this point the movement factionalized. There were many internal discussions about the increasing levels of militarism of the movement and many of the original squatters from the Groote Keijser and the Vondelstraat quit the scene.[145] Linus Owens's research into the decline of the squatters' movement in Amsterdam points to many complex reasons and fraught events that pre-cipitated the feeling that the movement was in decline by the mid-1980s.[146] He argues that the violence around the Lucky Luijk eviction and re-squat in 1982 was as a key turning point, during which internal ideological divides came to the fore.[147]

If the activities around the Lucky Luijk were a sign of decline, the death of squatter Hans Kok in a jail cell in 1985, after an eviction in the Staatslieden-buurt, provided a symbolic endpoint. After Kok's death, internal conflict consumed the squatters' movement in Amsterdam.[148] In the late 1980s, the

142 Mamadouh, *De stad in eigen hand*, p. 149. The fact that the city council earmarked the building for family dwellings rather than singles or young people—which would have pushed the existing squatters out—was one point of contention. Thus, it was not *any* social housing that the squatters demanded but rather social housing for themselves or people like them.
143 Mamadouh, p. 150.
144 Owens, *Cracking Under Pressure*, p. 103.
145 Mamadouh, *De stad in eigen hand*, p. 150.
146 Owens, *Cracking Under Pressure*; Evel and Geert, "Bluf!"
147 Owens, *Cracking Under Pressure*, pp. 89–130.
148 ADILKNO, *Cracking the Movement*, pp. 113–28; Duivenvoorden, *Een voet tussen de deur*, p. 280; Owens, *Cracking Under Pressure*, pp. 177–80.

PVK (*Politieke Vleugel van de Kraakbeweging*, Political Wing of the Squatters' Movement), a militaristic group of radicalized squatters, emerged from the war games of the Lucky Luijk and the retributive actions around Kok's death. They ruled the streets of the Staatsliedenbuurt with authoritarian zeal, through tactics of violence and intimidation.[149]

Despite the overall instinct toward movement and fluidity within the squatters' movement in Amsterdam, the PVK clung to the defense of particular buildings. In so doing, they failed to realize that the "territory" was not what was important but rather the temporary zones of resistance that were created in the cracks of the city. While their activities drew the "enemy" out, they also hastened the closure of the TAZ that had formed around the squatters' movement.

Combining graffiti with performance and installation, Stads Kunst Guerrilla (SKG) [urban art guerrilla] formed as a response to the militant tone of the punk and squatter movements, and their work delimited the boundaries of the cracked squatter territory. Active between roughly 1979 and 1981, SKG was primarily the brainchild of Erik Hobijn, who worked with a rotating cast of collaborators, mostly those who were part of the Handelsblad squat and the punk scene. Using the city as a platform, the group simultaneously embodied Constant's vision of a ludic *New Babylon* within the squatters' movement as well as the game of war and strategy, echoing Debord's fascinations. The idea was to create a parody of and a celebration of the aesthetics of leftwing terror organizations from the 1970s and Hobijn often labelled the activities of the group "artistic terror." Their mission was simple: they would try to bring art back to the streets in defiance of the elitism of the art world.[150]

SKG accomplished this through a variety of provocative performances and the use of graffiti. According to Hobijn:

> ...it was not important what you did, but the story, the myth [was important]. You didn't do documentation, that was very much rejected. Galleries or exhibitions were all totally uninteresting. It played out on the street and the trick was to get the story to go around.[151]

149 Seelen, *De stad was van ons*; Owens, *Cracking Under Pressure*, pp. 171–217. A detailed discussion of this period of the movement, featuring interviews with many of the main protagonists, can be found in the documentary *De stad was van Ons*.

150 Martijn Haas, *SKG* (Amsterdam: Lebowski Publishers, 2010), p. 34.

151 Geert Lovink, Interview met Erik Hobijn, accessed May 2, 2018, http://thing.desk.nl/bilwet/ Geert/HOBIJN2.txt.

This preference for the "subjectivity" of stories, as opposed to the "objectivity" of concrete documentation, is a key facet in Michel de Certeau's theory of spatial practice. It is also, in a broader sense, a constituent element of postmodern theory in that it seeks to move away from Enlightenment models of knowledge acquisition.

De Certeau sees stories as "tactics" of resistance, hallmarks of the "everyday" that counter the totalizing or geometricizing of space perpetrated by centralized systems of power (notably those modes of power initiated by the Enlightenment). He writes:

> ...the story privileges a 'logic of ambiguity' through its accounts of interaction. It 'turns' the frontier into a crossing, and the river into a bridge. It recounts inversions and displacements [...] it allows or causes the re-emergence beyond the frontiers of the alien element that was controlled in the interior, [...] to the alterity which was hidden inside the limits.[152]

De Certeau illustrates his point by outlining two models of space: "tours" and "maps." Tours are stories told through time, whereas maps present a static geometry, a marking of a place that bears no relation to time. He privileges the actions that bodies make through space—most notably, through walking—and the way that these actions form stories or narratives that create resistance to the strictures laid down from the established order or dominant systems.

Hobijn's performances and installations, since the late '70s, have often revolved around testing the limits of the body, particularly through the use of hazardous materials such as fire/pyrotechnics. The culmination of his experiments with fire and body-based performance can be seen in his work *Delusions of Self Immolation* (1993), in which a machine lights a participant, sheathed in fire resistant gel, on fire before extinguishing them. In the early to mid-'90s, Hobijn, like many of his former-squatter peers in the Netherlands, also tried his hand at creating internet art. The roots of both the danger and provocation of the fire machines and his experiments with internet art are rooted in the work he did with SKG in the late '70s and early '80s.

In addition to sporadic and often semi-spontaneous performances and installation, SKG were known for enigmatic white graffiti silhouettes that were prolifically painted around the city. Sometimes these silhouettes looked like the chalk lines of a crime scene, a lone cowboy or, as conflicts

---

152 De Certeau, *The Practice of Everyday Life*, p. 128.

Figure 5: SKG graffiti, 1980. Photo by José Melo. Internationaal Instituut voor Sociale Geschiedenis (IISG)/Staatsarchief, Amsterdam.

with the ME (the dutch riot police) heated up in 1980, rows of cartoonish riot police [Fig.5]. According to Hobijn, "A silhouette means that the police have been here and that a casualty has occurred."[153] All of the figures were accompanied by the letters SKG and sometimes also a star, mimicking the star logos of terrorist groups like the Red Army Faction (RAF) of Germany and the Red Brigades of Italy. For young people in Europe during the late '70s, as punk and anarchist subcultures were blossoming, these terrorist groups were tremendously attractive and many young people, at last superficially, sympathized with them.[154] According to Martijn Haas, students would often decorate their backpacks with pro-RAF doodles during those years, so it was not surprising that artists, too, were interested in using the aesthetic devices of those groups.[155]

In 1976 Hobijn and artist William Maghelhaes, reflecting on the popularity of the terrorist organizations of the day, came up with the idea to parody

153 Lovink, Interview met Erik Hobijn.
154 Michael Goddard writes that the RAF in particular was appealing to "marginalized youth subjects." Michael Goddard, *Guerrilla Networks: An Anarchaeology of 1970s Radical Media Ecologies* (Amsterdam: University of Amsterdam Press, 2018), p. 96. See also Diedrich Diedrichsen. "Geniuses and Their Noise: German Punk and the Neue Welle 1978-1982," in *Geniale Dilletanten: Subkultur der 1980er-Jahre in Deutschland* (Ostfilden: Hatje Cantz Verlag, 2015) p. 12.
155 Haas, *SKG*, p. 50.

the RAF logo as a way to "terrorize the tactics of the terrorists."[156] Dressed in combat clothing, they made the SKG star logo a kind of brand, painting it quickly in white paint on the walls all over the city. Maghelhaes soon abandoned the project, but Hobijn continued on with the sporadic help of artists Peter Giele, Marijke ter Rele, and David Veldhoen, all based in the squatted Handelsblad complex.[157]

The first major act of "artistic terror" that the group staged took place in September 1979. In August of that year, Tijmen Grootheest, the director of the Fodor Museum, a small museum affiliated with the Stedelijk Museum that was located in a seventeenth-century canal house on the Keizersgracht, was planning an exhibition of "young artistic talent" in Amsterdam to take place in September and October of that year. He received a request from a group calling themselves Stads Kunst Guerrilla with a proposal to participate in the show. The text read, "We are from the Stads Kunst Guerrilla and we want to barricade Fodor as a military fort, in order to portray the city at war."[158] The group proposed that they would blockade the museum with sandbags and barbed-wire fences, broadcasting fragments from Radio-Oranje—the World War II radio broadcasts of the Dutch government in exile in the UK. Meanwhile, artists dressed as soldiers would march back and forth. Grootheest and his colleagues ultimately rejected the SKG plan but did, however, showcase the work of many of their friends and associates, including Giele. The Fodor show also featured the work of neo-expressionist painters like Peter Klashorst and Maarten Ploeg and invited the pair to play a gig at the opening with their band Interior.

After hearing of their rejection from the event, SKG discussed ways they could disrupt the exhibition anyway. From a commune called the Leefwerk Kommune Keizersgracht, which happened to be adjacent to the Fodor museum and which was where Giele was living at the time, SKG planned their action. Giele's *official* project for the show was, incidentally, an installation of a Plexiglas window between Fodor and the commune, giving visitors a direct view into their way of life.[159] This official recognition and support from the organizers did not, however, stop Giele from helping plan the SKG intervention on the day of the opening.

156 Erik Hobijn, Pionieren in het buitenland: interview met Erik Hobijn, interview by Marianne Vollmer, De Nieuwe: kunstmagazine van Arti et Aemicitiae, June 2004, https://www.denieuwe. nl/Initiatief/artikelen/MarianneVollmer.html; Haas, *SKG*, p. 51.
157 Haas, *SKG*, p. 12.
158 Ibid., p. 11.
159 Ibid., pp. 14–15.

While SKG were busy preparing their action, the opening began to fill up with a mix of visitors, including everyone from elderly, middle-class art lovers to teenage punks in leather jackets. The graffiti artist Dr. Rat had already infiltrated the opening to staple some sheets of his own work, without permission from the organizers, onto an empty wall in the exhibition space.[160] As part of SKG's planned intervention, Hobijn and Veldhoen showed up to the opening, shuffling into the space, naked and wrapped in cellophane, with a plaster sculpture of a torso. The pair remained for a short period, attracting a bemused crowd of onlookers, before shuffling out again, leaving the torso behind. As soon as they were out of the building, a collaborator stepped forward to light a fuse on a firework positioned in the statue, which quickly filled the gallery space with clouds of smoke. Chaos ensued, as the police and fire department were called. Some of the visitors even tore through Giele's Plexiglas wall to escape the smoke. In the subsequent panic, an older woman fell down the stairs and had to be helped out of the building. She died a few days later.[161] Given that they now bore responsibility for someone's death (although they exculpated themselves by speculating that she was already ill), the SKG's "terrorist" antics had seemingly crossed the line from parody to reality.

Finding life in the commune difficult, Giele and Ter Rele began investigating carving out a piece of the Handelsblad building and making it livable in the summer of 1979.[162] This mega-squat was a collection of structures bordered by Paleisstraat on the north side, Spuistraat to the west, Keizerrijk alley to the south, and Nieuwezijds Voorburgwal. The centerpiece of the complex was the former offices of the *Algemeen Handelsblad* newspaper, which, shortly after merging with the *NRC-Handelsblad*, had moved out of the premises in 1977. Due to its association, in its last days, with the merger, many of the residents referred to the squat as simply the NRC.[163] The Handelsblad was originally squatted by a group of *lolkrakers* (squatters who did it for fun [*lol*]) named Oscar, Beer, Wouter, and Piet, who, while investigating an adjacent empty property, entered the labyrinthine space and discovered the insides of the complex were empty.[164] They told a bunch of friends about their find and, within a few days, it was filled. Expressing the ethos of the *lolkrakers*, one of the original squatters stated, "...we thought

160 Ibid, p. 15.
161 Ibid., pp. 16–17.
162 Ibid., p. 35.
163 Ibid., p. 19.
164 Martin Schouten, "De Wereld Is Een Kraakpand," *NRC Handelsblad*, March 3, 1979, Zaterdag edition, p. 193.

housing was something subordinate; having fun is much more important."[165] The maze of spaces, some still filled with printing machines and puddles of printers' ink on the floor, was christened "*speelplaats Keizerrijk*," the Keizerrijk Playground.[166]

Giele and Ter Rele were some of the original explorers to stake out space in the complex, following in the *lolkrakers*' wake. Over the years, Giele's attitude seemed to straddle the line between play and politics: he approached the task of building up and maintaining the space in a fun and playful way but was never attracted to the levels of all-out destruction that Hobijn and some of his collaborators executed in their work with SKG. Once a suitable spot in the complex had been found, Giele quickly pulled out a can of paint and scrawled a bed, a table, and a chair on the wall. In the re-telling of this origin story, Martijn Haas writes that, when a police officer arrived on the scene shortly after Giele had painted his symbols of a squatted space, Giele pointed the officer toward the drawing on the wall, declaring that he had legally squatted the premises.[167] This gesture, where the drawing becomes a viable stand-in for the three magical pieces of furniture that allow safe harbor within a squatted building, creates a poetic convergence of the game of squatting and the conceits of conceptual art. Squatting had become a fully ludic activity, and the symbolic significance of the table, chair, and bed was, effectively, enough to enter into the game. Recalling Joseph Kosuth's semiotic puzzle in *One and Three Chairs* (1965), the act of painting the furniture on the wall signaled that it no longer mattered whether the entry token was a representation of these objects or the objects themselves. The game or the frame was literally marked by drawings on the wall. In any case, the police officer, for whatever reason, decided that this was an acceptable enough proof of residency and left Giele and Ter Rele to their work.

After moving into the squat, Giele and Ter Rele busied themselves with constructing their own DIY spaces in the squat, starting with a gallery/ studio space Amok. Veldhoen also busied himself with other artistic projects. Although Hobijn remained close friends with Giele, Ter Rele, and Veldhoen after they had moved into the Handelsblad, the three did not remain SKG collaborators very long. According to Haas, "From their perspective, they interpreted the idea of a fictional artistic terrorist organization creating a unique public gallery space for themselves as, actually, wrong."[168] In a

165 ADILKNO, *Cracking the Movement*, p. 30.
166 Schouten, "De wereld is een kraakpand."
167 Haas, *SKG*, p. 36.
168 Ibid., p. 52.

later interview, Hobijn clarified that, despite the collective name, SKG was mostly a solo work. "It was actually not a group," he says, "For years I was alone. [...] I found that loneliness important because it was the era of the individual."[169] Even so, he still found many supporters and collaborators in and around the squatter and punk scene during the upheaval of 1980. Hobijn was an active part of the Handelsblad squat. As early as 1978, Hobijn was using the building to build sculptures and stage happenings, using DIY machines and fire as materials.[170] Like many of the punk-affiliated young people there, however, Hobijn was not involved in the day-to-day politics of the space. He says, "The squatters' movement was a big playground for us. The meetings were a blissful thing to hang around in, but you only did it two or three times because then it became boring."[171] Hobijn could, thus, be described as one of the *lolkrakers*.

Although SKG was very much Hobijn's project, he was able to harness a rotating cast of collaborators, particularly during the squatter riots of 1980. During the days of the Vondelstraat riot, Hobijn began painting little figures of ME agents around the city. The drawings were taken up by other sympathizers (not always known to Hobijn) and began to spread around the city, often with anarchy symbols or slogans such as "Housing is a right" (*"Wonen is een recht"*).[172] By the summer of 1980, Hobijn was joined in his SKG activities by Dr. Rat (Ivar Vičs) and Jos Alderse Baas, a frequent contributor to Handelsblad activities and the founder of the *NAP*[173] zine based in the building.[174] Like the event at the Fodor, the activities of SKG often took the form of a game of war, as groups of young men gathered to formulate militaristic plans.

One such dramatic plan was devised, and—of course—never executed, on the night before the coronation riots in 1980. Hobijn, together with Alderse Baas, organized a meeting at the Handelsblad on Queen's Night, which turned out to be a happening-*cum*-militia strategy session. They discussed plans to stage a coup and take as hostages the current Queen Juliana, the soon-to-be-crowned Queen Beatrix, and the prime minister, Dries van Agt.[175] Their hopes of attracting a large crowd for their wargames on that night, however, were thwarted by the lockdown of the building that the police

169 Qtd. Ibid., p. 53.
170 Ibid., p. 25.
171 Lovink, Interview met Erik Hobijn.
172 Haas, *SKG*, pp. 60–61.
173 Ibid., pp. 18–19. *NAP* mostly reported on the goings on of the Handelsblad residents.
174 Ibid., p. 103.
175 Ibid., p. 72.

had created in the lead-up to the coronation, which would take place just across the street at the Royal Palace at Dam Square.

Worried about the Handelsblad becoming a base for rioters, the police came into the building ahead of the coronation, registered the people living there, gave them ID cards, and blocked off the surrounding areas. The residents noted, with disdain, that this was reminiscent of the *Ausweis-passen* from World War II given to the Dutch by the German occupiers. The idea was that, on Queen's Night and the following day, officers would be able to check ID cards on who they would allow to pass into the area. In response to this move, SKG began to graffiti the war-era slogan *"Ausweis bitte"* ("ID please") around town.[176] Thus, due to the building being blocked off by police, only about ten people showed up to "play commando" at the SKG's "terror training" on Queen's Night. Haas describes the happening as "a sort of collective gestalt therapy, a manifestation of the subconscious dormant emotions through a pointed demonstration of the most intense feelings."[177] Despite the bluster of the SKG, there turned out to be a quite a gulf between these artists playacting militia activities and the reality of the riots the following day.

In preparation for the protest, the political wing of the squatters' movement had taken up residence in the attic of the Handelsblad to set up their radio broadcaster to communicate with those staging their protests around the city. According to Haas, "The upper world and the underworld of the squatters' movement—the 'real' squatters and the artistic squatters—lived, relatively speaking, side by side in the hours that followed."[178] On April 30, most of the participants in the happening the night before were off roaming the streets of Amsterdam. Hobijn, for his part, stayed in the area of the Handelsblad and the Royal Palace, staging a performance with fireworks that attracted a crowd of children.[179] Ironically, the would-be guerrillas, including Hobijn, were not actually present for the battle that took place around the corner from the Handelsblad on the Spui but, rather, arrived on the scene in time to observe the bloody aftermath.[180] They were more interested in harnessing the aesthetics of violence and destruction rather than actually participating in it.

Hobijn and his SKG collaborators regularly staged performance evenings in 1980, which they called Saturday Night Fevers. These semi-spontaneous

176   Ibid., p. 73.
177   Ibid., p. 75.
178   Ibid., p. 74.
179   Ibid., p. 76.
180   Ibid., p. 77.

events often incorporated costumes, elaborate constructions, and, in Hobijn's case, fire or fireworks. Hobijn regularly constructed large wooden towers, somewhat like rudimentary military watchtowers, covered in chicken wire. One such project, an installation he called the *Luxawam*, was meant as a comment on the housing crisis in Amsterdam and the luxury developments created by property speculators. This pyramid wooden living space was erected in the middle of the Handelsblad and, parodying corporate language, called The Tower Company.[181] In 1980, Hobijn abandoned the project and never came back to it.

Another tower, however, would arise in December of that year in Paradiso, a music venue established by the counterculture in the 1960s, whose staff had taken an interest in Hobijn and SKG. For the Paradiso performance event/party on December 20, 1980, Hobijn finally got to realize the pseudo-militaristic installation that he had proposed to Fodor the year before. Described as a *"terroristencongres"* ("terrorist convention"), a *"terroristennacht"* ("terrorist night") or a party in a *strafkamp* ("work camp")/*concentratiekamp* ("concentration camp"), Hobijn envisioned an event where there would be a jungle of tower constructions, piles of waste and rubbish, sandbag barricades, barbed wire, chicken wire, and loud noises echoing through the hall.[182] According to Hobijn, "The starting point would be a paradoxical thought: partying in a concentration camp, partying and dancing on a trash heap in an atmosphere of decay and destruction."[183] For the final event, Hobijn and his collaborators were able to acquire piles of animal manure from Artis, Amsterdam's zoo, and several cars from a local junk yard. They had plans to let live chickens loose around the venue, which were thwarted by animal rights activists, and to construct one of Hobijn's large fire displays, which was quickly nixed by the venue, but, as it stood, there were certainly enough elements of chaos and destruction on hand for the night. Instead of live chickens, the organizers came up with the idea of handing out eggs—without any real thought as to how those eggs would likely be used.

The program of the event consisted of performances by poets, punk/post-punk bands, and, even, a group of classical musicians, but it descended, predictably, into chaos in short-order. The young punks in attendance quickly got the idea to start throwing animal manure and eggs at each

181 Ibid., p. 91.

182 Paradiso, "Terroristencongres door Stads Kunst Guerilla," accessed May 6, 2018, https://www.paradiso.nl/nl/programma/terroristencongres-door-stads-kunst-guerilla/30417/.

183 Haas, *SKG*, p. 144.

other and the performers, flipping over the junked cars and playing in the
assembled rubbish. The bands performing in a cage-like construction Hobijn
had created within the tower were soon faced with a bombardment of eggs
from below and a shower of grain powder from above them in the tower,
as Giele and Alderse Baas dropped sack-loads of it.[184] According to Haas,

> For some young punks who were thirteen, fourteen, fifteen years old,
> this was Valhalla: a playground where you played little war games, with
> punk jackets as uniforms, shit as ammunition. They, of course, are already
> familiar with this. This is known territory. Vondelstraat was such an
> event. As was Queen's Day if you hung around the right places, like the
> Waterlooplein. There were already days like this in 1980, where they went
> out in the morning and, later in the day, encountered a destroyed world.[185]

In the end, the event at Paradiso was something of a finale for both SKG and
the upheaval of squatters' riots in 1980, a full expression of the evolution of
the movement into a fetishization of paramilitary aesthetics. The earnest
assimilation of militaristic aesthetics and war games within the confines of
both performance art and squatting was beginning to put pressure on the
boundaries that had been established, the frames and games that create the
magic circle. The magic circle where the space of play had been delineated,
was, through the wargames of artists and squatters in 1980, beginning to
look more like the chalk lines of the SKG silhouettes, marking a space of
death and stagnation. While militaristic tactics proved to be a dead-end for
the squatters' movement, there were still spaces of play, other temporary
autonomous zones, on the horizon.

For the squatters who opposed the more militant factions, such as those
connected to the squatter newspaper *Bluf!* and the group BILWET, squatting
was a synthesis of Debord's temporary strategies and Constant's timeless
play. As BILWET wrote, "Squatting was not a historical mission; it was
extra-historical space, with play as its fourth dimension."[186] The cracks
formed by the squatters' movement were closing, but new cracks were
beginning to appear. Increasingly, these cracks were formed in art and the
media, an immaterial space rather than physical urban sphere.

184 Ibid., pp. 175–97.
185 Ibid., p. 194.
186 ADILKNO, *Cracking the Movement*, p. 31.

2.   Cracking Painting

Abstract

This chapter addresses artist-squatters in the Netherlands, particularly the group of neo-expressionist painters known as De Nieuwe Wilden (The New Wild Ones). Although art schools around the country became important meeting places for artists during the late '70s and early '80s, rebellious young artists often dropped out or broke off from the more traditional curricula offered at these institutions in favor of pursuing collective DIY projects, such as starting their own bands and developing their own music/art venues in squatted spaces. Squatter venues like W139, Aorta, and V2_ focused on media art, performances, and anarchic exhibitions. At the time, artists in the Netherlands benefited from generous state subsidies and social benefits.

Keywords: Nieuwe Wilden, art school, squatting, neo-expressionism, social benefits, Netherlands

> *The Netherlands was not ready for it and New York wasn't either actually.*
> *The new art belief was a belief in non-new-art. We would make art*
> *that was not real art. Fake Art. Society and the authorities did not*
> *deserve any respect and neither did art history. No Future!*[1]
> — Peter Klashorst

In 1971 the teenage Peter Klashorst, together with a childhood friend, rode his motorized bicycle into the center of Amsterdam from nearby Haarlem, where he grew up. Telling his parents that he would stay with a cousin, Klashorst instead went straight to the Vondelpark, the central park of Amsterdam that had become a hippie campground in the late '60s and early '70s. The

---

1   Peter Klashorst, *Kunstkannibaal: Memoires van een beruchte kunstenaar* (Amsterdam: Prometheus, 2012), p. 77.

Wasielewski, A., *From City Space to Cyberspace: Art, Squatting, and Internet Culture in the Netherlands*. Amsterdam: Amsterdam University Press, 2021
DOI 10.5117/9789463725453_CH02

two teens wanted to get a taste of the counterculture life by sleeping out in the park among the young people who had flocked there from all over the world. Thanks to the Provo movement of the 1960s, Amsterdam had earned a reputation for liberalism and tolerance, as a center for youthful playfulness and hedonism.[2] The romanticism of the time left its mark on the next generation; the punk era kept the hedonistic playfulness while discarding much of the idealism of their predecessors. Klashorst, who dubbed himself a "New Dutch Master"[3], would go on to become one of the most infamous celebrity artists of the Netherlands. He was part of the Nieuwe Wilden painters ("new wild," after the German Neue Wilden), a short-lived neo-expressionist movement in the Netherlands from approximately 1980 to 1983. During this time, Klashorst and his peers were known for their sexually explicit expressive figurative paintings on disposable material and their provocative punk attitude.

The Nieuwe Wilden artists were vocally against conceptual art, which they saw as lacking expressive qualities. From a certain perspective, this was a period of macho painting, a wave of reactionary conservativism, and a rejection of the critical discourses around feminism, race, the media, consumer capitalism, and western imperialism that had been developed in and expressed through the art of the 1970s.[4] Although their work vacuumed up high and low cultural imagery indiscriminately, the only thing that was ostensibly off limits to the Nieuwe Wilden painters was high-minded declarations of art as idea (i.e., conceptual art). Likewise, the male-dominated return to painting could be seen an aggressive attempt to reassert the concept of western, male genius in art. Reflecting on his work from the early '80s in his autobiography, Klashorst says, "I was against everything. Against the established order, against museums, against galleries, but above all against conceptual art."[5] Within the limited scope of painting, therefore, the work of these artists could be categorized as purely

2   Ibid., p. 104.
3   Klashorst presented an exhibition of "New Dutch Masters" at Lucky Strike gallery at 16 Stuyvestant St. in New York City. The exhibition included installations and performance, curated by Christine Zounek and Hans-Peter Scholz and an "art sale by the inch" starting at midnight. He was mocked by the Dutch press for identifying himself as such. "Lucky Strike Art Showcase," May 23, 1983, Maarten Ploeg Knipselmap 16305, Stedelijk Museum Library; WvS, "Wilden," *Vinyl* 4, no. 7/8 (1984).
4   For a longer discussion of the problematic aspects of this work, see Amanda Wasielewski, "Between the Cracks: From Squatting to Tactical Media Art in the Netherlands, 1979-1993" (Ph.D., New York, City University of New York, 2019).
5   Monica Aerden et al., *Stop making sense: Nederlandse schilderkunst uit de jaren '80*, ed. Emine Kara and Loes Visch (Wezep: Uitgeverij de Kunst, 2013), p. 95.

reactionary, informed by a childish impulse to trash the progressive politics of their predecessors.

Seen a different way, however, the painting practices of the Nieuwe Wilden, which included the artists Klashorst, Rob Scholte, Maarten Ploeg, Sandra Derks, and Peter Giele, were but one facet of a complex constellation of media art practices that developed in tandem during this period. Despite their stance against conceptual art, much of the work they created contained elements of conceptualism. Moreover, they did not, at least initially, choose painting as their sole medium nor did they care about its triumphant return. Instead, the painters discussed in this chapter were, in the true sense of the word, media artists, toiling in multiple mediums simultaneously: painting, television/video[6], early computer/digital art, and installation. They did not limit themselves to painting, nor even to visual art, as many of them played in punk or post-punk bands alongside their artistic practices.[7]

These artists took a tactical approach to painting, cracking it open and occupying the spaces in between. If painting was an "abandoned" medium by the late '70s, not unlike the empty properties that squatters were claiming in cities around the Netherlands, then it could similarly be renovated and reconditioned under altered terms. As outlined in the first part of this book, the squatters' movement militantly "cracked" vacant property in Amsterdam in order to carve out autonomous platforms in the space of the city, creating what Hakim Bey has called temporary autonomous zones (TAZs).[8] For artists in the squatters' movement, this logic of occupation and squatting extended into their artistic practices. As Marja Bosma writes, "In the shortest time, painting, the bulwark of the establishment, was conquered, occupied, squatted."[9] Painting was not seen as an autonomous medium, separate from everyday life, but instead as autonomously occupied. Practically speaking, painting could no longer follow recognizable modernist rules, nor could it completely abandon its historical baggage. The way forward, then, was through the autonomy of the artists, not the artwork.

6   See chapter 3.

7   The theoretical relationship between German painters and musicians of the same era is theorized by Diedrich Diedrichsen in "Intensity, Negation, Plain Language" and "Geniuses and their Noise" in *Geniale Dilletanten: Subkultur der 1980er-Jahre in Deutschland* (Ostfilden: Hatje Cantz Verlag, 2015).

8   Hakim Bey, *TAZ.: The Temporary Autonomous Zone, Ontological Anarchy, Poetic Terrorism* (Brooklyn: Autonomedia, 2003).

9   Marja Bosma, "WEG met de steriele kultuurkathedralen! WEG met het ambtelijk kutkunstbeleid! op straat is onze strijd. de ESKAGEE leeft met u mee!," in *Peter L.M. Giele: verzamelde werken*, ed. Harry Heyink and Anna Tilroe (Amsterdam: Aksant, 2003), p. 147.

By the early '80s, a variety of image-making tools were easily accessible for artists—copying equipment, computers, video cameras, etc.—that gave them the ability to cut and paste/remix imagery copied from the mass media, but these new technologies were not the only tools artists used to remix images. The low-tech method of applying cheap paint to scraps of paper and cardboard also functioned as remix. It was an auxiliary way to participate in both the closed circuit of the media and the often-inaccessible contemporary art world without risking subservience to either one. In other words, painting could act, temporarily, as an autonomous zone. Artists took in the vast "image flow" of the mass media and, in turn, output their own flood of images, just as quickly but, often, with a roughness that stood in stark contrast to their source material. The autonomous space in which this outpouring of excess imagery was constituted was also a space where painting was *re*constituted as a media art practice.

The media art collectives that formed within art schools around the Netherlands in the late '70s gave rise to a variety of media art practices including those of the Nieuwe Wilden painters. These groups moved quickly to distance themselves from established institutions by organizing exhibitions and events in alternative, autonomous art spaces around the country in the early '80s. Their activities, in turn, were largely supported by a system of state subsidies for artists and unemployed youth that were deemed untenable by those in positions of political power by the mid-'80s. The Beeldende Kunstenaars Regeling [BKR, Fine Art Regulation], a welfare payment developed after World War II that offered support to visual artists in exchange for artworks, created a situation in which the government found itself responsible for a vast mountain of artworks piling up in storage facilities. The image flow of the artists discussed in this chapter, therefore, was paralleled by the literal image accumulation of the government. The early '80s were a breaking point for arts funding in the Netherlands, after which funding structures—and, consequently, the nature of artistic practice—fundamentally changed.

Art School as Laboratory

In the late '70s and early '80s, art collectives began to form in art schools across the Netherlands. A collaborative spirit took hold in these institutions and produced groups that engaged in music performance, publications/zines, painting, object making, and squatting. They forged their own galleries, bars, clubs, and music venues, and operated with a non-competitive spirit, which came more from a fatalistic punk attitude rather than an idealistic or unified political ideology. The Nieuwe Wilden painters studied primarily at the Rietveld Academy in Amsterdam, a group of multimedia and video artists came from the Jan van Eyck Academy in Maastricht, the punk art collective Kunstkollektiv Dubio (KK Dubio) came from the Academy of Fine Art in Rotterdam, and other artist-led initiatives popped up nearby other art schools in the Netherlands.[10] All of these groups, in different ways, were active in multiple mediums, had a relative disregard for traditional art institutions, and operated organically in collaborative ways. They all also relied on or took inspiration from the occupation of squatted property and the creation of alternative media and institutions seen within the squatters' movement of the time.

They frequently operated as bands as well as art collectives, and music was an essential part of this collaborative art scene. Between 1978 and 1981, both punk and a Dutch post-punk music movement known as Ultra (for "ultramodern") were flourishing.[11] The music scene in the Netherlands at the time was filled with art students from the Rietveld Academy in Amsterdam, the Kunstacademie in Den Bosch in the south of Holland, the Academie van Beeldende Kunsten in Rotterdam, and elsewhere. For example, one of the founders of the V2_ art collective, Joke Brouwer, was a drummer for the Ultra band Mini(o)on, Klashorst and Ploeg were part of the band Interior and then Soviet Sex, and Rob Scholte was involved with the bands The Case, The Young Lions, and Suspect.[12]

Several key figures in the Nieuwe Wilden movement, including Peter Klashorst, Maarten Ploeg, Rob Scholte, and Sandra Derks, studied at the Rietveld in the late '70s and early '80s, which served as a meeting place and staging ground for these artists to create their own DIY initiatives outside the institution. According to Klashorst, his time at the Rietveld was marked by a refusal to submit to a traditional art education. He says:

We started a club, a radio station, a pirate TV broadcast. I had PKP-TV with Maarten van der Ploeg and his brother Rogier, where we broadcast everything that we found interesting. [...] We were eighteen-year old boys with a TV broadcaster, it was crazy. [...] We were actually the forerunners

10   Tineke Reijnders, "Adressen van de autonome geest: kunstenaarsinitiatieven in de jaren tachtig en negentig," in *Peter L.M. Giele: verzamelde werken*, ed. Harry Heyink and Anna Tilroe (Amsterdam: Aksant, 2003), p. 178. See also Harold Schellinx, *Ultra* (Amsterdam: Lebowski, 2012).
11   Richard Foster, "'Afwijkende Mensen': Understanding the Dutch Ultra Scene," in *Postgraduate Voices in Punk Studies: Your Wisdom, Our Youth.*, ed. Laura Way and Mike Dines (Cambridge: Cambridge Scholars Publishing, 2017), p. 55.
12   Ibid, p. 58.

of MTV, which didn't exist yet. [...] We organized our own exhibitions in squats. [...] We didn't hold ourselves to the general rules of aesthetics. At the Rietveld total anarchy ruled. I had commandeered the gymnasium, which I used as a studio.[13]

As Klashort's description indicates, Rietveld students were eager to collaborate on projects across many different fields, with little care as to whether those activities fit neatly into the confines of traditional artistic practice. The work of Klashorst and Ploeg is a typical example of this collaborative spirit, as they, like many of their colleagues at the Rietveld, cooperated across media, both during their time at the Rietveld and shortly after they graduated. They were, at least initially, unconcerned with individual authorship and worked together to produce expressionist paintings that were exhibited, alongside their other media work, without individual attribution.[14]

The atmosphere of "total anarchy" at the Rietveld, as Klashorst describes it, had less to do with anarchist politics than with a general dissatisfaction with the status quo of the art world and a spirit of rebellion against it. This feeling was, in no small way, a reflection of the fact that, at the time, prospects for emerging artists in the small and quite traditional Dutch commercial art market were unfavorable, and youth unemployment was high. For the Nieuwe Wilden, therefore, the conceptual art of the previous decade came to symbolize everything that was wrong with contemporary art: buttoned-up, over-intellectual, elitist, and constrained.

Asked about the relationship between Nieuwe Wilden painting and anarchy, Sandra Derks says:

It was a completely natural state of affairs. So, it had nothing to do with anarchy. You just did what you did. [...] It was in that sense a sort of change in mentality that we had at the academy then. We were still in the academy, reckoning with conceptual art. [The stance against conceptual art] came out of that anarchy. So, it was not so much societal anarchy.[15]

The reckoning with conceptual art that Derks describes was, therefore, manifest in the rejection of its perceived "neatness" or mathematical

13   Robert Vuijsje, *King Klashorst* (Amsterdam: Vassallucci, 2003), p. 42.
14   These paintings were exhibited at Galerie Jurka while Klashorst and Ploeg were still students at the Rietveld. Not long after, they developed their own individual practices.
15   Sjarel Ex and Sandra Derks, interview by Maarten Westerveen, VPRO Radio, March 2, 2012, https://www.vpro.nl/speel~POMS_VPRO_186673~rom-87~.html.

regularity. In the Dutch context, "conceptual art" is typically defined (as it is elsewhere) as the pared-down, language and photography-based work of artists in the 1960s and '70s. This includes Jan Dibbets's photo montages, arranged around mathematical geometries, Hanne Darboven's installations of handwritten letters, numbers, and charts, and works like Stanley Brouwn's *This Way Brouwn* (1962), in which the artist asks people on the street to give him directions by drawing a map. Although conceptual art was itself a response to the limitations and constrictions of the art that preceded it, the Nieuwe Wilden artists felt that it had, in its simplicity and neatness, drained the life from artistic practice. In forming their reaction against it, they created work that was full of expression, figuration, and humor—all the qualities they felt their predecessors lacked. In order to achieve this, they employed an excess of media—old and new artistic practices as well as practices outside the confines of fine art.

At the Rietveld, the practice of making music together connected fluidly with collaborative visual art practices.[16] Perhaps more than any other art school in the country, the Rietveld Academy was a breeding ground for punk and post-punk bands in the late '70s and early '80s. Describing some of the musical experiments that happened during his time there, painter Rob Scholte says:

> ...there was Klashorst and there was Ploeg. They were in the same year as me. And we had no rehearsal space so we did it at art school. So there we met up with other guys in art school, and I remember an art school concert where two bands, we, the Case, and Klashorst and Ploeg with Interior, [I] think Peter Mertens had joined at that time [...] We had the idea of doing two live performances, two full sets, of two bands at the same time. We played our set and at the same time Interior played the other set; so we were completely concentrated on each other and at the same time trying not to hear the others. [...] So it was a conceptual performance.[17]

Scholte, in identifying the musical performances of these bands as "conceptual performance," highlights the ways in which the work of the Nieuwe Wilden was still connected to conceptual art while trying to develop a style

16   Richard James Foster, "'Afwijkende Mensen.' Formulating Perspectives on the Dutch ULTRA Scene" (Master thesis, Leiden, Leiden University, 2014), p. 38.
17   Rob Scholte, Digging Up Dutch Undergrounds – An Interview with Rob Scholte – artist – and of The Young Lions and Suspect, interview by Richard Foster, May 4, 2014, http://luifabriek. com/2014/05/digging-dutch-undergrounds-interview-rob-scholte-artist-young-lions-suspect/.

and ethos apart from it. Artists of the Rietveld, like Scholte, Klashorst, and Ploeg, were against conceptual art as a genre or style but not, seemingly, against developing their own chaotic form of process, concept, and ideas-driven work.

Tellingly, Klashorst and Ploeg choose to be in the audiovisual department of the Rietveld Academy (VAV), not the painting department. In an interview from 1984, published in the Rietveld's student newspaper, the two artists, who at that point had both won the most prestigious painting prize in the country for young artists, explained their rationale for joining the audiovisual department rather than painting. Klashorst says:

> Painting is not so very important in life [...] audiovisual [work] or glass-blowing is exactly the same thing—the technique is different. But the idea or the feeling that you work with can be exactly the same. I think that I could blow glass or sculpt just as well [as paint].

To this, Ploeg adds, "You choose the department where you can do the most things and that happens to be audiovisual."[18] It seems, then, that Klashorst, Ploeg, and other Nieuwe Wilden artists were primarily against the formal rigors of 1960s and '70s conceptual art rather than conceptual or process-based frameworks in general.

The role that art academies in the Netherlands played in the development of new media art, more than anything else, revolved around providing access to sophisticated media equipment as well as a central place for young creative people to meet one another. According to art historian Sebastian Lopéz, writing about Dutch video art in the 1970s and '80s, "The role of the art colleges has not been properly highlighted: as places for production and presentation, they provided the expensive hardware necessary for working in the new medium."[19] Jos Houweling, who was an audiovisual tutor for Klashorst, Ploeg, and Scholte, claims that it was the curiosity and inventiveness of the students of that era that transformed the role of the Rietveld, saying, "The Rietveld was no longer a school, it became a meeting place for like-minded people to exchange their thoughts."[20] He describes how he allowed the students to keep the

18   "Interview Met Peter Klashorst En Maarten Ploeg" (Gerrit Schoolkrant van de Rietveld Akademie Extra Editie no. 4, June 1984), Maarten Ploeg Knipselmap 16305, Stederlijk Museum Library.
19   Sebastián Lopéz, ed., *A Short History of Dutch Video Art* (Amsterdam: Gate Foundation, 2005), p. 15.
20   Vuijsje, *King Klashorst*, p. 44.

school's video recorder to use for their TV broadcasts, saying, "The school became a facilitating company."[21]

Houweling, in leading the audiovisual department with an open-minded attitude, was an ally and strong supporting presence for the artists of this generation. Reflecting on the role of the audiovisual department at the Rietveld in the development of his work, artist Walter Carpay, who was also at the Rietveld at the time, says:

> The free spaces in the city, the squats, already played an enormous role in cultural life at that time. You could experiment, make music, do performances, exhibit your own work, or have a beer there. My tutor at the Rietveld Academy, Jos Houweling, who ran the free department— in other words, the audiovisual department, for people that did not want to be stuck in *one* discipline—found it more important for the development of his student that they put time and energy into [their work] rather than come to school every time. So we were working in the squats more than we were present at the Rietveld.[22]

This official tolerance for experimentation and work outside the academy was not repeated in other cities, such as Rotterdam, discussed below, where the academy did not accept students' work on the street and in vacant properties as part of their course of study. Houweling, and thus the Rietveld, managed to maintain an intimate connection between the school and the activities outside of it in Amsterdam.

Commenting on the atmosphere in the art world in this era, curator Sjarel Ex says:

> I think that, in one way or another, more was shared. So, the squatters' movement was, of course, a kind of reflection of the artistic world in all the cities. The art academies were the real talent centers. They were cultivated there and were also always in communication with each other, so everyone that was important was immediately promoted and followed by everyone.[23]

For many of the artists of the era, the art academy was a launching pad for collaborative works. It made sense, given the lack of market competition

21   Ibid.
22   Harry Heyink and Anna Tilroe, eds., *Peter L.M. Giele: verzamelde werken* (Amsterdam: Aksant, 2003), p. 14.
23   Ex and Derks, interview by Westerveen.

for these artists, that they team up on projects rather than go it alone. Collaborative groupings emerged out of different art schools around the country and were often actively involved in the squatter activities of each individual city. Quickly, however, groups in different cities came into contact with each other and organized performances and exhibitions in each other's spaces.

For another group of artists, who were also active in Amsterdam in the '80s, the Jan van Eyck Academy in Maastricht was the initial "facilitating company" for their development as media artists. In 1971 artist Raúl Marroquin travelled to the Netherlands from Colombia, invited to study at the Van Eyck on a generous stipend. After achieving success with his work in Colombia and exhibiting in museums there from a young age, Marroquin decided to travel to the US to further develop his career. However, while Marroquin was making plans to go to New York, a museum administrator in Colombia, who supported the development of his work, applied to the Rijksacademie and Jan van Eyck Academy on his behalf, and Marroquin soon learned that he had been accepted into the Van Eyck. Not wanting to pass up the opportunity, he departed for the Netherlands, where he has lived ever since. Upon arrival, he was given an envelope of cash and sent straight to the academy, which was nothing like the art academies he was used to at home. He says:

> I arrived and I thought I was early. In Bogotá, the corridors were packed with people—packed! Here it was empty. Each one had his own studio or her own studio. I was very happy about it. No lessons, nothing. You just work. And I said, this is all very nice but where's the catch? So, I went to the administrative director and I said, everything is fantastic but what about the money? And he was like, 'Raúl, there are unlimited expenses.' Unlimited expenses![24]

Marroquin proceeded to use the resources of the school to the fullest extent, joking that he was the most expensive student that the Van Eyck Academy had ever had.

Several years after leaving the Van Eyck program himself, he guided other artists to the school. David Garcia and Annie Wright, a couple who arrived in the Netherlands in the late '70s from the UK, applied to the school at Marroquin's urging and had a similar experience of the institution. Garcia said:

> The Jan van Eyck Academy have an amazing printing operation there, where they can do very high-level printing things. And he'd [Marroquin]

24   Raúl Marroquin, interview by author.

studied there [...] so we did post-graduate at Jan van Eyck and, at the same time, we were building up in Amsterdam.[25]

Marroquin had been using the Van Eyck printing facilities to print his magazine *Fandangos*, a cut-and-paste publication that contained a variety of artist's works, photographs, and brief artist's texts often in a humorous or irreverent style. He enlisted Garcia and Wright to become its de facto editors so that he could continue to produce the publication at the school.

Apart from printing facilities, the Van Eyck Academy also allowed artists access to video equipment. According to Marroquin, when he first arrived in Maastricht, the Van Eyck was one of only two art academies in Europe that had video equipment, along with the Wuppertal Art Academy in Germany. Marroquin was introduced, via a friend at the academy, to the wealthy son of a Chinese restauranteur from Limburg, who happened to have the same video equipment as the academy. Using his new friend's equipment in combination with the academy's, Marroquin was able to copy tapes and create multi-channel videos as early as 1972.[26] He created a character called "Andy Dandy" who was shown engaging in mundane activities such as walking down the street or playing piano. The work he produced had an element of comic-book-like humor, eschewing the seriousness of other performance or conceptual art during the period. In *Monologue with Andy Dandy* (1974–5), thought bubbles appear over the character's head accompanied by cartoonish sound effects.

Aside from their connection to and collaboration with Marroquin on *Fandangos*, Garcia and Wright, who worked as an artist duo during those years, collaborated with two other artists at the academy, Lous America and Henk Wijnen. One of the first projects they did together was one in which they created posters and spread them around the city of Maastricht. After finding that their posters were amended and vandalized in interesting ways, they came up with the idea for another collaborative piece, *Posterama* (1980). Garcia, in the group's artist statement, says, "In fact, it was whilst working on this project that we became aware that, as interesting as our posters were, more interesting still was the response from local graffiti groups who attacked and undermined our work."[27] Staged in the central square of Maastricht, the Vrijthof, during the *Openbare Kunstwerken, Kunst 11 Dagen*

25 David Garcia, interview by author.
26 Marroquin, interview by author.
27 David Garcia et al., *Posterama*, 1980, http://www.li-ma.nl/site/catalogue/art/lous-america-david-garcia-henk-wijnen-annie/posterama/396.

[Public Art, 11 Day Art] festival in Maastricht from September 18–28, 1980, *Posterama* sought to harness the spontaneous public participation their earlier poster work elicited.

The set-up consisted of a simple wooden wall, positioned in the middle of the square, that the public was encouraged to alter and add to in any way they saw fit. In a video documenting the piece, a voiceover by Garcia delivers a statement from the group:

> In Maastricht, like any large town, there's a considerable subculture of graffiti and unofficial poster-making. What we wanted to do was take what is normally on the edge of people's attention and focus on it. Place it quite literally in the center as a wooden wall in the central square of Maastricht. [...] Quite apart from any social implications *Posterama* may have had, one of the main things we experienced was the sense of *Posterama* as a continually evolving painting. A painting that was forever making and re-making itself.[28]

The work was, thus, a way to formalize the process of graffiti into a sanctioned and certified fine art context (it was sponsored by an arts festival and explicitly defined as a work of contemporary fine art). The artists saw the work as a way to include those who might feel excluded from the inside of the museum or institutional space but, in so doing, also divorced graffiti from one of its essential qualities: its illegality.

While *Posterama* was inspired by the freeform irreverence of graffiti art, the form of participation that it solicited was largely artificial. The work was, in many ways, a formalized co-option or adoption of the aesthetics of the punk and graffiti scene by artists who were more interested in institutional connections and the official art world than some of their contemporaries. Given its open-ended format, *Posterama* invited a variety of responses, including at least one critical response: in the documentary video for the work, a group called the VIPs can be seen smearing "real bull shit" on the surface of the wall (i.e., painting the surface of the wall with excrement). According the artists' statement, "You could never work out whether it was a comment on *Posterama* or the festival as a whole."[29] This critical response was, nevertheless, well within the ethos of the work and the artists happily embraced it alongside other responses. The group—particularly Garcia—went on to create other platforms for public participation in the

28   Ibid.
29   Ibid.

years that followed. *The Underpass* (1983), which was inspired by pirate television in the squatter scene of Amsterdam, is described in more detail in chapter 4.

In Rotterdam in the late 1970s, the Academy of Fine Art produced another art and music collective, the Rondos/Kunstkollektief Dubio (Art Collective Dubio, KK Dubio), which was plugged into both the punk and squatter scenes in the city. The Rondos, the name of the group's punk band, was formed in March 1978 by a group of art student in the canteen of the school. According to Johannes van de Weert, none of the members of the band had any instruments nor had they composed any music when they agreed to perform their first gig for their tutor Sjoerd Buisman.[30] They went on to form KK Dubio, the visual art side of the collective, which they ran out of a condemned property they had discovered in the harbor area of the city. In a biography of the Rondos, Van de Weert writes:

> Most of us were fourth-year students and had no classes to go to. We were supposed to work independently in the studios. Which we did, to our heart's content. Most of our projects were meant to provoke, like the Art Collective Dubio and, at first, even The Rondos. One day we made a life-sized model of a tank and dragged it through Rotterdam. We took photographs of it in front of the town hall, the bridges over the River Maas ('Meuse') and the Euromast and left the thing on the station square, where it was attacked by a group of incensed members of the pacifist socialist party PSP. We loved the whole ruckus and exhibited the project in the academy under the name *Coming soon, German Panzerkampfwagen*. All of this to the great annoyance of many of our teachers and, to our pleasant surprise, many of our fellow students who wanted to be making serious art. Our goal was to get out of the stuffy atmosphere at the academy that we found blasé and lethargic.[31]

Like art students in other cities, the members of KK Dubio were drawn to a collaborative practice. Their work was playful, spontaneous, and provocative, and they were happy to work together.

The do-it-together attitude (or DIT, which is, perhaps, a more appropriate characterization for this collaborative spirit than DIY) was essential to the squatters' movement, where the practicalities of squatting vacant

---

30 Johannes van de Weert, "Rondos Biography: A Black & White Statement," 2009, http://rondos.nl/rondos_biografie/inhoud/RondosbioA4-EN.pdf.

31   Ibid., pp. 1-2

buildings necessitated a team effort: certain members of the community would specialize in plumbing, heating, carpentry, etc., and then help out where they were needed in other squats around the city. In 1979 KK Dubio had found the perfect base for their operations, a grand old vacant property in the Rotterdam harbor area, the Huize Schoonderloo. After threatening the local council that they would squat the building, which was slated for demolition, they convinced the council to temporarily rent it to them. This became the headquarters of their art collective. Van de Weert writes:

> At this time, we had our eye on a monumental white property, Huize Schoonderloo on the Tweede IJzerstraat in Delfshaven. Even the name of the street, 'Second Iron Street', was terrific. The building was empty and, as it turned out, had been so for five years. We rang the doorbell of the adjoining caretaker's house. The man rather unwillingly told us the property was due to be demolished and was in very bad condition. We glanced through the windows. It was just what we were looking for. We asked for more information with the Gemeentelijk Grondbedrijf, the municipal development department that turned out to be in charge of the building. 'In charge' being a bit of an overstatement. 'Neglect' sounded more like it. We got in touch with a man called Piet Slijkerman, a civil servant from the socialist party PvdA who worked at the Rotterdam Town Hall. We presented him with our plans. Saskia especially managed to keep Slijkerman's attention with her relentless perseverance. Rotterdam didn't have one of these yet: a living and-working collective of young artists. And just when Rotterdam wanted to present an image of itself as an 'art city'.[32]

Huize Schoonderloo quickly became a meeting point for the punks of Rotterdam. They started the zine *Raket* in September 1979 and produced, alongside it, books, fanzines, comic books, buttons, cards, stickers, and pamphlets at a frantic pace.[33] Their activity, like those of artists in other Dutch cities was a constant stream of imagery, produced as fast as possible.

The members of the art collective were so busy with the activities of their own operation at Huize Schoonderloo that they nearly forgot about their work with the art academy. The final year of their course did not require that they complete any coursework but was merely a studio year in preparation for the final end-examination exhibition. According to Van de Weert, they

32   Ibid., p. 3.
33   Leonor Jonker, *No Future Nu: Punk in Nederland 1977-2012* (Amsterdam: Lebowski Publishers, 2012), p. 83.

received a letter asking how their preparations for the final exam were going, and they then decided to do the exam as a group, as the Kunstkollektiv Dubio. As a response, they submitted a manifesto, in pamphlet form, that they had created in December of 1978 titled *Juliana Ja, Beatrix Nee*. Juliana was the Queen of the Netherlands until her abdication in 1980, when her daughter Beatrix took over the monarchy. In the beginning of the pamphlet, KK Dubio printed a *détourn*ed article on how television functions, replacing the word "television" with "KK Dubio."[34]

In October of 1979, they presented their end examination exhibition along with a publication that harshly denounced the close connection between the academy and the gallery system, art investors, museum conservators, etc.[35] They also denounced artists' reliance on the Beeldende Kunstenaars Regeling (BKR), a state program that was set up to buy artists' work in order to sustain the artistic output of the country after the Second World War and which, normally, ended up in large storage centers. They said, "It is, for us, unacceptable that our work often goes directly to the storage basements of the municipality via a BKR-regulation."[36] The exhibition consisted of their zine, *Raket*, posters and other print work, and a display of their music releases. They also proposed an alternative to the elite art of the gallery system: *stadskunst* [urban art]. They promoted "urban art that arises out of solidarity with the resistance to those structures in which one man oppresses the other."[37] The purest forms of these were not the expensive unique objects of the fine art world, but the anonymous graffiti on the walls of the city and the cheap reproducible videos, images, and music that KK Dubio produced. The group was ultimately denied their diploma for the project.[38]

Another artistic group formed around V2_, a space that began its life as a project of students from the Academy of Art and Design in the town of 's-Hertogenbosch (known as Den Bosch) in the south of the Netherlands. Although the connection between V2_ and the art academy was less pronounced than the relationships between the artists and art schools described above, it is unlikely that an independent art space like V2_ would have been started in this small Dutch town if not for the presence of the academy or,

34   Ibid., p. 87. *Détournement* is a Situationist term to describe the technique of subverting text or imagery by altering the existing material to function in another way.

35   KK Dubio, "Verklaring Bij Het Eindexamen," October 1979, http://rondos.nl/kunst_kollektief_dubio/index.php?id=abk.

36   Ibid.

37   Jonker, *No future nu*, pp. 89–90.

38   Ibid., p. 87.

for that matter, the presence of an active squatter scene.[39] Started by Joke Brouwer, Alex Adriaansens, and a loose collection of other young artists, V2_ was set up in a squatted property as a free, autonomous space, where artists could show the chaotic mix of multimedia visual art and music performances that they and their peers were making at the time. The idea of starting an independent art space was, at least partly, inspired by the censorious reaction they received for an exhibition they participated in at the University of Nijmegen. According to Brouwer and Adriaansens:

> In 1980, some young curators asked us to do an exhibition at the University of Nijmegen. We drove up there with a truckload of paintings and hung up large banners that said 'The university is occupied.' This rather alarmed them, as they felt that only students could occupy a university, not artists. The entrance hall of the building was covered in paintings that were either absurd or politically oriented. When the head of the faculty came to take a look, his first words were, 'This is not art!' He went on to say, on camera, 'My idea of art is a painting of 30 × 40 centimeters.' We edited the tape using the university's audiovisual department and then played it continuously on a monitor: this man crying, 'This is not art! My idea of art is...' Well, the audiovisual department was declared off limits to us and the tape was destroyed. Of course we then cut all of works down to this 'art size' and hung them all over the building. Things then quickly got out of hand so within two weeks the structures within the university were neatly exposed.[40]

Finding such preconceived ideas about art absurd, V2_ set no rigidly defined parameters for the type of work that would be shown there, which included a mix of performance art, painting, multimedia and video works, and performances by punk, post-punk, and industrial bands.

In summer of 1981, Joke Brouwer, Alex Adriaansens, Bart Domburg, and Roeland Rutten, who would later be involved with V2_, shared a studio space in Den Bosch at Guldenvliesstraat 4. They made a pamphlet of their work, published on June 17, 1981.[41] The pamphlet demonstrates the already burgeoning collaborative spirit among artists in the town

39   Reijnders, "Adressen van de autonome geest," p. 178. Schellinx, *Ultra*, p. 278.
40   Arjen Mulder and Maaike Post, *Boek voor de elektronische kunst* (Amsterdam: De Balie, 2000), pp. 81–82.
41   "Bart Domburg, Alex Adriaansens, Joke Brouwer, Roeland Rutten," 1981, R1997/0532 26 E 23, Stedelijk Museum Library.

and their desire to reach a broader audience. Shortly thereafter, on September 3–4, 1981, the first location for V2_ (and the inspiration for its name), Vughtenstraat 234, was squatted.[42] It was a raw, dark, cavernous space that was located across from a public square, which artists frequently used for projects that needed a larger outdoor space. According to Brouwer and Adriaansens:

> At first we didn't work interdisciplinarily but rather multidisciplinarily. All kinds of things were happening at the same time and we were overlapping each other. We painted, made Super 8 movies, and wrote. And we played in five different bands.[43]

Not content to remain in the relatively isolated confines of Den Bosch, the V2_ collective established connections to and collaborations with Belgian artists and bands such as Club Moral as well as other alternative/squatter art spaces in other parts of the Netherlands like W139 (Warmoesstraat 139) and Aorta in Amsterdam, which were both founded in 1982.

The collaborations outlined above were by no means the only artist collectives to form in and around art schools in the late '70s and early '80s. There were at least a dozen more independent artist spaces and groups that sprang up during the era, including De Ark in Enschede, an art collective founded in 1975 by students at the Academie voor Kunst en Industrie (AKI, Academy for Art and Industry).[44] Like the students at the Rietveld, a sympathetic tutor—in this case Geert Voskamp—supported the students who founded the collective, but not all art students found institutional support for their DIY and multidisciplinary impulses.[45] Facing grim economic conditions, where young artists had few prospects of either selling their work or finding steady employment, art students and recent graduates found the squatter lifestyle, with its DIY/DIT ethos, increasingly attractive. As a result, independent artist initiatives flourished during the period, and the attitude they embodied extended beyond occupying physical space. In the first few years of the '80s, the paintings of the Nieuwe Wilden

42 "Saturday 18 September," V2_, accessed October 19, 2017, http://v2.nl/events/zat-18-sept.
43 Ibid., p. 83.
44 Other notable initiatives were De Fabriek in Eindhoven, De Zaak in Groningen, Lokaal 01 in Breda, Archipel in Apeldoorn, Artis in Den Bosch, Planet Art in Hengelo/Enschede, Het Dropkollektiv in Hoorn, and Stichting ENNU in Tilburg, as well as Makkom, Sponz, Vol Sap, De Praktijk, Tetterode Complex, Stichting Edelweiss, and De Living Room in Amsterdam. See Geurt Imanse, "Kunstenaarsinitiatieven," April 6, 1984, Folder 1984, V2_ Archive.
45 Reijnders, "Adressen," p. 178.

exemplified both this squatter ethos and its attendant goal of autonomy from established institutions. The "abandoned" medium of painting, like the raw space at Vughtenstraat 234 or the decrepit Huize Schoonderloo, could be reclaimed and reimagined free from the associations that had once defined them.

Dancing on the Volcano

Part-subterfuge, part-sincere, the work of the Nieuwe Wilden was energetic, puerile, improvised, and ironic. Peter Klashorst called it "non-new-art" or "fake art," a characterization that simultaneously asserts and dismisses the idea that the work was "bad," naïve, or reactionary.[46] More to the point, as a statement against the ingress of critical theory and intellectualism into art, it became a kind of concept/theory of art in itself.[47] This internal contradiction was, evidently, an important facet of the work. The Nieuwe Wilden simultaneously decried conceptualism while pointing to the ir-relevance of medium in favor of ideas and expression. They celebrated total anarchy while renouncing the politics of anarchists. They lived and worked in squatted buildings and created their own galleries, clubs, and venues, but were also happy to link up with commercial galleries like Galerie Jurka in Amsterdam and pursue the spoils of commercial success abroad. Most of all, they ushered in a return of painting while toiling in many mediums at once.

Although their work reflected international trends in postmodern paint-ing, in that they disregarded distinctions between high and low culture and happily mashed together styles and genres, they went beyond rejecting image hierarchies.[48] They also, at least superficially, rejected the idea of intentionality in their work. The paradox in this was that, for the art market and the general public, a figurative painting did not need any high-minded declaration of intention to be accepted as a work of art and, thus, the return to figurative painting was, in some ways, a de facto conservative gesture. As Hal Foster writes:

46   Martha Tucker coined the term "bad painting" in 1978 for an exhibition at the New Museum and has become one of the terms used to describe postmodern painting of the 1980s.
47   Klashorst, *Kunstkannibaal*, p. 77.
48   Postmodernism in painting is associated with neo-expressionism, the return of figuration, and "bad painting" in the 1980s. Some scholars, such as Charles Jencks and Fredrich Jameson, place the beginnings of postmodern painting with Warhol and art in the 1960s, however. Charles Jencks, *What Is Post-Modernism?* (London: Academy Editions, 1986); Fredric Jameson, *Postmodernism or, The Cultural Logic of Late Capitalism* (Durham: Duke University Press, 2001).

...a basic opposition exists between a postmodernism which seeks to deconstruct modernism and resist the status quo and a postmodernism which repudiates the former to celebrate the latter: a postmodernism of resistance and a postmodernism of reaction.[49]

The work of the Nieuwe Wilden often balanced precariously on the border between these two postmodernisms.

Despite the creeping conservativism, the Nieuwe Wilden style in the first few years of the '80s was more resistance than reaction. Its execution was so forcefully improvisational that it was more akin to rude graffiti on a bathroom wall than traditional fine art—the artists often used trash and scrap materials, cheap paints, pencils, and crayons rather than canvas or fine art supplies. The paintings they produced were the polar opposite of conceptual art, with its sterile presentation, careful modes of display, and sophisticated ideas. Instead, the Nieuwe Wilden produced art in volume, taking a maximal rather than a minimal approach. These were not auratic paintings, works of individual genius laboriously and exactingly executed; they were rapidly produced, with little care given to the individuality of each work. The process of constant creation was often more important than the output or the exhibition of the work. Thus, it was the excessive materiality of their work that challenged the hegemony of art institutions and their methods of commodification and display, which was a complete reversal from the way immateriality in conceptual art of the previous generation had challenged the same institutions. The Nieuwe Wilden's radical counterpoint to intellectual conceptual art was dumb painting, carelessly constructed and produced in an endless stream that did not need to be labelled "art." As Ploeg said, "There must be a sort of contrast in it. A painting has to be very dumb and very intelligent at the same time, exciting and boring."[50] In place of neatness, emptiness, silence, constraint, small gestures, or geometry, they brought chaos and an ejaculation of material.

The work that Klashorst did for the punk club De Koer is indicative of these tendencies. In 1980 Eddy de Clercq opened a club on the Nieuwezijds Voorburgwal close to the NRC-Handelsblad building at Dam Square named after a Flemish slang word for toilet, koer.[51] Klashorst painted the interior

49 Hal Foster, The Anti-Aesthetic: Essays on Postmodern Culture (Port Townsend: Bay Press, 1983), pp. ix–x.
50 Leo Duppen, "De Implosieve Schilderkunst van Maarten Ploeg," Kunstbeeld, April 1985, Maarten Ploeg Knipselmap 16305, Stedelijk Museum Library.
51 Jonker, No future nu, pp. 218–21.

Figure 6: Peter Klashorst, poster for De Koer, 1980. Photo by Eddy de Clerq.

decoration and a poster for De Koer [Fig.6] that both feature the rough brushwork and vulgar yet cryptic figuration that was typical of his work during this time. The De Koer mural is an expressionistic city-scape with a large skull and prominent tribal-style mask on a cutout in the foreground, placed as a separate piece in foreground of what appears to be a stage set. A building with the word "Disco" is framed by other rough figures, painted with broad brushstrokes, dripping with paint in some areas. The floor is painted in a paving stone pattern (in Amsterdam, particularly in the old center where these squats were located, many of the streets are still paved with stones) and nightmarish creatures crawl up from the ground, imbuing the ordinary with an element of fantasy and danger. There is an improvised and automatic quality to the subject matter, composition, and execution, as if the artist was aimless doodling.

A similar stage-like painting can be seen in a video of Klashort's and Ploeg's band Soviet Sex that was broadcast on their pirate television channel, PKP-TV. The hour-long video from 1982 would have been aired on the PKP-TV late-night cable broadcasts, which are discussed in detail in chapter 3. The end of this particular video reel shows Klashorst touching up the paint on the homemade, roughly painted credits placards. He paints PKP's address and phone number before the camera pans away to scan the room and the video equipment, including a monitor showing the live video feed. The materials and process of both the painted sign and the video itself are thus irreverently exposed, both to document the action of making the work (as a more conceptually-minded artist might do) but also to express a nonchalant disregard for orderliness and professional production values.

The use of rough materials was not limited to the non-commercial or TV work that Klashort and Ploeg were doing; even their gallery work was presented without any polish or professional presentation standards. For their first joint exhibition at Galerie Jurka, Rob Jurka claims that the pair showed up with their work in rough form: "It was made on pattern-making paper, double folded, rolled up, rubber bands around it. It went up on the wall with pushpins, which was still very unusual at that time."[52] He subsequently asked the painters if they would paint on canvas instead of paper, since it would be easier to sell to buyers and easier to preserve. For Klashorst, however, paper was appealing precisely *because* of its cheap and disposable nature. He said, "I have only made a few paintings on canvas. We got that canvas from Rob Jurka. Otherwise we always paint on paper, the back sides

---

52   Rudie Kagie, "Klashorst En Ploeg," *VPRO Gids*, August 11, 1984, Maarten Ploeg Knipselmap 16305, Stedelijk Museum Library.

of posters for example. That works nicely. You can also quickly throw paper away. The investment has to be as low as possible."[53] Given the enormous outpouring of work for Klashorst and Ploeg at that time, the act of painting was more important than the result. In 1985 Ploeg asserted that "art is more than just the presentation."[54]

They sought to please themselves first and foremost, and their work was, as a result, un-mediated, un-filtered, and un-circumscribed. The attitude was, above all else, celebratory: a long party at the end of the world, or, as the press described the attitude of the time, "dancing on the volcano."[55] The group soon acquired a reputation for nihilism, a label that Klashorst rejected, saying, "The establishment may call what we do nihilism, but we don't call it that. Why don't they highlight the positive things? We are actually really positive, not constantly doom-mongering."[56] Despite his contention that he and his peers were not "doom-mongering," however, other statements he made at the time betray a deep pessimism about the state of society. In a 1982 interview after the release of his band Soviet Sex's single "Happy End," Klashorst said:

> I'm not at school anymore. I don't have unemployment benefits. It is, thus, a question of occupying yourself with staying alive. As a result, everything affects you very powerfully. It has to do with what I already said about that wild feeling. An idea of, we are just zero and the question of whether we ever become something more than zero remains. There is a wild feeling to go against the flow because, if I look around me, today's culture is still a very beautiful house with a beautiful façade and nice flowers in front of the window but it can, any moment, collapse because the foundations are rotten. [...] Like a sort of beast, we run against the flow to push back. Today or tomorrow the whole lot will collapse into itself, but I keep laughing [...][57]

This rebellious, youthful, "it doesn't matter anyway" attitude supported their unrestrained artistic production in that planning career moves or subscribing to accepted trends in art production did not hold them back from experimentation.

53   Cathérine van Houts and Jan Bart Klaster, "De Nieuwe Wilden!?," *Het Parool*, May 16, 1981, sec. PS Kunst.
54   Duppen, "Maarten Ploeg," p. 26.
55   Michiel van den Bergh and Maja van den Broecke, interview by author.
56   Houts and Klaster, "De Nieuwe Wilden!?," p. 23.
57   Joost Niemöller, "Een Wild Gevoel," *Plug*, April 1982, Maarten Ploeg Knipselmap 16305, Stedelijk Museum Library.

Rather than apocalyptic, the mood in Amsterdam's art scene at the time was somewhat *post*-apocalyptic, which fostered the impulse to build everything from scratch. The DIY spirit was tinged with a feeling of necessity and desperation. It was also largely collaborative; more DIT than DIY. Klashorst reiterates this stance, saying:

> We thought that we were going to form a new world order. Operating from squats, we did everything ourselves, we were totally independent. We kept everything in our own group. We read the books that we had written ourselves, we looked at the paintings that we had made ourselves, listened to the music that we had composed ourselves. [...] We didn't try to get on Dutch TV, we started our own TV broadcaster. We didn't try to get a house from the municipality, we squatted a place ourselves. We didn't go to the shop for books, we printed them ourselves.[58]

With their irreverent imagery, which often included phalluses, violence, and naked women, the Nieuwe Wilden was largely a boys club, and their work has been described by Sjarel Ex as containing a particularly masculine energy.

The poster that Klashorst created for De Koer, executed in grey-tones (most likely for reproductive purposes), exemplifies this dark, puerile masculinity. In the foreground of the poster, there is a figure with the grinning face of Mickey Mouse, standing in front of a skull and dressed in what appears to be a ruffled shirt and a plaid skirt (or perhaps Scottish kilt). The figure reaches down to lift the skirt with one hand while holding the other hand out to a dolphin (with one arm) who is half-submerged in a small pool, blowing water out its spout. As was typical of Klashorst's work, every figure in the composition is built on sexual innuendo. Penis projectiles rain down from the sky and a sun smirks overhead. Behind the dolphin are an assortment of figures: an electric guitar drawn in pen and which stands out from the rest of the painting with its thin lines and more detailed execution, a menacing muscular figure with a skull-like face next to an abstracted head with a beak-like protrusion, another spade-like shape, and another oblong figure that resembles a mushroom (or another abstracted penis) with a crude face painted on. The area around the figures is filled in with dark, rough brushstrokes applied in an uneven, patchy coating over the background with the words "De Koer" painted in white over the top. There does not appear to be any order or meaningful narrative surrounding the figures, some of which are rendered in great detail while

---

58   Vuijsje, *King Klashorst*, p. 45.

others are abstract cyphers. The combination of sexual, scatological, and pop cultural imagery was, however, representative of Klashorst's work at the time.

As Klashorst's involvement with De Koer demonstrates, clubs played an important role as meeting places and exhibition venues in the early 1980s, none more so than Mazzo, which was devoted to audiovisual experiments in the arts. It was home to both the younger punk generation as well as an older generation of media artists who had developed their work in the Amsterdam's alternative gallery and artist spaces of the 1970s. Mazzo opened its doors at Rozengracht 114, in the heart of the Jordaan district of Amsterdam, on June 6, 1980. The Jordaan, located on the western side of the canal ring, was a working class neighborhood for much of the twentieth century. In the '70s and early '80s, its vacant buildings were heavily squatted, thwarting redevelopment plans for the area. A group of young men, including Michiel van den Bergh, Michiel Romeyn, Hans Baaij, Ad van der Meer, Malcolm St. Julian-Bown, Bob Takes, Victor Tiebosch, and Fred Veldkamp started the club. Van den Bergh claims there was nothing like it in Amsterdam at the time—dance clubs open to a wider public simply did not exist in the city yet.[59] With contributions of about 4,000 Guilders from each member of the group, they rented and renovated the space.

Just before opening, Maja van den Broecke happened to wander into the club and Michiel offered her a job working the door. According to Van den Broecke, she was the first "door bitch." Van den Bergh says:

> We had articles in papers, 'dancing on the volcano.' And the volcano was the sign of the times. It could explode. The world could end. Which is totally ridiculous [...] But people seemed to think that. There's something always hanging in the air, disaster is coming. The whole punk movement came out of that.

Due to regulations governing liquor licenses, the club could not simply be open to the public, it had to be "members-only" in some sense. Van den Broecke came up with the idea to require that everyone who attended would be involved in audiovisual arts in some way. Asked why she choose this particular group, she laughed, saying, "Because there were Hells Angels in front of me and I didn't want to let them in!"[60]

---

59   Bergh and Broecke, interview by author.
60   Ibid.

For Van den Bergh and his cohort, Mazzo was not about commercial success or profits. He says, "Now everything's about start-ups [...] But this is commercial things. [...] We had to start up doing things, but in an artistic way. Why? Because there was a volcano and it would soon end all of this. It didn't matter." "—so let's have some fun!" Maja van den Broecke added.[61] The club became a hotbed of audiovisual experiments during the early years of the '80s. The club owned one of two video projectors in the country, the other being owned by the military. It was a massive, table-sized, expensive machine that was maintained by Fred Veldkamp, who was the technical wizard of the club. Experimenting with the machine, Veldkamp managed to concoct a connection between the early Apple II computer and the projector, which allowed artists to project early computer animations.

The club was one of the first venues to promote the emerging field of VJs (video DJs). Peter Rubin, who produced the majority of the slide and video shows in the early years of the club, was a pioneer of the medium. At any given time the room was filled with dozens of different slide projections, some doubled up on faders to give the impression of animation. The room was completely black and white so that the projections would form the decoration for the room, and the bar was a diamond-shaped light box with projections all around. According to Van den Bergh, the concept was simple—the décor could be constantly changing if they used slides instead of paint or permanent materials. Each week a new array of images could be projected. They even pumped odors into the room to accompany some of the imagery. Artists often came with hand painted or constructed slides to show as part of the club's program.

The space was also used for performances that required a larger space than other alternative art venues, in the days before Aorta, could accommodate. According to Van den Bergh:

> Galleries came. I had a connection with De Appel gallery for a couple of years. And they gave me connections for performances that were too big for them to handle, so they sent them to us. Josine van Droffelar and Wies Smals, the directors of [De] Appel. When they went down with the airplane in Switzerland, that more or less stopped the relationship. There was a very heavy connection. We also had a connection with someone who was taking care of photographers, agencies. They organized a gallery of photographers with slide projectors.[62]

61   Ibid.
62   Ibid.

Mazzo provided an early space in Amsterdam for larger scale multimedia installations. Once squats like Aorta and, to a lesser extent, W139 were established, artists had access to even larger alternative venues.

The club secured a variety of opportunities and funds through creative use of corporate backing. Companies were intrigued by the young artists and wanted to capitalize on the creative energy that was happening at the club. Van Den Bergh convinced the brewery Bavaria to prop up the club, and, due to its success there, helped Mazzo later secure bank loans for further development of the venue. Van Den Bergh says:

> Everybody had a little bit of money, but the biggest thing was the brewery. The guys from Bavaria, they wanted to have a foot on the ground in Amsterdam. And we told them what we were doing and I said I'm going to sell a million liters of beer. A year. I said, is that a good idea, do you want to invest? They said, yes, we want to invest. And we did, actually. [...] So that was a great thing. So we were top of the world. And they took that to the bank and said those guys want to borrow like 250,000 and we will back it up and the bank said, okay, here's the money. So we just started and we came up very much short.[63]

According to Van den Bergh and Van den Broecke, suddenly everyone wanted to come see what they were doing at Mazzo, and international magazines and people from abroad also came to see. Van den Broecke says, "And creativity was something back then. Nowadays everybody is creative, but at that point, it was really something special."[64] In addition to sponsorships from Canon cameras and other vendors that provided free building materials and equipment, Mazzo also received government subsidies from the Prins Bernhard Fonds, a cultural funding body.

After Mazzo opened and became the youth culture mecca of the city in the early 1980s, the PKP group of Klashorst and the Ploeg brothers decided to open their own more informal club in an adjacent squat, where the overflow crowd or the people who were rejected from Mazzo could hang out.[65] The less sophisticated or exclusive Disco Bizar at Rozengracht 149 was just up the street from Mazzo. As with Aorta, Disco Bizar was designed

---

63   Ibid.
64   Ibid.
65   Peter van Brummelen, "Kunstenaar Met Een Doe-Het-Zelf-Mentaliteit," *Het Parool*, February 21, 2004, Maarten Ploeg Knipselmap 16305, Stedelijk Museum Library; Houts and Klaster, "De Nieuwe Wilden!?," p. 23.

as an open-ended temporary venture. Peter Klashorst said, "Bizar is not a monument for eternity. Each Bizar evening is again a new evening [...]"[66] Like the squatted art institutions, the clubs of Amsterdam in the early '80s were primarily concerned with a quick-moving dynamism, producing a wall of imagery that was ever-changing. A growing art scene, propped up by ample government funding, was in a constant state of renewal and production.

Image Flow

> *I don't know if a painting that you work on for a year is better than just trying to make a hundred paintings.*[67]
> – Peter Klashorst

The Nieuwe Wilden seemed to enjoy their reputation as boyish pranksters and promoted themselves to a press that readily hyped their work and alternative squatter lifestyle. As Sandra Derks, one of the few women among the group, explains, "Maybe I have a little bit of a masculine attitude."[68] She elaborates on her involvement with the men in the group in another interview, stating:

> I had never realized that I was a woman because I only circulated in a man's world. But when I was 26, I came into contact with the 'official' art world and I was confronted with the fact that you are treated differently as a woman. That was really not a nice discovery. Now that I am a bit older, I hang around with women more. But in that time, I didn't because the people that I liked in the academy were men.[69]

The boyish attitude extended to the subject matter of the work. Between 1980 and 1984, the Nieuwe Wilden painters made work that was inspired by children's toys and characters from cartoons, films, and television, executed with quick, rough brushstrokes.

One work that was both a collaboration and a game in the spirit of the *cadavre exquis* was *Rom 87* (1981–1982) by Sandra Derks and Rob Scholte.

---

66 "Soviet Sex," *Vinyl*, June 1981, Maarten Ploeg Knipselmap 16305, Stedelijk Museum Library.

67 Houts and Klaster, "De Nieuwe Wilden!?," p. 23.

68 Ex and Derks, interview by Westerveen.

69 Cathérine van Houts and Pietje Tegenbosch, "Waar Blijven de Vrouwen?," *Het Parool*, December 31, 1993, sec. Kunst, Sandra Derks Knipselmap 04672, Stedelijk Museum Library.

It was an example of a more orderly, labor-intensive, and ambitious work from the period and has, since its creation, often been declared the masterpiece of the era. Originally shown at the squatted gallery space W139 in August 1982, the piece was inspired by a children's coloring book, which the artists purchased at Hema, a Dutch store that sells household goods, and displayed in a grid of eight by eight pages.[70] This was the first panel of an enormous nine-panel piece. For the second panel, the artists created a series of sixty-four paintings that incorporated the coloring book images, often adding a dark, science-fiction-like tone to the quotidian or cheerful objects in the original imagery. In one individual plate of this panel, where the coloring book showed a simple iron on a piece of cloth, the artists have painted the iron as it appears in the coloring book but with a swath of hieroglyphic-like symbols beneath the iron that look as if they are being somehow written by the iron, which is transformed into a kind of futuristic fax machine [Fig.7]. In an adjacent panel, a cheerful robot, depicted smiling and waving in the coloring book, is given a menacing grimace and a hammer. Each subsequent panel continues combining the imagery until the final panel breaks open the boundaries of the original coloring book pages as well as the rectangular geometric and mathematical conceit of the progressive panels, oozing out of the frame.

This formal dissolution in the progression of the panels, as well as the use of children's coloring book imagery, situates the work in opposition to (or, perhaps more accurately, in disregard of) the autonomy of painting. Even the title of the piece can be interpreted as a coded indication of the artists' disinterest in entering into a dialogue with either the modernist doctrine of medium specificity or more traditional forms of painting practice.[71] The title is taken from the text on a milestone that Derks and Scholte encountered while in Italy, which indicated that the city of Rome was 87 kilometers away. Riffing on the saying, "All roads lead to Rome," they decided to use "Rom 87" as a metaphor for the construction of the work.[72] The meaning of the phrase—that it does not matter what methods or means are involved in getting to the end, as the end result is the same—indicates a desire for openness or autonomy in the methods used to create the painting. In order to occupy or revive the practice of painting, as these artists did, it had to

70   Paul Groot, "Rob Scholte En Sandra Derks," *NRC Handelsblad*, August 20, 1982, Sandra Derks Knipselmap 04672, Stedelijk Museum Library.
71   Clement Greenberg, "Post Painterly Abstraction," *Art International* 8, no. 5–6 (1964): p. 63.
72   Adriënne Groen, "De Weg Naar Rome," *De Groene Amsterdammer*, March 1, 2012, https://www.groene.nl/artikel/de-weg-naar-rome.

Figure 7: Details, Sandra Derks and Rob Scholte, *Rom 87*, 1981–82, acrylic on paper, 44 sq. m. Rob Scholte Museum.

be open to hybrid processes in its execution—no more set rules on how a painting must be made. Furthermore, artists making paintings needed the autonomy or agency to create the final result—a painting—by whatever means they saw fit.

The work, then, reflects a stubborn refusal to engage with serious aesthetic theory. Its imagery is whimsical, surreal, and often darkly humorous, and the viewer is invited to play the game along with the artists, relishing the way various elements from the original images have been transformed and mutated over the panels. Although it takes children's imagery as its source material, it does not, ultimately, add adult-minded seriousness to those images.[73] Instead, the work takes the banal original plates of the coloring book and transforms them into an improvised fantasy. Due to their embrace of naïve or childish forms of expression, the Nieuwe Wilden have sometimes been compared to the Dutch CoBrA painters of the 1950s, such as Karel Appel, whose expressionist paintings also contained rudimentary figures and a child-like exuberance. Appel's work, however, reflected a primitivist impulse, containing colorful creatures and timeless, simple human figures. The subject matter of the Nieuwe Wilden artists, on the other hand, was darker and wholly entangled with the glut of mass media imagery surrounding them. Their work often depicted perverse or humorous combinations of family-friendly imagery, such as Mickey Mouse or coloring book images, engaged in violent or sexual behavior.

Although the Nieuwe Wilden artists were not keen to welcome the comparison between themselves and CoBrA, they found some things to appreciate about the older generation of artists. After visiting Appel in the US, Maarten Ploeg commented:

> He is not the very best painter of the era. I am more an admirer of his attitude than his paintings. He doesn't have any great stories or fantastic theories of his paintings. He is a normal person that continues seriously. He could, by his manner of speaking, as easily be running an auto body shop in the Jordaan.[74]

73   As is typical in primitivist movements in the modern era, this naïve posture is a reflection of a conscious decision by formally trained painters to "imitate" the untaught nature of children's work.

74   Rob Zwetsloot, "Maarten Ploeg: 'Je Moet Zorgen Dat Je Je Eigen Stroming Wordt,'" *De Waarheid*, January 26, 1985, sec. Kunst, Maarten Ploeg Knipselmap 16305, Stedelijk Museum Library.

The unpretentious, seemingly anti-intellectual attitude was, therefore, at least one point of continuity between the earlier expressionist and the Nieuwe Wilden.

Unsurprisingly, the artists of the Nieuwe Wilden did not find their way to painting through an admiration of national art heroes like Appel. For example, when Maarten Ploeg entered the Rietveld, he initially thought he wanted to be a cartoonist.[75] Although he turned toward the pursuit of fine art, Ploeg's work is as playful and irreverent as that of his peers in the early 1980s. During this time, he produced a zine titled *De hant* that was filled with comic strips and cartoon figures. Like Klashorst, Scholte and others, Ploeg painted freely on walls, cheap paper, and, even, scratched drawings on the backs of guitars, liberated from the need to construct discrete or orderly objects. While attending the Rietveld, Ploeg also spent a good deal of time repetitively painting cartoonish cars.

Ploeg's style was more abstract and unfocussed than Klashorst's during this time, but, given their close collaboration, strongly resembles his collaborator's work. His painting *Gevecht* [*Battle*], depicts a loosely rendered skeletal human figure on its knees with its hands in the air, a halo of fire surrounding it. Attacking the figure from all sides are crude phallic airplanes. Another untitled painting by Ploeg from 1981 depicts a human figure with a sword, spiky gritted teeth and closed eyes, apparently being washed over by a wave of white paint, a castle-like tower in the background. A snake with teeth, a bottle, a large apple and a smaller one, and a guitar sweep across the canvas to the left of the composition from the figure. Pencil doodles are scribbled into the white at the right of the composition. The work, like those of Klashorst, has an automatic, nightmarish quality. An uncontained mish-mash of symbols jostle for space on the page—childish, crude, and executed quickly with little compositional coherence. It is painting as nothing more than what the artist wills it to be: lived-in rather than vacant.

In 1982 Ploeg explored the life and death of painting more explicitly in an (unofficial) performance at the Stedelijk Museum, where twelve artists walked through the museum wearing painted masks [Fig.8].[76] Ploeg said, "The intension was to bring actually-living paintings into contact with other paintings."[77] The crude masks were reminiscent of Dada masks, cylindrical

75   Duppen, "Maarten Ploeg," p. 26.

76   Ed Wingen, "De Maskerade van Maarten Ploeg," *Telegraaf*, February 15, 1985, sec. Uit de kunst.

77   "Schilderijen Wandelen Door Museum," *Het Parool*, August 20, 1982, Maarten Ploeg Knipselmap 16305, Stedelijk Museum Library.

Figure 8: Maarten Ploeg and collaborators as living paintings in the Stedelijk Museum, 1982. Photo by Martin Grootenboer.

constructions made of crude materials with primitive faces painted on them. The artists wandered the museum for about an hour before they departed, and images of the performance appeared in the newspaper showing fellow museum-goers watching the performance with curiosity against a background of abstract color field painting. The performance, in a fairly transparent manner, critiques the status of paintings in museums as dead objects. In humorously communing with these dead objects as "actually-living" paintings, the work exemplifies the Nieuwe Wilden emphasis on vibrant creation, motion, and speed.

For the Nieuwe Wilden, two squatted art spaces gave spatial form to the chaotic outpouring of work they were producing: Aorta and W139. In both their commercial gallery exhibitions as well as exhibitions in these alternative spaces, the artists preferred to hang their work in the style of the nineteenth-century academy, stacked up the wall and right next to one another. They found it "pretentious" to hang painting one by one in a row.[78] While the mathematical constraint of *Rom 87* was an outlier in the image production of this group of painters, who were often unconcerned with neat, orderly, discrete works of art, its ambitious overproduction of imagery was typical, and the piece happened to be showing at W139 in August of 1982,

78   Ibid., p. 23.

at the same time as the inaugural exhibition at Aorta, *Beeldstroom* (Image Flow). While the space of Aorta was somewhat more polished than W139, both were characterized by a desire to create opportunities for young artists who were often struggling to find venues to show their work.

In the late '70s and early '80s, artist Peter Giele was living in the Handelsblad squat, an enormous complex of interconnected properties close to the Royal Palace and Dam Square that had formerly been the headquarters of the *Algemeen Handelsblad* and then the *NRC Handelsblad* newspapers. The first space that Giele set up there was a small workspace/gallery called Amok (as in "running amok").[79] As detailed in chapter 1, Giele and his collaborators at the Handelsblad squat had a penchant for provocation, and his opening day performance for the gallery was no exception. On Feburary 8, 1980, Giele planned to pose nude in the street-facing window of the gallery, offering "free life drawing" to the public. The performance, which was intended to last two hours, from noon until 2pm, was cut off after only half an hour by the police.[80] As a key member of one of the largest squats in the city, Giele was more connected to the squatters' movement than some of the other Nieuwe Wilden artists. After the Vondelstraat squatters' riots, in March of that year, Amok organized a photographic exhibition of the events of the riots.[81] By 1982, however, Giele was ready to launch a larger, more ambition space—Aorta.

In that year, William Lindhout, a tutor at the Rietveld, approached Giele and one of his students, Aldert Mantje, about using the space to construct and show a large-scale artwork. Inspired by this request to transform the squat into a larger art exhibition space, Giele began renovating the space with the help of eight of Lindhout's students; it was finished three months later.[82] The huge, cavernous space was called Aorta, as it was at the very heart of the city of Amsterdam, and the inaugural exhibition, in July and August of 1982, was titled *Beeldstroom*— "Image Flow". The poster for the exhibition [Fig.9] shows the space as the beating heart in the center of the map of the city with main arterial roads branching out in all directions from it. The idea of this beating heart pumping out images—an arterial stream of images—was very much in line with the working methods of the Nieuwe Wilden, who were producing imagery with little care to neatly packaged formulas or even to its preservation or preciousness.

79   Heyink and Tilroe, *Peter L.M. Giele*, p .10; Bosma, "WEG," p. 145.

80   Heyink and Tilroe, *Peter L.M. Giele*, p. 13.

81   Bosma, "WEG," p. 145.

82   Anneke Oele, "Jonge Kunst in Amsterdam: Aorta En The Living Room," *Ons Erfdeel* 29, no. 1 (February 1986): p. 350; Heyink and Tilroe, *Peter L.M. Giele*, p. 35.

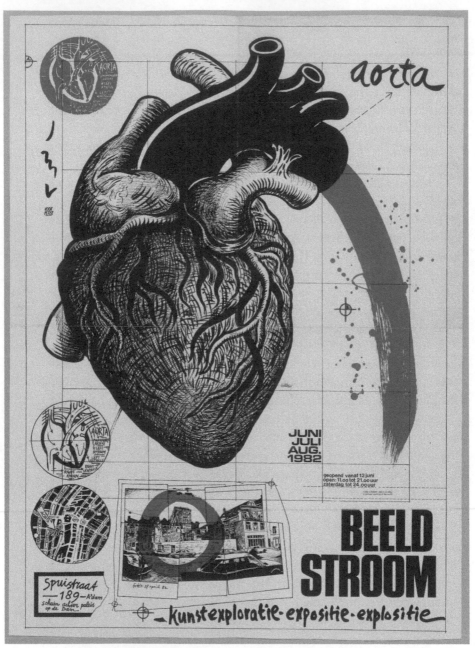

Figure 9: Jan Marinus Verburg, poster for *Beeldstroom* exhibition at Aorta, July-August 1982,
62 × 44.5 cm. Internationaal Instituut voor Sociale Geschiedenis (IISG)/Staatsarchief, Amsterdam.

Installation images from *Beeldstroom* show posters and paintings hanging *en masse* along the support beams on the ceiling as well as covering the walls of the atrium space [Fig.10]. Sculptures, performances, and videos were ongoing, and the exhibition changed throughout the summer. As artist Pjotr Müller described it, "Our point of departure is [always] different, so you can see an artwork grow here. Every ten days, the exhibition changes."[83] Aorta, as the beating heart at the center of the city, was in this way pumping life into not only painting but other media as well. For artists showing at Aorta, what was at stake was more than just output, it was having their work seen. At that time, the availability of the BKR meant that artists were earning money through selling their work to the government. The government, however, was accumulating vast warehouses of this work that never saw the light of day. Therefore, artists felt the need to establish their own spaces where their work could be shown, if not to a wider public, then at least to their friends in the community.

The task of clearing the space in the NRC-Handelsblad building was an enormous undertaking, as the building had never been cleaned up after it stopped being used as a printing facility for the newspaper. According to Harald Vlugt:

> Everyone was mobilized to deal with that building because it was a gigantic job: the concrete floor had to be poured, machines dismantled, in some spaces there was still a decimeter of ink, we had to build movable podiums. It was worked on for months. Eighty percent of all Amsterdam galleries were full of ugly etchings by Anton Heyboer and commercial prints by Corneille. Only the gallery of Helen van der Meij had an international outlook. For a young artist, it was almost impossible to land in a gallery. So there was an enormous need for our own artist's place.[84]

According to artist Walter Carpay, Aorta provided a much-needed counterpoint to the focus on conceptual art of the 1970s, saying, "Aorta, where hundreds of people were involved, is, of course, always a better breeding place for talent than the dead, academic hinterland of the seventies, where everyone was only busy trying to top Jan Dibbets."[85]

Apart from building exhibition spaces, Giele was also a painter and a performance artist who used his body as a medium in a variety of works he

83   "Een Eiland van Anarchie: Galerie Aorta in Het Oude Handelsbladgebouw," *NRC Handelsblad*, October 9, 1982, sec. Cultureel supplement.
84   Heyink and Tilroe, *Peter L.M. Giele*, p. 36.
85   Heyink and Tilroe, p. 56.

Figure 10: Installation view of *Beeldstroom* exhibition at Aorta, Amsterdam, Summer 1982. Photo by Fred Schoonberg.

performed at Aorta. For the opening of *Beeldstroom*, he performed a work titled *The Artist Dreaming of His Own Reality*, where he slept on a suspending door dangling across the central atrium. For the closing evening of the show on September 18, 1982, Giele performed once again, doing a cleaning ritual with his body smeared with paint, while suspended on a slim raised platform, high along the wall, again above the central atrium. In another performance by Giele at the space on January 29, 1983, he pedaled a bicycle for three and half hours while suspended from the ceiling with a sign saying *"De Hoop"* ["The Hope"] dangling in front of his face.[86]

Giele would later pour his energy into the iconic Amsterdam club RoXY. Even in the early '80s, he had an entrepreneurial impulse that sometimes struck his colleagues in the scene as a betrayal of the anti-establishment attitudes they held. One of the first acts that Giele initiated, along with William Lindhout and Aldert Mantje, shortly before the opening of Aorta, was the establishment of the Aorta Foundation on March 15, 1982, which made it possible for the initiative to seek government subsidies to fund its exhibitions. This was "something that W139 and V2 despised because you don't want to be eating out of the palm of an enemy's hand."[87] W139, for its part, claimed not to have received a cent of subsidies.

86 "Aorta Beeldstroom: De Enige Stijl Is Een Dynamische," *De Waarheid*, August 31, 1982, sec. kunst.
87 Bosma, "WEG," p. 148.

The line that organizations like W139 drew, however, was relatively arbitrary in that many of the artists of the scene were already receiving individual subsidies for their work from the BKR or, in the case of Klashorst and Ploeg, already earning money from showing in commercial galleries. According to Marli Luyten, briefly interviewed while hard at work in Aorta:

> For us, this gallery is an island. We all think anarchically, to just name something, and we hate rules, organizations, though you can't get around it. Not here either. Yeah, most of us have the BKR or have unemployment benefits. It is a luxury island. But we are not sitting around, cashing in, we don't do that. We give a lot back for it.[88]

The ethos of Aorta, more so than other spaces, was entirely open-ended. There was no dominant ideology, art theory, or agenda beyond providing a place where all work, including music, dance, and theater, was welcome.

Unlike V2_, for example, there was little curatorial discussion among the organizers over which artists would be included or excluded in the program. Although V2_ would often collaborate with Aorta, there were certain rivalries and differences in outlook between the two squatter spaces. For instance, the artists of V2_ thought they were taking their work far more seriously than those of Aorta.[89] They also felt, according to Bart Domburg, that Aorta was trying to be too neat and professional in its presentation. Domburg says:

> Those of us from V2 in Den Bosch were invited to take part in *Beeldstroom*, the opening exhibition of Aorta in June 1982. We had already been busy for a year [with V2] and always discussed what we thought would be interesting to show. 'Beeldstroom' was pretty disappointing despite the energy and the number of different things there were to see. I thought it was very non-committal. And when I saw that certain artists were vacuuming before the opening, I totally got it. [I thought that] Aorta [should not be] a gallery or museum where the presentation is more important than the work itself! [If] you are, with all of them, busy creating a free place, in order to show that it can be different, with a different energy, from the ideas and vision of the artist, then, I think you shouldn't be vacuuming. I was a co-organizer of V2, a really intensely political art center [...] We had an exhibition, bands and performances every weekend [...] I thought Aorta was relatively calm and stuffy. We also had real discussion in V2

88   "Een eiland van anarchie," p. 9.
89   Bosma, "WEG," p. 146.

whether we really had to show PKP, the circle of Peter Klashorst and the Ploeg brothers. We actually found it to be bourgeois art, CoBrA-like shit, old-fashioned. But we did it anyway. They made television, painted, played in bands. All things considered, we thought it was really good to show it all.[90]

Despite these rivalries and differences of opinion, however, there continued to be a strong connection between artists working in the numerous alternative art spaces around the country.

Ultimately, Aorta provided an open-ended platform—a space in the cracks or the margins of the city—at a time when many struggled to find venues to show their work. Asked to describe his vision for Aorta at the time, Giele said:

> We want a revolution in art-making. What I mean is to cultivate another mentality towards your work. That you, as an artist, think more of the totality rather than sit in a corner. In this building, anyone can show whatever style or concept. [...] We have our own little school here and we learn from each other. [...] There is no strict organization or agreed-upon ideology. It is altogether still early days and we would actually like to keep it that way. Art must dare to be temporary. Yes, Aorta is also temporary.[91]

Aorta was, thus, a quintessential temporary autonomous zone. As it turned out, the space ended up lasting for four years. It closed in June 1988, at which point Giele went on to found RoXY and pursue other ventures. Discussing the design of squatted spaces, artist Willem de Ridder has asserted that many squatted spaces, including Aorta, could be considered works of art. Giele himself came to see the building of Aorta—and later RoXY—as an extension of his own artwork, even though some of the artists involved in Aorta would have preferred that Giele spend the money he had for the space on the works shown within the building rather than the building itself.[92] Nevertheless, as artist Aldert Mantje, puts it, "Aorta was an artwork, the model for RoXY."[93] Although squatted spaces were acquired with no stake

90   Heyink and Tilroe, *Peter L.M. Giele*, p. 43.
91   "Aorta Beeldstroom."
92   Marina de Vries, "Wat is er nou lekkerder om te scheppen, om een beetje god te zijn," in *Peter L.M. Giele: verzamelde werken*, ed. Harry Heyink and Anna Tilroe (Amsterdam: Aksant, 2003), p. 171.
93   Heyink and Tilroe, *Peter L.M. Giele*, p. 36.

on legal ownership of the premises, there was an enormous desire to invest in the renovation and aesthetic renewal of these vacant structures, and Giele was one of the great builders of the era.

Not far from Aorta, on the other side of Dam Square, a group of artists from the Rietveld academy— Guus van der Werf, Marianne Kronenberg, Martha Crijns, Reinout Weydom, and Ad de Jong—started another alternative art space, W139 (short for Warmoesstraat 139). In the spring and summer of 1979, the group spent time touring Europe, trying to get their work shown in galleries and museums outside Holland. Since they had little luck in the endeavor, they decided that it would, perhaps, be better to focus their efforts on showing their work in their own city, and, in October of that year, they squatted the space on Warmoesstraat, a former theater adjacent to the Red Light District.[94] Although they began using the space to exhibit their own work in 1980, there was no formalized exhibition program until January of 1982. According to De Jong:

> The space in the Warmoesstraat was used as storage for the Bijenkorf [a high-end Dutch department store on the Dam Square], that was almost bankrupt at that time. We got the key from the manager, actually we got it 'with permission' and squatted the whole block. That made an impression. The political power of the squatters was very strong in those times. It wasn't much in the beginning. It was not even pretending to have a gallery. We cleaned the lobby, hung the work up, and sat behind a table from twelve in the afternoon until ten at night with a heater nearby and that was it. We didn't make any invitations, you called some people and then they came along. And we hung a note up saying, 'Come in.' Then the neighborhood children, people living in the neighborhood, and people who happened to pass by from the Red Light District came in to see. We also did not call it an artist's initiative in the beginning. It was also not an extension of the studio, that came later. Only when we got the backroom did the idea arise: you can paint and build things here. Only after the first large group exhibition in January 1982 did it get on a roll. That exhibition was called '30 Man Art' and a large group of people came down for that. For the first time, a sort of consciousness of the artist arose. The feeling that you were free to show the things that you wanted to show.[95]

94   Gijs Frieling, "Desire and Relevance: Curating for the Many at W139," *Manifesta Journal*, no. 10 (2010 2009): p. 29.

95   Heyink and Tilroe, *Peter L.M. Giele*, p. 10.

Like Aorta, the space provided artists with a free and autonomous space to show their work. As De Jong's description shows, W139 was, at least initially, more inward-looking than Aorta. Shortly after Aorta opened, Giele bragged that fifty people a day would show up to his space, while galleries could only expect about three.[96] W139, on the other hand, took several years before it evolved into a fully public exhibition venue.

Although Aorta was as huge and spectacular as W139 was small and subdued, both were nevertheless instrumental in showing the full range of work produced by the Nieuwe Wilden artists. Like Aorta, W139 saw itself as a place where artists could critique one another and learn from each other, a satellite school of their own making. De Jong says:

> At W139 your friends came to look. That was our goal. We wanted to show the work to each other and were ruthless, diehard in our critique. Nothing was good, we shamelessly broke each other down. I was, for example, in what Peter Klashorst called 'the worst band in Amsterdam' at the time […] The critique of each other's work was very fruitful. It gave an energetic impulse to continue working, to develop yourself.[97]

Like Aorta, W139 became a space where the image flow—the messy excess of production—could find expression.

One of the first exhibitions at W139, in January 1981, *Container Art* by Anno van der Heide, addressed both the flow of image production as well as the attendant government accumulation of artwork. Critical of the BKR and the careless way the government was treating the work it was collecting through the regulation, Van der Heide said, "The work that was bought went to the government, where it was meanwhile in large part stored. First in warehouses, later in containers, where especially a lot of graphic art molded and disappeared for good."[98] She goes on to point out that, via the BKR, the government was able to cheaply acquire museum-quality work and that many well-known artists from the latter half of the twentieth century including Karel Appel, Jan Dibbets, and Constant made use of the BKR at some point in their career.[99] For the exhibition, Van der Heide acquired a large dumpster, which was filled with her drawings and paintings. In

96 "Een eiland van anarchie," p. 9.
97 Heyink and Tilroe, *Peter L.M. Giele*, p. 44.
98 Anno van der Heide, "W139 – Container Art," accessed October 24, 2017, http://w139.nl/en/article/17404/container-art/.
99 Ibid.

addition to the dumpster installation, the artist included drawings, comics, and large abstract paintings. Like the work in *Beeldstroom* and the output of the Nieuwe Wilden, the exhibition was characterized by excess. The excess, in this case, came with the message that the government was not adequately respecting the artwork it collected via the BKR.

The work in the exhibition responded not only to the government's art policy but also to the increasing tensions around squatting in the city. One painting Van der Heide showed is interesting not only for its commentary on squatter evictions but also for its involvement of the viewer. It depicts the figure of a lone squatter facing off against a row of cartoonishly-rendered riot police, with a circular hole cut out in the surface of the painting where the squatter's head should be. Like a seaside or carnival attraction, viewers are invited to stand behind the painting and put their heads through, becoming comically implicated in the scene.[100] Rather than a typical "wish you were here" vacation text along the bottom of the painting, the text reads, "Holland über alles," echoing German fascism. This work, like others of the period, portrays a dark subject—the militarism of the police force—in a light-hearted and irreverent way. While it would be classified, in the broadest sense, as a painting, this work is also a platform for (albeit, limited) viewer participation. As such, it becomes a series of nested occupations. Aside from playing a part in the revival of painting during the era, which is already a form of squatting or occupation, this work is also *literally* occupied by the viewer. The role that the viewer occupies in the tableau is the role they have already played upon entering the gallery, which is itself a squat. The occupation of the gallery space is then reflected back within the scene of the painting as part of the broader occupation of the city around it.

After an initial period of sporadic shows, including Van der Heide's, W139 began putting on regular exhibitions in January 1982, beginning with *30 Man Kunst,* a group show that included work by thirty artists including Peter Giele, Rob Scholte, and Sandra Derks.[101] During the run of the exhibition, the exterior of the gallery space was decorated with a mash of sloppily applied graffiti and paint with the word *"tentoonstelling"* (exhibition) scrawled on the façade of the front of the building. The interior installation shows a

100 Ibid.

101 The full roster of artists who participated in the show were: Peter Giele, Marijke ter Bee, Martha Crijns, Harmen Dijkstra, Walter Carpay, Guus van de Werf, Marianne Kroonenberg, Bart Wils, Jan Verburg, Lies Gronheid, Rob Scholte, Sandra Derks, Merkjan Oosterhof, Koen de Keyzer, Maarten van Loon, Bas Oudt, Reinout Weydom, Tom Santfort, Ans van Campen, Harm Wallast, Mark [last name not listed], Ronald Heiloo, Ad van der Zee, Joep van de Bijl, Paula Witkamp, Alfred Banze, Bernhard Ingversen, Eric Holbein [possibly referring to Erik Hobijn], and Ad de Jong.

space filled to the brim with a chaotic mix of sculpture, painting, drawing, and a video work on a monitor. Judging by the photo documentation of the show, W139 was left in a raw state for its exhibitions, with unpainted walls and debris on the ground that melded contiguously with the sculptures and installations in the space.

While W139 still exists as an exhibition space today, it has gone through a number of permutations in the last four decades. In an attempt to survive the changing structure of arts funding in the mid-'80s, they put in their first government funding application around 1985. Shortly thereafter, they began paying rent on the space they were occupying.[102] While the rallying cries of the day were autonomy and solidarity, the government funding that propped up the young art scene was a constant source of tension.

Aorta and W139 were by no means the first alternative art spaces to pop up in Amsterdam. In the 1970s, several independent spaces, such as the In-Out Center[103] and De Appel Arts Centre, were set up to create opportunities for artists to show print work, performance, and video. Many of the artists who had been involved in those spaces, such as Raúl Marroquin, were active in Amsterdam in the early '80s alongside the younger generation of squatter-artists. Although those in Marroquin's circle, which included artists like David Garcia and Annie Wright, were initially unimpressed by the macho hijinks of the Nieuwe Wilden, in a small art scene like Amsterdam's, they often came into contact with each other. Despite a fair amount of mutual animus between the two groups, both benefited from the same system of alternative spaces and funding during the time.[104] Indeed, many of non-Dutch artists were in Amsterdam in the first place due to the presence of generous subsidies, funding, and educational stipends offered.

Land of Milk and Subsidies

On March 10, 1966, Provo activists made the front pages of international newspapers for setting off smoke bombs during the wedding procession of

---

102 Frieling, "Desire and Relevance," pp. 30–31.

103 The In-Out Center was an alternative art space that was active from 1972 to 1974, started by a group of international artists. See Tijmen van Grootheest and Frank Lubbers, eds., *Amsterdam 60/80: twintig jaar beeldende kunst* (Amsterdam: Museum Fodor, 1982), p. 92; Lopéz, *Dutch Video Art*, p. 15; Christophe Cherix, *In & Out of Amsterdam*, ed. Jennifer Liese (New York: Museum of Modern Art, 2009); De Appel, "In-Out Center" (De Appel Arts Center, Amsterdam, December 15, 2016), https://deappel.nl/en/exhibitions/in-out-center.

104 Marroquin, interview by author.

then-Princess Beatrix. Within a few years, the antics of the Provos, combined with the societal changes they pushed through, had made Amsterdam an unlikely international hippie hotspot. By the time John Lennon and Yoko Ono famously decided to promote world peace by spending their 1969 honeymoon in bed at the Hilton Hotel in Amsterdam, the city was well-established as an international countercultural mecca. Amsterdam's reputation for open sexuality and marijuana/drug-use attracted a growing international crowd of both tourists and transplants. Meanwhile, artists, including many openly gay artists, were attracted to the atmosphere of tolerance that was fostered in the wake of the Provo movement.

A decade after Lennon and Ono spent their honeymoon in Amsterdam, another couple—David Garcia and Annie Wright, two young English artists—decided to come to Amsterdam during their honeymoon and ended up making the city their new home. Wright, through her involvement with the feminist publication *Spare Rib,* had some connections to artists there, and the couple, short on money, got in touch with them to see if they could find somewhere to stay during their trip. Video artist Nan Hoover, herself a transplant from the US, was delighted that the couple were on their honeymoon and invited them to stay with her. She introduced them to Raúl Marroquin, who, in turn, urged them to apply to the Jan van Eyck Academy. After studying at the Van Eyck, they made Amsterdam their base.[105]

By the early '80s, therefore, Amsterdam was already a very cosmopolitan city, having attracted a vibrant mix of artists and countercultural types over the course of the previous decade. When asked why international artists were attracted to the city, Garcia answers that they came "for many reasons, including money." He explains:

> ...at that time, you know, it was the land of milk and subsidies. And, also, it was a very different—you can't imagine a more different political climate—because people from outside the Netherlands were welcomed with open arms. And, actually, if I'm honest, it was almost like international people were fetishized. And I think the Dutch people could be forgiven for getting resentful that maybe they were not getting the same degree of attention, and if you were somebody from outside Holland, you were by default more interesting [...] of course, for us foreigners it made it very interesting. And England, you know, Margaret Thatcher had just come in and it was a tough environment to be an artist there. And it

105 Garcia, interview by author.

was—wow—what's not to like? It's a complete no-brainer. And then we had all these friends and contacts, so we could segue into a scene here and then become part of it.[106]

While many of the artists in the art scene of the early 1970s and '80s were not Dutch, they nevertheless participated in a scene that was flush with state subsidies and money for artists and projects, courtesy of Dutch funding bodies as well as state subsidies for artists. This access to arts funding for international artists often started with postgraduate institutions like the Jan van Eyck Academy.[107]

In this book, the work under discussion is categorized as Dutch, even if it was produced by artists who came from abroad. This seems appropriate given that it was the scene in the Netherlands that fostered the kind of work they did rather than attachments to their respective countries of origin. Art historian Sebastian Lopéz similarly categorizes the international video artists he discusses in his research as Dutch. He writes:

> ...they are sometimes called international, at other times, Dutch, and more recently, migrant. [...] If we explicitly call it Dutch, it is to question, by contrast, the current situation in the Netherlands, and by extension in Europe, in which the national is negotiated between the colonial past, migration, the broadcast of constructed identities, and segregation.[108]

Indeed, much of the work of these artists, regardless of their national origin, sexual orientation, or gender, eschewed identity politics and instead focused on consumer culture and a globalized media landscape. The Dutch scene was a place to explore universals rather than specific identities, despite (or, perhaps, due to) the international character of the scene.

Even though the scene attracted a relatively large number of international figures, it was still extremely locally-oriented. Although it is the capital city of the Netherlands, Amsterdam still felt like a small community in the early 1980s. According to Michiel van den Bergh, one of the founders of Mazzo, "Everybody, who is now in our age, came to Mazzo. Everybody." Both Van den Bergh and Maja van den Broecke, who worked the door at Mazzo, insisted that, since there were no other options in 1980–82, an entire generation

---

106 Ibid.
107 The the other two of the big three two-year residencies in the Netherlands that attracted international artists were the Rijksakademie and De Ateliers (formerly Ateliers '63).
108 Lopéz, *Dutch Video Art*, pp. 9–10.

met in Mazzo.[109] Speaking about his role in the Ultra music scene, painter Rob Scholte says:

> When people discuss my historical position or what I've done with my art and my music, I always say, we are pre-internet. What ULTRA is, is a pre-internet movement; and that is very, very important. So as a characteristic, it has something local, it has something small, it has something that is not spreading like wildfire because it couldn't spread like wildfire, because you had to invite people by mail. In 1980s we had the first fax machine; ten years later we had the first email. But we are 1978, 1979, 1980. I mean we printed posters, and put them up in the city [...] it is pure, it is local, it is limited, it is human in a sense that it is just there if you're there, and nothing else. [...] And the same with my art career, because my art career is before the internet even though in a way my art is about the internet, about reproduction about copyright and so on.[110]

While the international figures entered the scene from the outside, they quickly became part of a small local community that rarely reached an audience outside of the Netherlands. While a few artists in the Dutch scene attempted to break into galleries in other countries, the majority of them were content to produce work within the Netherlands, where government funding provided a level of comfort for artists that was largely unmatched in other countries that were turning toward the neoliberal economic policies of Reagan and Thatcher.

The normalization of being on unemployment benefits was an important facet of culture in the arts in the early 1980s. According to Van den Bergh, "At that moment in time, it was still good if you had an *uitkering* [unemployment benefits]. If you were on the dole, no one cared. You were modern, you were hip. It has totally changed in the culture now. Now, you're a loser if you're on the dole."[111] Not only did the prevalence of unemployment benefits provide for the material needs of the art scene's denizens but it also created an atmosphere of collaboration and non-competitiveness. Hardly anyone at the time was overly interested in commercial gains. Maarten Ploeg says, "We did everything; there was no commercial idea behind it. We made music, set up a pirate TV station. Money played no role, the unemployment benefits

109 Bergh and Broecke, interview by author.
110 Scholte, Digging Up Dutch.
111 Bergh and Broecke, interview by author.

were high. The movement that we set in motion, that was important."[112] According to curator Sjarel Ex, "For a long time... at that time, I thought we were not in competition with each other. The artists weren't either."[113] He goes on to say that that, by 1985, that lack of competition and collaborative spirit had dissipated. Sandra Derks also places the turning point around 1984 or 1985, saying, "What I think happened [in '84] is that all those movements were very quickly incorporated into all sorts of other movements. So, you also get a turnaround in the whole thinking. [...] You get the yuppie coming up in that time, '85, '86. So, everything went. The punk went out and the slick suit came in. And it was an enormously quick turnaround."[114] The change in funding structures, commercial dynamics and the housing market undoubtedly affected the level of collaboration that artists had in the latter part of the 1980s.

Geert Lovink, founder of the squatter newspaper *Bluf!* and pioneering new media theorist, lived on unemployment benefits for nine years. He said, "There were no jobs anyway. There were no jobs in the Netherlands. So it was really a very dark period. It was a period of mass unemployment."[115] While the unemployment was real, there was also no incentive to get off unemployment benefits, which according to Lovink were easy enough to maintain if one knew how to navigate the bureaucracy. Indeed, many in the squatters' movement and the alternative culture scene became experts in legal means of gaining government funding. As pirate TV pioneer Menno Grootveld puts it, "We had a universal basic income. That's what I always say."[116] The small amount of unemployment benefit money that young people received, therefore, helped facilitate a whole range of creative activities.

Apart from unemployment benefits, which artists and squatters took full advantage of in the 1970s and '80s, artists of the time also benefited, as mentioned, from the Beeldende Kunstenaars Regeling (BKR). This government regulation subsidized artists via purchase of artworks by the local government of each municipality. After the Second World War, when the Netherlands was freed from Nazi occupation, art and the work of artists were seen as important building blocks of post-war democracy and freedom of expression. Through better access to education, the number of artists was increasing, and many of them found that they were not benefiting from the

112 Vuijsje, *King Klashorst*, p. 65.
113 Ex and Derks, interview by Westerveen.
114 Ibid.
115 Geert Lovink, interview by author.
116 Menno Grootveld, interview by author.

rising prosperity that other Dutch citizens saw during the post-war years.[117] The Beroepsvereniging van Beeldende Kunstenaars (BBK) [Professional Association of Fine Artists] was established on May 15, 1945, a mere ten days after liberation, and it lobbied for artist subsidies and benefits, including the BKR, emphasizing the educational role and function of art for society.[118] It was founded by artists who had been active in the artists' resistance during the war and had been members of socialist, leftist, and anti-fascist groups prior to the war.[119]

Between 1949 and 1956, the ministry of social welfare—notably *not* the ministry of culture—developed a subsidy package for artists that would keep them working and out of poverty by buying artworks from them. This essentially created a social welfare benefit specifically for artists. The BKR was fully instituted in 1956 and the program started to be dismantled in 1984, when its budget, which was part of the Ministry of Social Affairs and Employment (Sociale Zaken en Werkgelegenheid), was siphoned off into the Ministry of Welfare, Health, and Culture (Welzijn, Volksgezondheid en Cultuur, WVC). By 1987, the transfer was complete, and the WVC had gained an additional 36 million Euros as a result.[120] In 1960, there were 200 artists registered with the BKR, and, by 1983, that number had climbed to 3800. Artist and social scientist Hans Abbing argues that the presence of the BKR and other state subsidies artificially increased the number of artists while the demand for artworks did not increase in turn.[121] He thus concludes that state subsidies are detrimental to artists and contribute to the relative poverty of those in artistic professions in the Netherlands. Many of the artists who participated in the BKR, however, saw it as an essential lifeline to independence from the galleries and museums and, thus, a force for innovation in artistic production during financially difficult times in the late 1970s and early 1980s.

In 1976 the Dutch government began to float the idea of producing a research report on the BKR as it considered possibly restructuring the regulation; the motivation was the exponential growth in its use during the

117 Roel Pots, "De Nederlandse overheid en de beeldende kunsten in historisch perspectief," in *Second opinion: over beeldende kunstsubsidie in Nederland*, ed. Lex ter Braak et al. (Rotterdam: NAi Uitgevers, 2007), p. 241.
118 Ibid., p. 240–41.
119 IJdens, "Van Kunstenaarsverzet Tot Politieke Vakband," p. 82.
120 Currency reported in Euros. Pots, "De Nederlandse overheid en de beeldende kunsten," p. 244.
121 Hans Abbing, *Why Are Artists Poor? The Exceptional Economy of the Arts*. (Amsterdam: Amsterdam University Press, 2008), p. 133.

previous decade. The push for research was then led in 1978 by the secretary for the Ministry of Social Affairs (Sociale Zaken), Louw de Graaf, and the research was commissioned in November 1981.[122] As artists across the Netherlands reported, the BKR remained an important source of income for them in the early 1980s up until its demise. Artist Rob Malasch says, "Everyone had the BKR. And you could always borrow money from someone who was also in the BKR. And everyone borrowed from you, that was no problem because in six months you'd get your BKR again. There was always money for everything you wanted to do."[123] As noted, the existence of alternative spaces such as Aorta and W139 in Amsterdam, as well as spaces elsewhere in the country, is indebted to the supply of funding that the BKR and other subsidies provided. Thus, it was perhaps a force not only in increasing the number of people participating in the arts and creative fields but in facilitating artist-led spaces and alternative art exhibition venues as well.

The criteria for acceptance into the BKR were largely social rather than based on artistic quality. Each municipality was responsible for enrolling applicants and determining whether their work qualified for the program. The policy document for the regulation states that in order to qualify, the artist had to be a Dutch citizen between 25 and 64 years old; this would have, in theory, excluded those who were still in art school. For examples, Klashorst and Ploeg did not turn 25 until 1982 and 1983 respectively. However, the policy gave discretion to the minister or the central committee to grant permission for artists under 25 or who were not Dutch to be granted the provisions. The artists also had to demonstrate that they had insufficient resources available to them and were clearly established in the profession of fine art, based on education or professional activities. Furthermore, they had to ensure that they had done everything possible to earn income from work in their profession or another profession where their professional abilities were valuable. Those under 35 were compelled to demonstrate that they had done everything possible to secure work outside of the profession of fine art. In short, these rules established an unemployment benefit *specifically for artists*. Luckily for artists who applied, it seems that the rules outlined above were not very strictly followed.[124] Amendments to the regulations

---

122 George Muskens, *Beeldende kunstenaars, beeldende kunstenaarsregeling: eindverslag van het onderzoek naar het functioneren van de BKR* ('s-Gravenhage; Tilburg: Ministerie van Sociale Zaken en Werkgelegenheid; IVA-Instituut voor Sociaal-Wetenschappelijk Onderzoek, 1983), p. v; Roel Pots, *De BKR: kunst- of sociaal beleid? ontstaan, groei en resultaten van de contraprestatieregelingen* ('s-Gravenhage: VUGA, 1981), p. 49.

123 Heyink and Tilroe, *Peter L.M. Giele*, p. 53.

124 Muskens, *Beeldende kunstenaars, beeldende kunstenaarsregeling*, p. 130.

between 1971 and 1982 show a relaxation of these principles. In 1974, the requirement to seek work outside of the artistic profession was qualified to specify that such work should not prevent the artist from continuing their artistic work, and the age requirements were clarified to reassert that exceptions could be made, as per the provisions.[125]

One question that arises out of the history of the BKR is what effect the regulation had on the mediums chosen by the artists who participated in the program and their artistic output. It is evident from the research that painters and graphic artists made up the overwhelming majority of the artists in the program.[126] According to a report commissioned by the government and published in 1983, "The terms that govern the acceptance of fine artists [into the program] are difficult. [...] In particular, with regard to practitioners of modern disciplines of fine art, the wording [of the regulation] is one of both yes and no."[127] As is true in the commercial art market, unique and compact works rather than multimedia or installation works seemed to have been more readily collected by the municipality. The report comes to the following conclusion:

> Of all the fine artists, the practitioners of the classic disciplines distinguish themselves the most of the three [versus modern and craft/applied disciplines]. This could be an effect of the BKR: the professional practice of fine art that is most fitting (concentrated work) is made possible via this regulation and, through the selection criteria of the regulation, transfers to the practice of classic disciplines. [...] Nevertheless, practitioners of craft, modern and applied disciplines make sure that, with all the problems, and with less support from the BKR, they maintain a level of professionalism [...][128]

The conclusion was, therefore, that although support for non-traditional mediums was somewhat more difficult, it was not excluded or impossible.

The 1974 amendments to the guidelines for the regulation also made clear that work other than paintings, drawings, graphics, and sculptures would qualify as fine art, including work where "elements of light and movement play a role."[129] The committee for the BKR felt it necessary to issue a memo in

---

125 Ibid., pp. 155–56.
126 George Muskens and J.M.A.G. Maas, *Materiele afhankelijkheid, beroepsmatigheid, autonomie: de leefsituatie van Nederlandse beeldende kunstenaars* (Tilburg: Katholieke Hogeschool Tilburg, IVA, Instituut voor Sociaal-Wetenschappelijk Onderzoek, 1983), p. 34.
127 Muskens, *Beeldende kunstenaars, beeldende kunstenaarsregeling*, p. 90.
128 Muskens and Maas, *Materiele afhankelijkheid, beroepsmatigheid, autonomie*, p. 90.
129 Muskens, *Beeldende kunstenaars, beeldende kunstenaarsregeling*, p. 157.

February 1982 that clarifies how to handle photographic or reproducible work with regard to valuation.[130] Another problematic clause in the regulation was that artworks should be purchased, when possible, without "damaging the free market," which was difficult to measure, especially within the small art market of the Netherlands.[131] There is no evidence that this particular criterion was given much weight by the municipalities, though critics of the BKR would later raise the issue of its effect on the art market as justification for reconfiguration of the funding.

As the previous sections have shown, the BKR factored heavily in supporting the alternative art and culture scene in the Netherlands, although it was certainly controversial in the late '70s and early '80s, as Anno van der Heide's *Container Art* and the Kunstkollektiv Dubio's manifesto demonstrate. Critics of the BKR argued that the artwork was merely accumulating unseen in warehouses and was not sufficiently recognized and valued. When the BKR was instituted in the 1950s, many of the artworks that were collected were hung in public buildings around the country, but, as the number of artworks and artists increased, works collected in the 1980s were often sent straight to storage.[132] While the budget for the BKR increased from 0.6 million Euros to almost 2.8 million Euros in 1982, it did not, judging by the reactions of the artists who participated in it, provide enough for the maintenance and preservation of their work.[133] Beginning in 1992, the government sought to offload warehouses full of art. Of the 220,000 works collected, 93,000 were deemed not museum quality or appropriate for other venues. The government decided to return the leftover works to the artists or their relatives, but few of the artists responded to the call to collect their works and around 50,000 of the works, many of them on paper, remained. Although slated to be thrown away, they were in the end given to an art-lending foundation in Amsterdam in 1997.[134]

The impression among artists, particularly the few that were more commercially successful, was that the BKR and subsidies were making artists lazy, although this assertion does not seem to be borne out by the sheer volume of art activities and artworks created during that time. People were equally ambivalent about subsidies for music. In 1985, Rogier van der Ploeg, who was a member of the band Blue Murder along with his brother Maarten,

130 Ibid., p. 193.
131 Ibid., pp. 133–34.
132 Pots, "De Nederlandse overheid en de beeldende kunsten," p. 241.
133 Ibid., p. 243.
134 Angela Dekker, "Nuis Geeft de Laatste Resten BKR-Kunst Weg," *Vrij Nederland*, September 27, 1997, p. 16.

said, "Subsidies make people lazy. You see that at youth centers too. If they are in a good financial place, sometimes they don't make any more posters to announce a performance."[135] Jan Worst, another painter in the Nieuwe Wilden circle, was on the BKR for six years. Only after the demise of the BKR did he have his first gallery exhibition in 1985.[136] The BKR, therefore, was always a counter-balance for a relatively weak private gallery sector, but it is unclear whether that weakness was, in part, an effect of the BKR and system of government subsidies or whether it was determined by other economic and social factors. As artist Rik Lina points out:

> You did not have to worry about fashion or the demands of gallerists. [Willem] Sandberg did not purchase the Cobra painters, the BKR did that. The pluralism of Dutch painting is a result of the BKR. And the Zero group, the post-Cobra, the minimalist paintings and much later the After Nature came out of that period.[137]

It would be impossible to know whether the styles that Lina mentions would have flourished without the BKR, but it is clear that the subsidy facilitated a wide range of artistic styles and practices during the decades of its existence.

The more commercially successful artists from the era often scorned the reliance of some of their peers on the BKR. And, indeed, it provided unique problems. In 1997, the squat, punk, and graffiti artist Hugo Kaagman said, "Artists are asocial. The profession has been ruined by the BKR."[138] The BKR fostered a highly experimental but very introverted art scene in the 1970s and '80s, and it could be argued that the BKR funded the work that galleries were unwilling to show. Galleries in the early '80s were excited that artists had returned to painting, as this work was easier to commodify than television broadcasts, multimedia installations, or works on delicate or disposable material, and they were, thus, mostly interested in showing and promoting paintings. If an artist was working in multiple media—video, prints, street art, painting, etc.—major commercial gallerists, such as Rob Jurka, would only ask them to show their paintings. Aorta and other alternative spaces, on the other hand, were far more interested in showing

135 Peter Koops, "Yoghurt En Pop, Met Excuses," *De Volkskrant*, April 6, 1985, sec. Vervolgens., p. 1.

136 Rutger Pontzen, "De Verleden Toekomst van de No Future-Generatie," *Vrij Nederland*, January 18, 1997, p. 42.

137 Dekker, "BKR-kunst weg," p. 17.

138 Pontzen, "De verleden toekomst van de No Future-generatie," p. 40.

the breadth of the artistic output that was going on around them. One of
the biggest criticisms of the BKR from artists and art professionals was
that the government was accumulating a mountain of artwork that was
of poor quality and unambitious.[139] The conventional wisdom remains
that subsidies produce lazy, boring work from unchallenged artists. The
standard by which the artwork was accepted into the collection and thus
accumulated were quite low and the ability of the government to maintain
those works was equally limited.[140]

Scholars and government researchers began, in the late 1970s and early
1980s, to suggest that the government should focus more on the artistic
quality of the work. Roel Pots suggested that if government buildings do
not want to show a work of art, it has no value for the community and thus
should not be accepted into the BKR program. He recommended:

> There could, in principle, be selection based on artistic and not social
> criteria. The work collected in this way could then eventually be accom-
> modated in art-lending centers or in a state lending system for government
> buildings. The work that is found to be unsuitable [for these venues]
> should not be accepted. After all, it does not have a single value for the
> community as an artistic product.[141]

The suggestion that artwork that is not adopted as appropriate decoration for
government buildings does not have *any* value for the community is quite
narrow in its focus; it shifts the valuation of art to a specific use function
in much the same way that the commercial market does.

Artists at the time were split between those who disapproved of the BKR
and those who saw any change in funding as a threat to their "social gains."
The latter group argued that the government could not possibly decide the
artistic quality of work because "everyone had to decide for themselves what
art is and what it is not."[142] It is certainly true that, as the recommendation
above suggests, a narrowly defined use-valuation of artwork would severely
limit the type of artwork supported by such a government program. The
issues that arose in the relationship between government purchases and
the art market, however, also presented a less than ideal scenario for some
artists, particularly those who relied on the market. According to Pots:

139 Reijnders, "Adressen," p. 178.
140 Abbing, *Why Are Artists Poor?*, p. 133.
141 Pots, *De BKR*, p. 73.
142 Ibid., p. 69.

On the other side, artists who supported themselves mainly through the existence of the free market had totally different objections to the BKR. This group felt that it was unfair that, via the BKR, amounts were paid for artwork that would not, by a long shot, be achieved on the free market. Lower quality work was, in their eyes, thus, rewarded more [than it should be] based on improper grounds (i.e., social criteria). The objection from this group against this course of events does not mean that they [did not want to] grant their colleagues an acceptable income, but that, via the BKR, the purchased work drains a not-insignificant part of the market.[143]

Speaking about the workings of the BKR assessment committee Rik Lina, who served on a BKR commission for two years in the 1970s, says:

Quality was the only criterion. [...] At a given moment, we had over-full, unmanageable depots. We bought increasingly less and paid increasingly more for a painting because someone had to live for a year on that. We sometimes gave ten thousand guilders for a painting that a gallery would give three thousand guilders for. The ratios [between the works and their prices] were lost. It became an indecipherable puzzle. It was not arts policy but a social policy that dealt with artists.[144]

This was the crucial distinction between the BKR and subsequent merit-based public arts funding.

The BKR provided an easy way to make a living as a practicing artist when commercial galleries were not willing to show the work artists were producing, but it also perhaps kept artists comfortably in the Netherlands. Dutch artists of the early 1980s were not forced to try their luck in the international art market, and, besides Klashorst and Scholte, few of them sought out international recognition merely for fame or increased income. Because of this, the international artists that were attracted to the Netherlands became important connections to the outside world for the rather insular Dutch art scene. As individual subsidies declined, exhibitions like *Talking Back to the Media*, discussed in chapter 4, and several other adjacent media festivals shifted the focus to new media and a more international outlook.

143 Ibid., p. 69.
144 Dekker, "BKR-Kunst Weg," p. 27.

3.   Cracking the Ether

Abstract

This chapter explores the earliest artist-led pirate TV project, PKP-TV, as an example of how squatter tactics were applied to the media. The illegal channel, which was created by the artists Maarten Ploeg (né van der Ploeg), Peter Klashorst, and Rogier van der Ploeg, made it its mission to crack open the closed medium of television. PKP and pirate cable TV in the Netherlands are situated within a longer history of both alternative TV projects internationally—such as the Videofreex and TVTV—as well as video and film-based artworks shown on television both in the Netherlands and abroad. Artist-led pirate television in the Netherlands, like squatters in urban space, cracked open the media space of television and created temporary autonomous platforms.

Keywords: pirate television, squatting, autonomy, platforms, PKP-TV, Netherlands

> *The sea-rovers and corsairs of the 18th century created an*
> *'information network' that spanned the globe: primitive and devoted*
> *primarily to grim business, the net nevertheless functioned admirably.*
> *Scattered throughout the net were islands, remote hideouts...*
> – Hakim Bey

Artists in the early 1980s reacted strongly against the minimalist and conceptual artwork of the 1970s by producing a material stream of imagery in multiple media at once—painting, TV, video, music, and others. Although they were inspired by the legacy of the counterculture in the 1960s, the artists of the punk era were less idealistic, influenced by the depressed economy and high youth unemployment of their era. As noted in chapter 2, the art scene in the Netherlands between 1980 and 1984 was closely connected and locally-oriented, and the work they produced was characterized by collaborative

Wasielewski, A., *From City Space to Cyberspace: Art, Squatting, and Internet Culture in the Netherlands*. Amsterdam: Amsterdam University Press, 2021
DOI 10.5117/9789463725453_CH03

practice. Although the neo-expressionism of the Nieuwe Wilden painters would later be celebrated as a return to painting, these artists fluidly moved between mediums and helped found pioneering new media art projects.

In the late '70s, new opportunities for media experimentation arose in Amsterdam. At the time, the municipal government was embarking on an ambitious plan to connect all the residencies in the city to a unified cable television network. Before the installation was halfway complete, young hackers devised ways to access the system. The first cable TV pirates broadcast hardcore pornography—a choice they thought would attract the most attention—which would appear late at night on the dead air after the channels ended regular programming for the day. The punk and anarchist youth culture of the time—the 'no future' generation—was loosely united by widespread unemployment and the practice of squatting disused or vacant property. These young people were some of the first TV pirates in Amsterdam.[1] Once they had sought out autonomous living in the squatters' movement, it was a small step to imagine creating autonomous media in the form of newspapers and zines as well as pirate radio stations and cable TV broadcasts. The young artists among them were quick to realize that pirate TV had potential well beyond late-night porn. Beside the vandalistic interruption itself or the provocative spectacle of pornography, pirate television provided the opportunity for open-ended, free distribution of DIY content and the possibility to create an ad hoc community around music videos, video art, tapes of performances, and experimental videos. In essence, it opened a gateway to create a pirate utopia.

Cable pirating was possible in Amsterdam in the late '70s and early '80s due to a unique combination of progressive technological infrastructure and lax government enforcement of broadcasting regulations. In 1975 the municipal government put a plan in motion to connect all official residences in the city to a cable system so that individuals would no longer need aerial antennas and could receive the ordinary Dutch channels, plus a host of foreign ones, via the superior cable signal. Unlike the cable infrastructure in the United States, for example, the system in Amsterdam was completely publicly owned. The country's flat geography and relative proximity to its neighbors in Germany, Belgium, and the UK allowed a few centralized receiving points to pick up three German television channels, the UK's BBC1 and BBC2, and two Belgian channels, which then sent out the signal

---

1   They were quickly joined, however, by other TV pirates who were affiliated with the "real" underground (i.e., those involved in organized crime and drug trade). Menno Grootveld, interview by author; Rogier van der Ploeg, interview by author.

to individual homes via the cable network. These channels provided an astonishingly large array of content for a European city in the mid-1970s.

Meanwhile, the large receiving dishes located in the harbor area to the west of the city, on top of the Okura Hotel in the south, and other locations around the city were vulnerable to hacking. The receivers were, at that time, left active throughout the night, so that, when they no longer received their regular broadcasts, they were still open to receive signals from elsewhere. Another effect of the switch to cable was that Amsterdam was suddenly full of discarded aerial transmission receivers. The would-be pirates quickly discovered that a large number of sophisticated aerial receivers could be hacked to act as transmitters instead. These DIY transmitters could then be pointed toward the dish and initiate a pirate broadcast.[2]

Many artists in the '60s and '70s, such as Nam June Paik, Wolf Vostell, Dan Graham, Bruce Naumen, Joan Jonas, Lynda Benglis, and Vito Acconci, experimented with the reflexivity of video and television. Although artists had envisioned television as a potentially interactive medium almost from its inception, these early experiments were usually only ever able to *simulate* interactivity in the closed system (and the closed-circuit) of the studio, gallery, or exhibition. Meanwhile, advocates of guerrilla TV in New York City like the Videofreex, Global Village, People's Video Theater, and the Raindance Corporation (who produced *Radical Software*, a magazine that articulated the theoretical position of that community) were never able to seize complete control of broadcast or cablecast as they envisioned.

This chapter looks at the artist-led pirate TV channel PKP-TV and its successor Rabotnik. These pirate TV channels succeeded in creating illegal television broadcasts that were true to the vision of these earlier TV experiments: they were democratic, participatory, and free from the mandates of gatekeepers or authorities. For this reason, Rogier van der Ploeg of PKP-TV and Menno Grootveld of Rabotnik look back on this era as, "the last free media in the West." Van der Ploeg characterizes their broadcasts as totally free, meaning not only that the initiative came from the grassroots but that the authorities had no control or oversight. They were essentially allowed to do whatever they wanted to do.[3] But the cost of this freedom was criminality, and they were always careful to have someone keeping watch at the window while they were broadcasting to make sure they were not caught by the authorities.

The appearance of PKP-TV on cable television in Amsterdam opened a rift or a tear—a crack—in the infrastructure and created a space within it.

---

2   Grootveld, interview by author.
3   Ploeg, interview by author.

While they were not the first to break into the afterhours broadcast signals, they were the first to form a pirate utopia within it. Anarchist writer Hakim Bey describes pirate utopias as the erstwhile "free" islands or smugglers' coves of sea pirates, where, he imagines, the rule of law did not exist and which may have constituted early Temporary Autonomous Zones (TAZs).[4] According to Bey, the TAZ is a nameless, hidden, impermanent site of pure freedom within Baudrillard's "simulation" or Debord's "spectacle,"[5] He states, "As soon as the TAZ is named (represented, mediated), it must vanish, it *will* vanish, leaving behind it an empty husk, only to spring up again somewhere else, once again invisible because undefinable in terms of the Spectacle."[6] Once it is opened, the TAZ provides an autonomous space within the fabric of the existing order, submerged and out of sight. After a certain amount of time, however, its effect starts to be felt by the whole, destabilizing it enough to draw the notice of authority, which closes it down/fills in it/erases it and re-establishes rule of law. But the forces that create TAZs are canny: they quickly mutate and open new cracks elsewhere.

If the enemy, for Bey, is what Debord describes as the integrated spectacle of liberal democracy, then Bey's "poetic terrorism" and "art sabotage" are the tools he proposed to combat it.[7] The criminal element is essential to the endeavor: subversiveness or transgression is not enough. PKP-TV was not only a space for the artists who created it to show their art and music but also for their viewers, whomever they might be, to get their work on TV. The community was not defined by a top-down ideology or program but rather by the audacity of its own appearance. It was a dark mirror of "official" television, an upside-down punk world. At the same time, the formal aesthetic of their programs was similar to other local cable artists in other countries, such as Paper Tiger Television, which began slightly after PKP in 1981 on New York cable access TV. PKP's broadcasts were composed of roughly-hewn, hand-drawn, low-fi sets and hand-held, reality-TV/gonzo-style videography.[8] These aesthetic choices were eventually formalized on MTV, albeit with smoother edges.

4   Hakim Bey, *TAZ.: The Temporary Autonomous Zone, Ontological Anarchy, Poetic Terrorism* (Brooklyn: Autonomedia, 2003) pp. 95–97.
5   Bey, *TAZ*, p. 99; Guy Debord, *Comments on the Society of the Spectacle*, trans. Malcolm Imrie (London: Verso, 2011); Jean Baudrillard, *Simulacra and Simulation*, trans. Sheila Faria Glaser (Ann Arbor: University of Michigan Press, 2014).
6   Bey, *TAZ*, p. 99.
7   Debord, *Comments on the Society of the Spectacle*.
8   The rough and DIY look of the sets was something that PKP and Paper Tiger Television (PTTV) shared. Deedee Halleck, the founder of Paper Tiger, writes, "If there is a specific look to the series,

Pop Art Pirates

In late 1980 artists Maarten Ploeg, his younger brother Rogier van der Ploeg, and Peter Klashorst began investigating the possibility of setting up their own broadcast and found that the concept, at least, was relatively simple: get close to one of the TV receiving dishes, point a homemade transmitter at it after midnight when the regular broadcast finished, and create a platform for art, free from any restrictions or oversight.[9] Already part of a group that was experimenting with making videos, making music, and making their own music videos, they were interested in showing their own output as well as facilitating other artists' and musicians' work. As noted in chapter 2, Maarten Ploeg and Klashorst were students at the Rietveld Academy and had secured video equipment from the school's audiovisual department to play with, mostly black and white U-matic video. They began investigating pirate television together with Maarten's brother Rogier, who was two years younger than Maarten and enrolled in the Dutch Film Academy.

Rogier recalls that the Rietveld was far more open-minded about the students' illegal broadcasting than the film school:

> I had to come to the board of directors [of the film academy] and they said, 'If we ever notice that you *ever* use any of the official film school equipment for this illegal activity, you're out.' I said, 'I don't get your stuff and I don't need your stuff. I have my own stuff.' Whereas the Rietveld Academy, the art school, they were cooperative, they gave us everything.[10]

it is *handmade*: a comfortable, nontechnocratic look that says *friendly* and low budget. The seams show: we often use overview wide-angle shots to give the viewers a sense of the people who are making the show and the types of equipment we use." Compared to PKP, PTTV implemented a far more professional, studio-style of videography. The first broadcast of PPTV was on October 28, 1981, so PKP aired earlier, though neither was aware of the other at the time. Beyond the shooting style of Paper Tiger, its form of dissemination was also fundamentally different to pirate TV in Amsterdam. Paper Tiger began on New York public access cable and, despite the relative freedom allowed there, was connected to a formalized and legal form of broadcast. They later expanded into other cities but began as a local-based public access program. Even if the format was not completely radical, the content of Paper Tiger was highly politically-charged. See Deirdre Boyle, *Subject to Change: Guerrilla Television Revisited* (New York: Oxford University Press, 1997), p. 207; Deedee Halleck, "Paper Tiger Television: Smashing the Myths of the Information Industry Every Week on Public Access Cable," *Media, Culture & Society* 6, no. 3 (July 1, 1984): pp. 315–16.

9   Maarten Ploeg (né van der Ploeg) and Peter Klashorst (né van de Klashorst) both profession-ally dropped the *tussenvoegsels* in their names for the sake of simplicity. Rogier van der Ploeg, Maarten's younger brother, maintained the original formulation.

10   Ploeg, interview by author. Ploeg recalls that the PKP crew quickly purchased their own equipment: "So the first thing we did was buy a montage VHS so we could actually make edits,

Being the most technically inclined member of the group, Rogier tried, at first, to teach himself how to build a DIY transmitter by consulting radio and electronic hobbyist manuals and magazines. He figured out that they needed to get their transmitter as close as possible to the receiving dish, in a direct line of sight. The only limitations were finding a close enough broadcasting location and building a working transmitter—two significant hurdles to overcome for the young DIYers. Maarten lived on the eighth floor at Van Nijenrodeweg 466 in the Buitenveldert neighborhood of Amsterdam at the time and, noting the presence of TV stations not far from there in Amstelveen, the brothers went about testing their equipment.

The Ploegs' and Klashort's initial broadcast, which was called Bizar-TV, was assumed to be a failure. It was a combined effort by two local bands: Soviet Sex (their band) and the members of Necronomicon (Jan Willem Vaal, Ernst Vos, Bob Pieck, and Kareltje). Although they had no way of actually checking whether the broadcast worked as there was no cable connection installed at their transmission location, they suspected that the equipment was not powerful enough and the location was not quite right.[11] After the initial failed broadcasts, the Ploegs and Klashorst began investigating ways to broadcast on their own. Having reached the limits of their DIY skills, they enlisted the help of a squatter pirate radio veteran– Vincent L.—to help tweak their equipment.[12] According to Rogier, Vincent was "stoned out of his head [...] but he actually had the knowledge."[13] He had previously helped build transmitters for some of the porn pirates as well as the radio pirates at the Vrije Keijser squatter radio station. With new and improved equipment, they prepared for another attempt at broadcasting at a new location: in the attic of artist Peter Mertens's anti-squat apartment at Van Hogendorpstraat 81 in the Staatsliedenbuurt of Amsterdam.[14] The property

---

and a camera and portable VHS recorder. I think we made the money by doing live concerts with our band and put everything together to buy that." A conflicting report from the time, however, claims that they secured money from the Ploegs' father to purchase the equipment. See Susanne Piët, "Televisie-Piraten Wapenen Zich Tegen Invallen van Opsporingsdienst," *NRC Handelsblad*, July 25, 1981, Dag edition, Maarten Ploeg Knipselmap 16305, Stedelijk Museum Library.

11   Ploeg, interview by author.
12   Vincent L. requested that his full name not be used.
13   Ploeg, interview by author.
14   Anti-squat [*anti-kraak*] properties, also known as property guardianship, are living quarters that are often rented to students or low-income residents for lower rates with the condition that they will receive no maintenance of the living space (which might be a commercial building not normally suitable for living) and may have to move out on very short notice. This is generally seen as a way for building owners to protect their property from being squatted and is, thus, a

was selected by Vincent L. and was perfectly situated for broadcast.[15] After midnight in June 1981 they aimed their new transmitter toward the receiving dish for Duitsland 3 (WDR, West Germany 3) located in the harbor area of Amsterdam. Still without a cable connection, the boys phoned up a friend to see if they were finally on air. This time, they were live.

After the first few erratic transmissions, they began broadcasting biweekly on Sunday and Wednesday nights under the name PKP-TV for Ploeg-Klashorst-Ploeg or *Pop Kunst Piraten* (Pop Art Pirates) and enlisted a crew of friends and associates to help. In August of 1981, they dropped down to one broadcast per week on Sunday nights, as they were increasingly busy touring with their post-punk band Soviet Sex. The typical PKP-TV broadcast was a rough and anarchic mix of clips from live music performances, tongue-in-cheek news segments, *dérives* around Amsterdam with artists and musicians, and a variety of tapes that viewers had made to be aired on the program. They kept their broadcast open to both local and visiting musicians and artists who would pass through their studio, get airtime for a live concert, or appear in their broadcasts in impromptu interviews and segments. What sets PKP-TV apart from earlier television art is not its use of TV itself or even its relationship to video art, but its focus on and success in creating, from the start, a totally independent platform for viewers' content that was accessible to everyone within a major metropolitan area. In the process of creating the platform, they also created an ad hoc participatory community.

The show that PKP produced for air on September 9, 1981, the seventeenth episode, came after the PKP crew had honed their broadcast style over the previous six months. It provides a fully-formed example of the shape their pirate utopia took. The episode begins with a twang of distorted guitars—the intro to The Pop Group's 1979 song, "Thief of Fire." A figure—PKP (and later Rabotnik) TV presenter Jos Alderse Baas—is dressed in a crude paper facsimile of a tribal mask and a geometric cloak with PKP printed on it [Fig.11].[16] He gyrates with arms raised like claws as the camera jerks in and out. The wall in back of him is adorned with the gothic lettering of

practice frowned upon by squatting and housing activists. Rogier van der Ploeg, "PKP-TV Text," February 9, 2018.

15   According to Rogier, PKP moved to another place two streets down in October of 1981, shortly before they concluded broadcasting. It was the home of Tante Jopie, a drag queen and performance artist.

16   Alderse Baas, a recurrent figure in the punk and squatter-art scene of the early 1980s, was associated with SKG (Stads Kunst Guerrilla), PKP, Rabotnik, De Reagering, and many of the other art/media experiments of this time.

Figure 11: Stills from PKP-TV, September 9, 1981 broadcast. Courtesy of Rogier van der Ploeg.

the PKP-TV logo and, as the camera gets closer to the masked face, the viewer sees that PKP's lettering is also written on the surface of the mask.[17] The mask itself is constructed from a piece of decorative packaging paper, similar to the paper used to wrap food items like cheese, with a repeating pattern of a windmill in a traditional Dutch landscape. It is a piece of trash

17   The same style of gothic font used by PKP was previously used in the graffiti scene by Ivar Vičs (Dr. Rat) and the SKG (Stads Kunst Guerrilla) led by Erik Hobijn, who also used the font in their graffiti and posters.

repurposed as useable material. The camera then zooms into Alderse Baas's hands as he holds up a sheet of paper to his chest. With a marker, he scrawls PKP awkwardly upside down so that the letters are facing the camera. The paper he writes on has a crudely-cut hole like the ones on the paper mask he is wearing—it is perhaps another discarded attempt at a mask that was nonchalantly plucked from the floor to serve as a station identification card. Every element of the scene is unapologetically makeshift, using disposable materials in an improvised way.

As the rhythm of the drums from "Thief of Fire" accelerate, Alderse Baas points to the viewer and then back to the paper. By reaching out through the television toward the viewer and then back to the station logo, he is not only implicating the viewer in the broadcast but also bringing the viewer into complicity (or camaraderie) with the pirate outfit. This breaking of the fourth wall, which is nothing new for either theater or television, should not be conflated with the more self-reflexive gestures of pointing in early close-circuit video art, an example of which, Vito Acconci's *Centers* (1971), is explored by Rosalind Krauss.[18] Acconci's piece consists of the artist pointing toward the camera while watching himself in real time on a close-circuit video monitor, attempting to maintain the pointing finger in the center of the screen during the approximately twenty-minute video. Krauss writes:

> As we look at the artist [Acconci] sighting along his outstretched arm and forefinger towards the center of the screen we are watching, what we see is a sustained tautology: a line of sight that begins at Acconci's plane of vision and ends at the eyes of his projected double. In that image of self-regard is configured a narcissism so endemic to works of video that I find myself wanting to generalize it as *the* condition of the entire genre.[19]

Krauss's essay remains perhaps the most often cited argument in scholarship that address '70s video art, if only because so many feel the need to rebut or correct what they find are mischaracterizations contained within it. In one such essay, Anne E. Wagner argues, "For, if *Centers* records the artist's pointing at himself, he also points at the viewer. As long as he has an audience, his gesture aims to find and fix it in its line of force."[20]

18   Rosalind Krauss, "Video: The Aesthetics of Narcissism," *October* 1 (1976): pp. 50–51.
19   Ibid., p. 50.
20   Anne M. Wagner, "Performance, Video, and the Rhetoric of Presence," *October* 91 (2000): p. 68.

Acconci's own writing on his work also speaks to his concern for the viewer. He writes, "Starting point: Where am I in relation to the viewer—above, below, to the side? Once my position is established, the reasons for that position take shape..."[21] Commenting on the gesture of pointing specifically, he says, "The result (the TV image) turns the activity around: a pointing away from myself, at an outside viewer—I end up widening my focus onto passing viewers (I'm looking straight out by looking straight in)."[22] The paradigm of close-circuit television (CCTV) in a gallery setting or elsewhere is fundamentally different to the broadcast paradigm of cable television, in whatever form it might take. Where a CCTV video is a closed loop between camera input and screen output, the distribution model provided by cablecast is very different. Early video art might implicate the viewer (as the artist implicates themself) but it is always an after-effect of a reflexive relationship of feedback between artist, camera, and screen in the limited circuit. This setup is, therefore, not at all the same as using a cable network to draw in a wider public, as PKP-TV did.[23] The broadcast public created by cable is not part of a closed feedback loop, which might later be shown to a gallery audience on tape or performed for a limited audience. Cable creates a more open-ended ad hoc community of primary television receivers.

As the PKP broadcast continues, the camera zooms closer and closer in on the backlit paper that Alderse Baas is holding, the reverse side of which is visible as another copy of the PKP logo [Fig.11]. He throws the paper to the ground and the scene cuts to him wearing the geometric PKP cloth from the previous scene over his nose and mouth, bandit-style. Throughout the program, he transitions through a variety of makeshift masks and face-coverings and presents many of the segments while seated next to a monitor with a live feed of himself. In the first such scene, he greets the viewers and then turns to the TV next to him, peering into the regress of images of himself [Fig.11]. Again, this could be read through the lens of Krauss's characterization of video as narcissistic, but I would like to

---

21   Vito Acconci, "10-Point Plan for Video," in *Video Art: An Anthology*, ed. Ira Schneider and Beryl Korot (New York: Harcourt Brace Jovanovich, 1976), pp. 8–9.

22   Lori Zippay, *Artists' Video: An International Guide* (New York: Electronic Arts Intermix, 1991), p. 12.

23   Yvonne Spielmann defines the concept of "reflexivity" (and "feedback") in video in a slightly more complex way than I use it here, arguing that this quality of video (i.e., video art, in particular) stems from its position as a medium in between the physicality of analog film and the immateriality of digital media. Yvonne Spielmann, *Video: The Reflexive Medium* (Cambridge, MA: MIT Press, 2008), p. 103.

suggest an alternative reading focusing on the regress as not infinite mirror reflections of a singular figure but as a way that video creates the effect of a mass or a crowd. The combined effect for PKP is that of a multitude of anonymous masked figures at first doubled on screen but then exponentially repeated ad infinitum. The program is then presented by a pirate army that is infinitely multiplied rather than just one identifiable individual.

Contrary to the many works of 1970s video art that use and manipulate the presentation of identity on the television screen, the endless multiplication of the figure in this context stands in for an electronic and potentially limitless public, the telepresence of the multitude implicated via the pointed finger. For Michael Hardt and Antonio Negri, who delimit the concept of a multitude as a force against the power of the empire of global capitalism, "The multitude is not formed simply by throwing together and mixing nations and peoples indifferently; it is the singular power of a *new city* [emphasis original] [...] the movements of the multitude designate new spaces, and its journeys establish new residences."[24] The autonomous activity of the multitude, in the case of both squatters and pirate television, is a collective gambit toward spaces of freedom within an all-encompassing power structure, toward pirate utopias, however short-lived.

As noted above, Alderse Baas wears a variety of masks and face coverings at various points during the broadcast. In one later segment of the episode, he wears a mask that covers his entire face while reading the "NAP" news [Fig.11].[25] Looking through the slits of the mask, he seems to be having a hard time reading from the paper in front of him, so he holds it up and traces along the words with his finger, reading in an unsure, halting manner. The camera zooms into the paper and then back out and then into his face in the mask. The happenstance of this incident is incorporated unabashedly into the segment; chance and "mistakes" are embraced. The NAP news reading is periodically interrupted by spontaneous bursts of guitar, further fracturing the segment. The fragility on display releases the pirate broadcasters from the constricts of control, neatness, and professionalism. The small oddities of unreadiness and spontaneity are each micro-acts of rebellion. In the

24 Michael Hardt and Antonio Negri, *Empire* (Cambridge, MA: Harvard University Press, 2000), pp. 395, 397. The term is developed from Negri's prior discussion of Spinoza in *The Savage Anomaly: The Power of Spinoza's Metaphysics and Politics*, trans. Michael Hardt (Minneapolis: University of Minnesota Press, 1991).

25 Martijn Haas, *SKG* (Amsterdam: Lebowski Publishers, 2010), pp. 18–19. NAP was the name of Alderse Baas's DIY zine and stands for, variously, Nieuw Amsterdam Piraat [New Amsterdam Pirate], Nationaal Amsterdams Peil [National Amsterdam Poll], and Nieuw Amsterdams Persbureau [New Amsterdam Press bureau]

next segment, Alderse Baas wears yet another mask, this time constructed from a cutout of a fashionable woman's face from a magazine ad. After announcing a performance by Joy Division, he playfully sticks his tongue through the mouth hole of the mask while the camera lingers. Again, the ludic quality is paramount, and nothing is more than minimally planned, so nothing can be taken too seriously. The use of masks obscures identity rather than performs it.

According to Hakim Bey, "poetic terrorism" consists of the aesthetic activities conducted illegally or in unauthorized spaces; they are works that do not announce themselves as art and are encountered, perhaps, at random. It is exemplified by Dada, graffiti, pirate radio transmissions, raves, and vandalism.[26] Bey writes, "Dress up. Leave a false name. Be legendary. The best PT [poetic terrorism] is against the law, but don't get caught. Art as crime; crime as art."[27] The use of masks, disguises, and symbols in this PKP broadcast aligns with Bey's definition of poetic terrorism. In the 1970s, a number of leftist terrorist cells in the US and Europe—the Weather Underground, the Red Army Faction, the Symbionese Liberation Army, and others—romanticized mayhem and deployed aesthetic devices such as makeshift flags, symbols, and regalia to prop up their subversive and illegal activity, creating layers of spectacle, mystique, and myth.

This sort of terrorism is, in a contradictory sense, both improvised and carefully planned. It disavows the liberal sense of orderly individuality in favor of the paradoxical individuality of collectivist anarchism. Tiqqun, a French anarchist/autonomist collective from the early 2000s, investigate this suspension between the individual and collective, writing: "Does one ever escape alone from the prison of the Self? In a squat. In an orgy. In a riot. In a train or an occupied village. We meet again. We meet again *as whatever singularities*. That is to say not on the basis of a common belonging, but of a *common presence*."[28] Masks, in a way, help navigate this paradox between the singular and the collective. They are just as often the tools of terrorists, revolutionaries, and criminals as they are of actors and artists. As Bey writes: art as crime, crime as art.

Dada, cited by Bey as an approved method of poetic terrorism, is certainly a pertinent antecedent for PKP-TV. The artists of Zurich Dada during the 1910s—notably Marcel Janco, Jean Arp and Sophie Taeuber—made masks

26   Bey, *TAZ*, p. 5.
27   Ibid., p. 6.
28   Tiqqun, *Introduction to Civil War*, trans. Alexander R. Galloway and Jason E. Smith (Los Angeles: Semiotext(e), 2010), pp. 204–5.

a key facet of their anarchic work. Influenced by the geometric, abstracted masks and figures of Africa and the Pacific Islands that entered Europe as a result of colonial expansion, they were primitivists, enticed by a belief that these objects had a spiritual purity that the art of corrupted, "civilized" Europe, enmeshed in a senseless and destructive war, did not. Based in neutral Switzerland during World War I, this group of exiles created their own pirate utopia at the Cabaret Voltaire. Their retreat was part of desire to escape into an imaginary primordial humanity, pre-linguistic and performative.

Like the PKP masks, Marcel Janco's masks, for example, were made out of rough materials like cardboard. They were used to transform the wearer in the act of performance but not to perform identity itself. They facilitated not only transformation but a descent into madness and anarchy, a loss of identity. Hugo Ball, a key member of the Zurich Dada group, wrote:

> We were all there when Janco arrived with the masks, and each one of us put one on. The effect was strange. Not only did each mask seem to demand the appropriate costume, it also called for a quite specific set of gestures, melodramatic and even close to madness.[29]

Similarly, this descent into madness has an antecedent in the use of masks in the pre-Lenten carnivals of Northern Europe, where the rigid structures of medieval society could be temporarily relaxed and dissolved in collective anonymity. Like the Dada or carnival masks, the masks in the PKP broadcast divorce the wearer from his own individual subjectivity. The masks transform Alderse Baas into an avatar of PKP as a collective. While the collective was more important than the individual players, the individual's freedom to create superseded any collective forms of control. According to Rogier van der Ploeg, "We felt this should be a collective of more people and it didn't matter if that would devalue the quality."[30]

Although I use the term "avatar" in the above paragraph in a general sense, it resonates with David Joselit's theoretical use of the term. Joselit defines and utilizes a methodology labelled "eco-formalism" in his treatment of video and television works from the 1950s to the '70s. For this methodology, "image ecologies" rather than individual artworks are analyzed as connected visual systems. Joselit sees art as catalytic, not revolutionary (viz. modernist) nor

29   Qtd in Naima Prevots, "Zurich Dada and Dance: Formative Ferment," *Dance Research Journal* 17, no. 1 (1985): pp. 3–8.
30   Ploeg, interview by author.

subversive (viz. poststructuralist), and outlines three methodological tactics for artists and art historians to "act" rather than "interpret": feedback, virus, and avatar.[31] Summarizing the idea behind the avatar in the manifesto at the end of the text, he states, "LOSE YOUR IDENTITY! Don't believe that you're a piece of property, a 'gay man' or an 'African American' whose 'subject position' is the product of market research. Use icons opportunistically, and share them with like-minded people. Make an avatar!"[32] Indeed, PKP's use of masks and collective anonymity are a manifestation of this tactic: dissolving identity behind an avatar.[33]

Furthermore, like the Dada artists, the PKP-TV artists had primitivist inclinations, not only creating wearable masks but also mask-like representations of faces and figures in their expressionist paintings. As noted in chapter 2, Maarten Ploeg organized a performance in 1982 in which artists walked around the Stedelijk museum in Dada-like masks as "actually living painting" [Fig.8]. The primitivist impulse for art in the first few years of the 1980s in Amsterdam was born out of a reaction to the strictures of 1970s conceptual art as much as the freedom and anarchy of the DIY scene. Poor and unemployed, young people built their own homes, collected rubbish and cheap materials for their work, and operated simultaneously in whatever activities took their fancy. They were not bound by a professional trajectory of any kind, as opportunities were very limited. According to Rogier van der Ploeg:

> Art students were people who have not necessarily set out, 'this is going to be my job.' They set out on exploring themselves and, if you explore yourself, then you don't even know if you are a painter or a sculptor— you could also be a musician. And it could also be that you do four hours of sculpting and then eight hours of music and then maybe four hours of painting and then maybe a little writing too. It's people who want to express themselves, in a way, and not by expressing themselves by talking all the time but by doing things. And, in a way, that's also the essence of art. I think a lot of people ask, where does art end and where does a

31   David Joselit, *Feedback: Television against Democracy* (Cambridge, MA: MIT Press, 2007), pp. xii, 40, 45, 171.

32   Ibid., p. 171.

33   The other terms used by Joselit, "feedback" and "virus," can likewise be applied to PKP. If feedback is the "noise" that "opens the circuits" then PKP certainly accomplishes this by cracking the cable infrastructure and interrupting the parameters of sanctioned broadcast. Similarly, the concept of virality applies to PKP in that the pirate broadcast inhabits the system, perpetrating "diversification" and "distortion." See Joselit, *Feedback*, pp. 5, 48–50.

good job start. I think, if people are trying to express themselves, then it is artistic. But, in a way, you see even the arts now, sometimes these people are not expressing themselves, they have a concept and they want to build on it.[34]

For PKP, who participated in the Nieuwe Wilden movement of neo-expressionist painting, getting in touch with the expressive quality of art often meant working spontaneously in many different formats at once. It also meant doing away with the circumscription of conceptual art and the orderliness of minimalism.

The impulse was bigger than the art world, however. As I argue in chapter 1, squatters were busy building a city within a city in Amsterdam, opening their own hang-outs and galleries and creating their own media, which was something akin to starting a new civilization from scratch, from within the fabric of the existing structure. No one was telling them not to or curbing their activities, so what they built became an increasingly elaborate facsimile of the "outside" world as time went on, using whatever materials they could find in their surroundings. The youth culture scene was an "island in the net" (to use Bey's terminology)—no future except the one you created yourself. These pirate islands, therefore, maintained a hedonistic and post-apocalyptic sense of starting over again—a wild freedom. The appearance of ritualistic primitivism was a facet of this world-building impulse.

Despite their attempts to distance themselves from their immediate predecessors in the art world, PKP-TV is, as noted, contiguous with 1970s video art in its exploration of the reflexivity of the televisual medium. The work of Joan Jonas, Lynda Benglis, Vito Acconci, Dan Graham, Peter Campus, Marina Abramovic, Douglas Davis, and many others in the 1970s dealt with the televisually-mediated body in diverse ways that often exploited feedback loops between body, camera, and screen. In the case of PKP-TV, this impulse does not appear as a "narcissistic enclosure inherent in the video-medium," as Krauss would have it, but rather as a gambit for autonomy within the *televisual* medium.[35] The broadcasts of PKP operated on different levels as they contained pre-recorded as well as live feedback loops. At the end of the broadcasts, PKP-TV would sometimes switch to a live feed from inside the studio. For example, the end of one of the PKP broadcasts goes live and pans around the studio to show the PKP crew lounging around amid the various equipment, exposing the mechanics behind the scene. According to

34 Ploeg, interview by author.
35 Krauss, "Video," p. 64.

Richard Lorber, writing on video art in 1974, "The dematerialized intimacy of the video monitor image and the medium's reflexive properties in live feedback systems have tended to make video art something of a 'final solution' for handling all the epistemological ironies (harking back to Duchamp) in the art of the last 10 years."[36] Apart from providing a "solution" to the tangled discourse of twentieth-century artistic practice, however, video also presented a wider ontological solution to the struggle of autonomous individuality against the closed system of broadcast media.

Put another way, video was, for artists, not an opportunity to *make* TV but to *be* TV, to enter into and participate inside the frame of television in real time, to merge with the medium rather than interact with it from afar or tinker with it on the receiving end. In Nam June Paik's piece *TV Bra For Living Sculpture* (1969), for example, Paik's collaborator Charlotte Moorman performs on the cello with her naked body literally enveloped or covered in television(s). This was, in some ways, a crude attempt to overlap and embody television and a tongue-in-cheek reversal of the political position of the viewer in relation to TV. In the words of Gregory Battcock, "instead of 'being on television,' the televisions were, in fact, on Charlotte Moorman."[37] There was room, however, for video artists to take the idea of *being* television further. Since broadcast was, at least metaphorically, a black box, it became the Holy Grail for artists of the early 1970s. These multi-faceted artistic experiments with television outside of pirate TV, as much as they aimed for independence, were only mere representations or riffs on the televisual rather than television itself. They fall into roughly three categories: manipulation of or interventions with existing hardware, pre-recorded or live video art and video art installations in gallery or exhibition settings, and pre-recorded or live video art on network television. Paik's work at various points fell into all three categories. Most of the canonical video art from the artists cited above, including Joan Jonas, falls in the second category.

Before addressing the third category—art on network television—it is worth pausing to compare Jonas's work, as an example of the second category listed above, to PKP. Her use of masks and video reflexivity has some superficial similarities to the Amsterdam pirates but, in its form of delivery and concerns, it is quite different. In *Organic Honey's Vertical Roll* (1972) and *Organic Honey's Visual Telepathy* (1972), Jonas wears a mask of a woman's face and show-girl-like costumes to embody an ostentatious,

36   Richard Lorber, "Epistemological TV," *Art Journal* 34, no. 2 (1974): pp. 132–34.
37   Qtd. in Joselit, *Feedback*, p. 62.

hyper-sexualized female identity. The work is not a meditation on gender alone but on *mediated* gender. It operates within and points to the formal qualities and constraints of analog television via its glitches: scan lines and rolling picture bars. Jonas gets inside the bars, merging with the image on the screen rather than existing separately from it. Whereas television was, at first, only a means of receiving representations of identity, video gave artists like Jonas the ability to overlap their own bodies with these received tropes so that they could now participate in and take control of them and attempt to *be* television rather than merely receive television. This is, then, not so much a reflection of narcissism as a desire for autonomy within the broadcast medium, a desire that pirate TV was able to achieve on another level, stripping back the layers of close-system artificiality.

The third category, art on network television, is a better point of comparison for PKP-TV than the work of Acconci, Jonas, or other artists in the second category. While many artists in Europe and the United States—including the Netherlands—were actively working with television stations to bring artworks to the public via broadcast, the Videofreex and TVTV in the United States were interested in producing guerrilla documentary forms of television with the goal of opening up and democratizing the closed broadcast system of the late '60s. US television at that time was dominated by only three major networks, which had considerable power over the messages the American public received.[38] These politically-minded artists and theorists contributed to the publication *Radical Software* in the early 1970s and hoped to speak truth to power through the new medium of video.

The New York-based radical video group that called themselves the Videofreex came together in the summer of 1969 at the Woodstock music festival. David Cort, who was already an active member of the New York video underground, met Paul Teasdale there, who was independently experimenting with video. Together with artist Mary Curtis Ratcliff, they formed a video collective in Cort and Curtis Ratcliff's SoHo loft.[39] Louis Brill, who worked in the mailroom at CBS, had also met Cort at Woodstock and, impressed by the work they were doing, put them in touch with Don West at the network. Working as the assistant to the president of CBS, Frank

38 Boyle, *Subject to Change*; Parry D. Teasdale, *Videofreex: America's First Pirate TV Station & the Catskills Collective That Turned It On* (Hensonville, NY: Black Dome Press, 1999); Nancy Cain, *Video Days: How Street Video Went from a Deep Underground Phenom to a Zillion Dollar Business. From Pirate TV to YouTube, What Was Gained and Lost along the Way and What We Saw through the Viewfinder* (Palm Springs, CA: Event Horizon Press, 2011); Jon Nealon and Jenny Raskin, *Here Come the Videofreex*, 2015.
39 Boyle, *Subject to Change*, p. 15.

Stanton, West secured approval to spearhead a new kind of television show that reflected late '60s youth culture, "The Now Project"/*Subject to Change*.[40] After enthusiastically viewing their Woodstock footage, West began pumping money into the project. The Videofreex were given an RV, a large budget, and equipment to go out and capture the counterculture throughout the United States. David Cort recalls, "They were treating us like a rock band, that's the model that they had of us."[41] According to Parry Teasdale, they did not particularly care whether the support of CBS left their "ideological pedigree" less than "politically pure."[42]

Unlike PKP a decade later, the Videofreex had no way to access television without network approval and, hence, were at the mercy of CBS to broadcast their videos. Although they parted ways with CBS before making it to air, the Videofreex managed to take many of their tapes and the pricey video equipment with them when they left. Prior to pirate cable hacking, artists had to either ask for permission to broadcast from the gatekeepers of the broadcast television (including local cablecast providers), limiting the inherent freedom of the endeavor, or create a close-circuit version of television within galleries or performance spaces, limiting their claim to televisuality.

Obsessed with finding a way to broadcast, the Videofreex went about setting up a pirate station. They were pushed in this endeavor by radical activist and provocateur Abbie Hoffman, who enlisted them to figure out how to pirate TV so that he could publish details about it in his activist manual *Steal This Book* (1971). Hoffman and the Freex initially dreamed of setting up a New York City-wide mobile TV transmitter, but they soon discovered that aerial pirate TV (i.e., terrestrial transmission) would not be possible in the city due to inadequate broadcasting conditions and the limits of their technical capabilities.[43] It was, however, possible in a more rural location, and they succeeded in setting up the first pirate aerial TV station in the US in 1972, based in tiny Lanesville, New York.[44] They were able to achieve this feat thanks to a transmitter supplied by Hoffman and $40,000 of funding from the New York State Council on the Arts. Their upstate New York residence operated as a commune and a collective. True to this form of cooperation, they insisted on being identified or quoted in

40 Boyle, *Subject to Change*, p. 17; Cain, *Video Days*, pp. 14–16.
41 Nealon and Raskin, *Here Come the Videofreex*; Teasdale, *Videofreex*, p. 16.
42 Teasdale, *Videofreex*, p. 17.
43 Teasdale, *Videofreex*, pp. 29–30; Cain, *Video Days*, p. 34; Nealon and Raskin, *Here Come the Videofreex*.
44 Cain, *Video Days*, pp. 49–51; Teasdale, *Videofreex*.

the press as a collective rather than individuals, which was a practice shared with the collective endeavors of the late '70s and early '80s in Amsterdam.[45]

In 1972 Michael Shamberg, author of the radical television manual *Guerrilla Television* and founder of Raindance and *Radical Software*, started a video collective called TVTV (Top Value TV). Members of the group included Megan Williams, Allen Rucker, Hudson Marquez, and Tom Weinberg.[46] The group's first major activities were creating video documentary of the Democratic and Republican National Conventions in Miami Beach, Florida in 1972.[47] TVTV was, from the start, more business-oriented and organized than many of the other guerrilla TV outfits. Shamberg and his collaborators recruited other video groups like the Videofreex to help them shoot, and they negotiated with cable channels in Manhattan, Ohio, and elsewhere to fund the endeavor.

Their documentary style was more like a "video collage," roughly shot right in the middle of things, where they were able to move smoothly in and out of the various groups within the conventions.[48] Unlike the independent work of the Videofreex, who were still trying to realize their dream of live, participatory television after falling out with CBS, the Shamberg-led TVTV embraced commercial deals for their projects, including—eventually— broadcast deals with Westinghouse. The Westinghouse deal meant that the aesthetics of guerrilla television had become palatable to broadcast TV.

In addition to the three categories of video enumerated above—manipulation of or interventions with existing hardware, pre-recorded or live video art and video art installations in gallery or exhibition settings, and pre-recorded or live video art on network television—there was a fourth category (which was closely related to the third): art on cable television. Although the development of cable infrastructure began in the 1960s in the US, it was only expanded to major metropolitan areas in the mid- to late 1970s and was thus not really used by artists until later, by which time video camera technology had become far more banal.

Early cable television was not the space of democracy and freedom that guerrilla television activities in the late 1960s dreamed it would be. Cable technology was developed not with the goal of allowing broader participation in television but to facilitate larger, joint aerial reception and perhaps access to a few more professional, commercial channels—as was the case

45   Sami Klein, "Everybody Will Be On Television," *Rolling Stone*, March 18, 1971.
46   Boyle, *Subject to Change*, p. 72.
47   Cain, *Video Days*, pp. 64–73.
48   Boyle, *Subject to Change*, p. 39.

in Amsterdam. These early cable networks were, thus, community antenna systems that could more effectively get television to non-urban communities shrouded by mountains or other obstructive geography. Additionally, satellite reception was used (in place of local terrestrial reception) in cable television practically from the moment it became widespread in the late 1970s. The cable system in Amsterdam, which still relied on terrestrial broadcast in the early 1980s, used cable primarily as a broadcast distribution system.[49] While laws in the United States required that local cable networks provide community access channels, these were not closed circuits between the viewer and the screen—like gallery-based video art– but rather a form of broadcast on a much smaller scale (a narrowcast, so to speak).[50] What is interesting about pirate television is that it disrupts the broadcast flow. It interrupts the network at the intermediary point of group reception (i.e., the receiving dish), and thus carves out a space in between.[51]

Despite a shared belief in the liberatory and democratic nature of DIY media, there are several other elements that set PKP apart from the more optimistic and idealistic television experiments of the late '60s and early '70s. For one, groups like the Videofreex and TVTV saw themselves as the vanguard reporting the truth of the social movements of the era, on the ground, in unadulterated form. Although the handheld camera work of the Videofreex and TVTV was far more immediate, fluid, and spontaneous than anything being shown on network television at the time, they still aspired to a professionalism in their reportage that groups like PKP actively eschewed. Apart from the use of anonymizing masks in their broadcast, other elements of PKP-TV, such as the interruptive music, the shaky, puerile, constantly moving or zooming camera work, and the amateur sets, all guide the viewer out of the legally sanctioned space of professional television into their pirate utopia, their crack in the net. Gone was the desire to use video to record the unadulterated "truth" on the ground—the stated goal of the Videofreex and TVTV—and, in its place, was a relativistic and subjective notion of truth.

49   Fransje Klaver and A. van der Meer, *Kabel en satelliet: een onderzoekscollege* (Amsterdam: Universiteit van Amsterdam, Vakgroep Massacommunicatie, 1984), p. 38; F. J Schrijver, *De invoering van kabeltelevisie in Nederland.* ('s-Gravenhage: Staatsuitgeverij, 1983); F. Klaver et. al., *Visie op kabeltelevisie* (Amsterdam: Stichting Moderne Media, 1973).

50   Boyle, *Subject to Change*, pp. 33–34. The term narrowcast describes a broadcast that is tailored to a specific audience. For pirate television, the audience will by default be narrower in a rural setting than an urban one. See Amanda D. Lotz, *The Television Will Be Revolutionized* (New York: New York University Press, 2014), p. 37.

51   In the late 1980s, Amsterdam cable developed a similar initiative called SALTO. See chapter 4.

While PKP still maintains a glimmer of a connection to professional television in that it has a presenter who introduces the clips and, later, presents the "news," it is a twisted parody of the format, like a children's make-believe game. The news itself, although it is labelled national and international, as in a serious newscast, concerns mainly the mundane going-on in their immediate milieu. For example, one absurd "news" item during the "international" segment of the seventeenth PKP broadcast reports that the Peugeot car belonging to the members of PKP/Soviet Sex broke down in Germany and they need a mechanic. Though this broadcast happens to be interspersed with clips of bands, including Joy Division, the Sex Pistols, and Deutsch Amerikanische Freudschaft (DAF), that are all ripped from professional recordings, PKP also made many of their own tapes at local gigs or art exhibitions (which were often not separate events). For example, another clip from this episode shows a performance by artist Peter Giele from the opening of the V2_ art space in Den Bosch. Shot in the darkened space on black and white U-matic video, the footage of Giele's performance is relatively unclear but shows the artist wrapped or bundled in fabric, moving along a rope on the floor of the space. For PKP, it made no real difference where the footage came from or whether the quality was consistent throughout; the clips varied between color, black and white, and appropriated professional footage.

Another segment that was aired during the broadcast is also indicative of the difference in attitude between PKP and the Videofreex or TVTV. It is a report from Waterlooplein, which was a huge construction pit at the time, partially occupied by punks.[52] The clip consists, again, of black and white U-matic footage by a group calling themselves Vlo-TV, in collaboration with PKP-TV. As is typical of the outside contributions to PKP-TV's broadcasts, each group that aired segments came up with their own collective moniker. The footage shows young children and punks building piles of rubbish up on the site. A large tower of old TVs has been assembled [Fig.11] and each has a number painted on (as well as one with PKP written on it). It becomes clear that this is a kind of makeshift carnival game, as young people and children are then seen shown throwing stones at the screens, trying to break them

<hr />

52   A group of young people, including Diederik de Savornin and David Elders, built a treehouse at the site, which protested the razing of trees for the construction of the Stopera complex. Stopera was a portmanteau of the two proposed functions for the site: city hall "stadhuis" and the opera/ballet. The treehouse activists used the slogan, "These trees will stay, Stopera will not go through" ("Deze bomen blijven staan, Stopera van de baan"). See Martijn Haas, *Bibikov for president: politiek, poëzie & performance 1981-1982* (Amsterdam: Lebowski Publishers, 2012), pp. 82–86.

and, one would assume, score the corresponding points. Once all the TVs are shattered and knocked down, the footage shows them piled up and set on fire, the clouds of smoke billowing into the sky. This segment is reminiscent of the San Francisco art collective Ant Farms's 1975 performance/film *Media Burn*, in which a Cadillac car is driven into a tower of flaming television. By creating their own mass media spectacle, Ant Farm critiqued both American post-war consumer behavior and the ways in which consumption was promulgated by the mass media.

In the case of the Vlo-TV segment, the playful destruction on display has no clear social or political rationale—at least nothing as overt as *Media Burn*— and, so, indicates a willful childishness that the self-serious guerrilla TV crews of the early '70s generally steered away from. Any irreverence that appeared in counterculture videos was always focused on serious experimentation and inquiry or "speaking truth to power" whereas PKP was focused on play and anarchic freedom. When asked if there was something political about their broadcasts, the PKP boys replied, "There has to be a little madness in it. It may have something to do with politics but not in an informative or serious way."[53] They were not really concerned with challenging an amorphous power structure per se. The powers that be, in turn, did not seem to care much about them. In this way, the clip of the destruction of the TVs in the middle of an urban wasteland has more in common with not only Zurich Dada but also Neo-Dada and Fluxus in the 1950s, during which Wolf Vostell and Nam June Paik got their start with TV installations, than the guerrilla television of the late '60s and early '70s.

PKP-TV were not the first artists to work with television in the Netherlands.[54] In the early 1960s, Dutch artist Wim T. Schippers, along with

53   Mart Roegholt, "Nee, Geen Porno Meneer," n.d., Maarten Ploeg Knipselmap 16305, Stedelijk Museum Library.
54   Although outside the scope of this discussion, many visual artists made work for broadcast television during the late '60s and early '70s. See Gene Youngblood, *Expanded Cinema* (New York: Dutton, 1970); Fred Barzyk et al., *Fred Barzyk: The Search for a Personal Vision in Broadcast Television* (Milwaukee: Patrick and Beatrice Haggerty Museum of Art, 2001); Małgorzata Jankowska, *Wideo, wideo instalacja, wideo performance w Polsce w latach 1973-1994: historia, artyści, dzieła* (Warsaw: Wydawn. Neriton, 2004); Dieter Daniels, "Television—Art or Anti-Art?," February 15, 2007, http://www.medienkunstnetz.de/themes/overview_of_media_art/massmedia/; Łukasz Ronduda, *Polish Art of the 70s* (Warsaw: Centrum Sztuki Wspoczesnej Zamek Ujazdowski, 2009); Sarah Hollenberg, "Art on Television: 1967–1976" (Ph.D., Los Angeles, University of Southern California, 2012); Robyn Farrell, "Network(Ed) TV: Collaboration and Intervention at Fernsehgalerie Gerry Schum and Videogalerie Schum," *Afterimage* 43, no. 3 (December 11, 2015): p. 12; Laura Leuzzi, "Interventions, Productions and Collaborations: The Relationship between RAI and Visual Artists," *Journal of Italian Cinema & Media Studies* 3, no. 1–2 (March 1, 2015): 155–70.

several of his peers in the art world, seized on television as a novel way to disseminate art to the public. Rather than approach the medium critically, as the guerrilla TV makers in the US had, Schippers asserted approvingly that, via television, "I exhibit in the biggest gallery in the country."[55] Part of the disjunction in attitude here may be due to the difference in broadcast control between Europe, where broadcasters were government funded and more tightly controlled, and the US, where network TV was highly commercialized and public television was underfunded and ultimately forced to rely on corporate sponsorship.

Nevertheless, in 1962, Schippers and Willem de Ridder produced a television program about contemporary artists called "*Signalement, kunst na 1960*" [Report, art since 1960] focusing, in particular, on Pop Art, which was not well-known in the Netherlands at that time. The program featured work by George Brecht, Stanley Brouwn, Roy Lichtenstein, Henk Peeters, and Andy Warhol, as well as a notorious piece, *Adynamic Action* (1961/63) [also called *Signalement* (1963), after the program that aired the work] by Schippers himself, which documented him emptying a bottle of fizzy lemonade into the sea. The TV program annoyed the general public and art aficionados alike, as it presented the artworks on the show in an irreverent, joking manner. The ludic nature of Schippers's work and the impulse for irreverent experimentation resonates with the punk hijinks of the Nieuwe Wilden/PKP group and demonstrates that there was an established aesthetic tradition of irreverence in Dutch art-TV, which they followed.

In 1967 Schippers, Wim van der Linden, Willem de Ridder, and Hans Verhagen produced the short-lived *Hoepla* for VPRO (the Dutch liberal protestant broadcaster), a playful and subversive program for young people at the height of the Provo era that featured nudity and colorful language in an unprecedented way. The show only lasted for three episodes but went down in the annals of TV history for being the first television show to feature a fully nude woman.[56] The set up was more comic than erotic: the woman, Phil Bloom, was shown casually reading a newspaper which at first covered her body before the shot moved to reveal her naked beneath it. Schippers's work for VPRO during the 1970s, like that of PKP, had a deliberately cheeky, low-fi vibe. Not unlike PKP, Schippers' TV shows demonstrate, according to Jeroen Boomgaard and Bart Rutten, a "deliberate amateurism" in which

55 Noemi Smolik, "Very Funny: Wim T. Schippers on His Long and Diverse Career," *Frieze*, February 2017, p. 126.

56 Hans Verhagen, *De gekke wereld van Hoepla: opkomst en ondergang van een televisieprogramma.* (Amsterdam: de Bezige Bij, 1968).

the "cardboard sets, the almost constant presence of an audience, the errors and mistakes" give the programs "the atmosphere of domestic intimacy and presence."[57]

Another key moment for Dutch artists on TV came in 1969, when German artist and video art gallerist Gerry Schum and Dutch conceptual artist Jan Dibbets teamed up to produce Dibbets's *TV as a Fire Place* to air after the end of WDR's programming during the Christmas period. As the name implies, by showing a roaring fire on the screen, the TV was transformed into the gathering place and hearth of earlier generations. The piece was a tongue-in-cheek reminder that flickering TV had come to replace the hearth as the center of domestic life. Schum was an important early promoter of television and video art in the 1960s. He initiated the Television Galley in 1968 with Ursula Wevers, a "virtual" gallery to show works on television, and, in 1971, started Video Gallery in Düsseldorf to distribute artists' tapes.[58]

Also in 1971, Dutch artists Marinus Boezem, Stanley Brouwn, Dibbets, Ger van Elk, and Peter Struycken participated in a series titled *Beeldende kunstenaars maken televisie* [Fine Artists Make Television], which aired on NOS (Dutch Broadcast Foundation). Marinus Boezem's work for the program, *Het beademen van een beeldbuis (Breathing on a Picture Tube)* (1971), shows the artist breathing onto a glass sheet in front of the camera, creating the effect of condensation on the television screen. While the video's interaction with the viewer and attempts to break the fourth wall are not dissimilar to some of the American video art examples discussed above, Boezem's work was actually shot on 16mm film rather than video. Like Dibbet's TV fireplace, it creates an awareness for the television viewer that their TV is an object present in their homes and not just a picture window to a fantasy world.

In light of these early expositions of contemporary art on television, the Dutch public was primed to see avant-garde and artistic experiments on television. Despite their sometimes controversial nature, however, these

57   Jeroen Boomgaard and Bart Rutten, "Early Days: Dutch Video Art in the 1970s," in *The Magnetic Era: Video Art in the Netherlands 1970-1985*, ed. Jeroen Boomgaard and Bart Rutten (Rotterdam: NAi Publishers, 2003) p. 43.

58   Edith Petten and Robertus Dettingmeijer, *Beeldende kunstenaars en televisie: de aktiviteiten van Gerry Schum* (Utrecht: Utrechtse Kring, 1972); Dorine Mignot and Ursula Wevers, *Gerry Schum* (Amsterdam: Stedelijk Museum, 1979); Benjamin H. D. Buchloh, "From Gadget Video to Agit Video: Some Notes on Four Recent Video Works," *Art Journal* 45, no. 3 (1985): 217–27; Ulrike Groos, Barbara Hess, and Ursula Wevers, *Ready to Shoot: Fernsehgalerie Gerry Schum, Videogalerie Schum* (Köln: Snoeck, 2004); Chris Wahl, "Between Art History and Media History: A Brief Introduction to Media Art," in *Preserving and Exhibiting Media Art: Challenges and Perspectives*, ed. Julia Noordegraaf et al. (Amsterdam University Press, 2013), p. 41; Farrell, "Network(Ed) TV."

earlier art broadcasts used television in relatively conventional ways: either as an alternative method of disseminating film and video art (or documentation of works in other mediums such as land art) or, in the more avant-garde cases, by turning the viewer's television into a prop serving an alternative purpose *à la* Dibbets's fireplace. Although PKP-TV follows in the tradition of these early TV experiments, their broadcasts differ in their clandestine nature. These autonomous pirate broadcasts were a new form of art on television and followed not only the irreverent spirit of the Dutch artists that came before them but also a tradition of pirate media in the Netherlands.

Pirate Media, Pirate Politics

Just as art on television was already established in the Netherlands, pirate media was also already something of a mainstream institution for the Dutch public at the beginning of the 1980s. Illegal media was a revered symbol of freedom, rooted in the German occupation of the Netherlands during World War II. Especially in Amsterdam, the material and psychological effects of the occupation lasted for decades afterward. Over 100,000 Dutch Jewish citizens were killed in concentration camps during the war and, so, many of the houses in the old Jewish quarter of the city, particularly the Nieuwmarkt, Waterlooplein, Plantagebuurt, and Weesperplein areas, were left empty. After the war, squatters occupied many of these neighborhoors. The government, hoping to ease the economic hardships of the post-war era, passed a law in 1947 that allowed these squatters to legally remain.[59] Nevertheless, the ramshackle state of these areas after the war precipitated a number of *tabula rasa* urban planning initiatives in the following decades, as the government sought to modernize the city by building new highways and metro stations. Squatters and residents vociferously protested these changes and, in so doing, preserved portions of these historic areas from redevelopment. These protests were noteworthy in that they also spawned the first squatter/neighborhood pirate radio station in Amsterdam: Radio Sirene. The station was started in 1971 to protest the proposed demolition of the Nieuwmarkt neighborhood.[60]

---

59 Caroline Nevejan and Alexander Badenoch, "How Amsterdam Invented the Internet: European Networks of Significance 1980-1995," in *Hacking Europe: From Computer Cultures to Demoscenes*, ed. Gerard Alberts and Ruth Oldenziel (London: Springer, 2014), p. 193.
60 "Illegale 'Sirene' Bewaakt Nieuwmarkt," *Het Parool*, April 10, 1971, Dag edition; "Geheime Zender Buurtwapen Tegen Slopers," *De Volkskrant*, April 10, 1971, Dag edition; "Sirene," *NRC*

The Second World War delivered another legacy—a strong tradition of illegal alternative media within the Dutch Resistance. Important national newspapers such as *Trouw* (Loyalty), *Het Parool* (The Password), *Vrij Neder-land* (Free Netherlands), and *De Waarheid* (The Truth) were founded as illegal resistance papers during the 1940s and continued as successful national newspapers in the postwar period.[61] Illegal and guerrilla radio broadcasts also played an important role for the resistance during the war years, as they did in many of the occupied countries of Europe. In the '60s and '70s, illegal and alternative pirate radio stations flourished throughout Europe—notably in the UK and Italy—and served as an important communication channel for leftwing and anarchist movements.[62]

Despite the changes to media brought about by the German occupation during World War II, the Dutch media landscape still largely reflected the careful balancing act in Dutch society between competing religious and political groups. Government policy was determined, throughout much of modern Dutch history, by tolerance of this plurality. The different factions co-existed via a system of social stratification that was labelled *verzuiling* (pillarization) by Dutch sociologists after World War II. This meant that Dutch media and society were divided into different segments including Protestants, Catholics, Liberals, and, later, Communists, and each of these pillars maintained their own institutions and media.[63] During the early days of radio in the Netherlands in the 1920s, the Dutch debated whether a single unified national broadcast system could protect the interests of the various pillars or whether broadcast media, like periodicals, should be divided along pillarized lines. In 1930 regulations were passed in the Netherlands that sided with those in favor of pillarization and stipulated that licensed broadcasters

---

Handelsblad, May 1, 1971, Dag edition; "Aktiegroep Nieuwmarkt 1968-1973," 1973 1968, SAVRZo28 Doos 001B Map 1, Instituut voor Sociale Geschiedenis – Staatsarchief.

61   Hans van den Heuvel and Gerard Mulder, *Het vrije woord: de illegale pers in Nederland 1940-1945* ('s-Gravenhage: SDU-Uitg., 1990), pp. 23–49.

62   Michael Goddard, *Guerrilla Networks: An Anarchaeology of 1970s Radical Media Ecologies* (Amsterdam: University of Amsterdam Press, 2018), pp. 174–191.

63   Jakob Pieter Kruijt, *Verzuiling: een Nederlands probleem al of niet voorzichtig benaderd* (Zaandijk: Heijnis, 1959); Hans Daalder, "The Netherlands: Political Opposition in a Segmented Society," in *Political Oppositions in Western Democracies*, ed. Robert A Dahl (New Haven; London: Yale University Press, 1966), pp. 188–236; Arend Lijphart, *The Politics of Accomodation: Pluralism and Democracy in the Netherlands* (Berkeley, Calif: University of California Press, 1968); Ken Gladdish, "Opposition in the Netherlands," in *Opposition in Western Europe*, ed. Eva Kolinsky (London: Croom Helm, 1987), pp. 195–214; Cees van der Eijk, "The Netherlands: Media and Politics between Segmented Pluralism and Market Forces," in *Democracy and the Media: A Comparative Perspective*, ed. Richard Gunther and Anthony Mughan (Cambridge: Cambridge University Press, 2008), pp. 303–42.

must meet the cultural or religious needs of a particular segment of society (i.e., one of the pillars) and offer broad programming content that covered the cultural, educational, and entertainment needs of the pillar it serviced.[64]

In the 1950s and early '60s, Dutch television was also limited in the programming and content it could broadcast in order to conform to pillarization. As the country and media landscape rapidly modernized in those decades, however, Dutch cultural commentators increasingly called for depillarization. Concurrently, illegal radio and television broadcasters began to establish themselves in the waters off the coast of the Netherlands to avoid strict circumscription within these pillars and, thus, due to their illegal activities at sea, were called pirates.[65] Rather than pirating material goods, they were stealing the airwaves, or the "ether." One of the first of these was Veronica, which was based on a ship off the coast of the Netherlands. In 1964, TROS established itself on REM-Eiland, a World War II-era military platform that was positioned off the coast, so that they were not subject to the land-based broadcast rules. At the same time, illegal pirates began to establish themselves on land and broadcast locally on empty airwaves.

As noted, due to its flat geography, Dutch viewers had long had access to television and radio from neighboring countries—provided the weather conditions were favorable—but the presence of tall structures in larger cities like Amsterdam could still disrupt the quality of the terrestrial transmissions. By the late '60s and early 1970s, the government began to look into cable infrastructure on both the local and national level. The manner in which cable television developed in the Netherlands (i.e., the creation of unified public infrastructure coupled with tolerance of community use of these networks) set up ideal conditions for local TV piracy in the 1970s.

Following the alternative media spearheaded by the Dutch Resistance in the 1940s and the sea-based pirates of the post-war years, grassroots community cable television initiatives appeared in Amsterdam almost as soon as the first cable networks did. In 1971 the Lokale Omroep Bijlmermeer (LOB, Local Bijlmermeer Corporation) was set up in the newly-built Bijlmermeer housing estate in the southeastern suburbs of Amsterdam, which paved the way for pirates at the end of the decade. A massive high-rise housing complex built in the International Style, the Bijlmermeer, which broke ground in 1966, was designed to house working class Dutch families that were, at the

---

64 Eijk, "The Netherlands," p. 306.
65 J.H.W. Lijfering, *Illegale recreatie: Nederlandse radiopiraten en hun publiek* (Wageningen: Landbouwuniversiteit, 1988).

time, living in derelict older housing stock in city center neighborhoods like the Jordaan. Due to unforeseen rises in construction costs, however, the completed apartments, which residents began moving into in 1968, were initially too expensive for the Dutch lower-income families they were designed for and, thus, attracted higher income residents or those willing to share the units, such as students and foreign workers.[66] The heightened political atmosphere of the late '60s and early '70s did not pass the Bijlmer by, and, on October 31, 1971, local community organizers and activists there figured out how to connect their own DIY television studio to the centralized cable system installed in the estate [Fig.12].[67] During the subsequent decade, the area saw a rapid influx of ex-colonial subjects from the Dutch Antilles, which had become an autonomous country within the Dutch kingdom in 1954, and Suriname, which achieved independence in 1975. The Bijlmermeer, thus, gained a lasting reputation as a "foreign" enclave, and the LOB became a central point of information and organization for immigrant communities in the area.[68]

In the early '70s, municipalities around the Netherlands drew up plans for cable television and radio networks, but the most ambitious network would be in Amsterdam, where plans were made to connect the entire city—approximately 300,000 residences—to one unified public cable network. On September 3, 1975, the Amsterdam city council voted in favor of initiating the project, which was forecast to take approximately five years to complete and, eventually, provide at least twelve channels from the Netherlands, Belgium, Germany, and the UK.[69] The network, Kabeltelevisie Amsterdam (KTA), was publicly owned and controlled until 1995, when it was sold to private interests.[70] During the gradual installation

---

66   Nicholas Warren Jankowski, "Community Television in Amsterdam: Access to, Participation in and Use of the 'Lokale Omroep Bijlmermeer'" (Amsterdam, University of Amsterdam, 1988), pp. 46–49.

67   Ibid., p. xii.

68   Ibid., p. 69.

69   "Met 26 Tegen 17 Stemmen Amsterdam Krijgt Kabeltelevisie," De Volkskrant, September 4, 1975, Dag edition; "Amsterdam Begint in Januari Met Kabel-Tv," NRC Handelsblad, December 18, 1976, Dag edition; "Kabel-Tv in Hoofdstad," Het Vrije Volk: Democratisch-Socialistisch Dagblad, September 4, 1975, Dag edition; "Raad Besluit Tot Project van f 127 Miljoen Amsterdam Krijgt Kabel-Televisie," Nieuwsblad van Het Noorden, September 4, 1975, Dag edition; "Bij Kabel-Tv Vergoeding Aan Het Buitenland," Het Parool, September 5, 1975, Dag edition.

70   René Bogaarts, "KPN En Philips Stevenen Af Op Fusie in Kabel-Tv Van Onze Verslaggever René Bogaarts AMSTERDAM," De Volkskrant, September 30, 1995, Dag edition; "Interesse Philips Voor KTA," Het Parool, January 12, 1995, Dag edition; "Amsterdam Gaat Kabel-Tv Verkopen," De Volkskrant, June 30, 1994, Dag edition.

Figure 12: Stills from Lokale Omroep Bijlmermeer (LOB) broadcast, late 1971. Stadsarchief, Amsterdam.

of the system, the city council mandated that all outdoor aerial antennas be removed in areas connected to the cable network. The new system cost residents 8.50 guilders per month, and many complained that they were given no choice other than to pay the fee if they wanted TV access.[71] By May 1979, half of Amsterdam—around 150,000 residences—were on the network.[72]

As the system expanded, pirates began exploiting it. In summer of 1978, it was announced that improvements to the antennas would be made so that users could get better quality English and Belgian channels.[73] The first documented episode of piracy on KTA was during a test of the British BBC2 channel in December 1978. The broadcast was interrupted between ten and eleven o'clock in the evening by a hardcore pornographic video. Officials in charge of KTA speculated that the pirate signal came from Amsterdam-West, where PKP-TV would later operate, as the affected antenna was in that part of town.[74] A few weeks after the incident, the newspaper *De Telegraaf* published an interview with a young man claiming responsibility, described as a "skinny eighteen-year-old."[75] He details how he and a group of six guys between eighteen and twenty years old were active pirate radio hobbyists before they turned their attention to television hacking. They choose to broadcast pornography, he says, because of the extra attention it would attract and the conversation it would start. During the short interview, he explains that while some boys get their kicks playing with fireworks, they were getting theirs from the danger of illegal pirate broadcasting.

In the years that followed, more groups joined the ranks of pirate TV, finding it safer—and less controversial—to broadcast after the normal programming of the day rather than interrupting the scheduled programming. Most of them began to show commercials during the programming to fund their operations. The different pirate groups were self-organizing, meeting up occasionally to discuss who would have the late-night slots on

71 "Antennes Verdwijnen Voor Aanleg Kabel-TV," *De Waarheid*, March 22, 1977, Dag edition.

72 "Helft Amsterdam Aangesloten Op Kabeltelevisienet," *Nieuwsblad van Het Noorden*, March 24, 1979, Dag edition.

73 "Nog Dit Jaar Twee Engelse Zenders Erbij," *De Waarheid*, June 20, 1978, Dag edition.

74 "TV-Piraat Zendt Harde Porno Uit," *NRC Handelsblad*, December 14, 1978, Dag edition; "Porno-Piraat Uur Op Tv," *Het Vrije Volk: Democratisch-Socialistisch Dagblad*, December 14, 1978, Dag edition; Bert Voorthuijsen, "Hoofdstad Verrast Televisiepiraat Bracht Pornofilm," *De Telegraaf*, December 14, 1978, Dag edition.

75 "'Ik Ben de Pornopiraat': Illegaal Zenden Is Altijd Mijn Hobby Geweest," *De Telegraaf*, December 30, 1978, Dag edition.

various channels and solve any disputes among them. According to Menno Grootveld:

> This is one of the most important and interesting aspects of the whole era because everybody thinks that, as soon as you leave things like this out in the open, it becomes a Wild West situation. You know, everybody's going to kill each other and they will fight and whatnot. That didn't happen. What happened was that there were maybe not regular, but there were meetings of all the different pirate stations. [...] These were usually quite friendly and cooperative. [...] it's interesting because most of the other stations were all commercial pirates and some were linked to the underground. The real underground— the mafia. They were really heavy guys, not very nice people usually, but, in these meetings, they were very friendly and cooperative towards us, even if we were from a totally different planet. They didn't care.[76]

The early years of pirate broadcast on KTA were, thus, an anarchist success story, where despite lack of government oversight, all the pirate stations lived in cooperative harmony. The increasingly provocative content on pirate television, however, coupled with a period of unrest in the city of Amsterdam in 1982, soon brought the Wild West era to a close.

Prior to the opening of Mazzo on the Rozengracht on June 6, 1980, the only dance clubs in Amsterdam (due to restrictive liquor licensing laws) were underground gay and "student" clubs at Leidseplein, the old Provo and counterculture stomping ground. According to Menno Grootveld, everyone in the underground art and music scene got together at clubs like COC and Dansen bij Jansen in the late 1970s. He surmises that he first came into contact with people involved in PKP, namely Jos Alderse Baas, at Dansen bij Jansen. He explains:

> My surname is Grootveld and Grootveld is, of course the name of one of the people from Provo [Robert Jasper Grootveld], and, I mean, as far as I know, I'm not related to him, but everybody thought I was. So I went there and there was this guy hanging around there all the time and he would always greet me like, 'Hey, Grootveld! Good that you are there.' And I always thought, okay, but why? [...] And he was actually, he was involved with PKP. He was the anchor man of PKP. So after a while he asked me, don't you want to come and play along?[77]

76   Grootveld, interview by author.
77   Ibid.

And so, Grootveld was soon put to work shooting concert videos, drawn in by the creative, anarchic energy of PKP.

By November 1981, the Ploegs and Klashorst were growing too busy with other activities and decided to pass their pirate television operation over to Grootveld and anyone else who wanted to continue the broadcasts.[78] For a short while they continued operating under the PKP name but soon decided that a new name would be more appropriate, since the Ploegs and Klashorst were no longer actively working with them and the PKP name consisted, after all, of their initials. Grootveld, unable to think of a suitable name, began asking friends in the bars and clubs around town if they had any suggestions. Someone suggested Rabotnik and, after some time thinking about it and taking informal polls of his friends, the name grew on him. Grootveld says, "And nobody knew what it meant, that was the funny thing [...] it sounded nice."[79] The name, in fact, is Russian for worker [работник], which gave it a fashionable sense of irony in the waning years of the Cold War. The broadcasts that appeared under the name Rabotnik started in February 1982.

Although initially similar in format to PKP, Rabotnik was somewhat more conventional in its reports and less anarchic in its presentation. Simultaneously, though, Rabotnik often edited shows together in a more narratively abstract way than PKP had, queuing up seemingly disparate clips in quick succession. The broadcasts were still hosted by Alderse Baas but placed somewhat less emphasis on viewer-submitted content and more emphasis on politically-oriented reporting and video/music collages. One episode, from May 30, 1982, begins with a long segment of a man in a cowboy hat driving a car around Amsterdam with "Rabotnik Oil" written on the side of the vehicle, passing housing estates and industrial areas while the theme song from the TV show *Dallas* plays. Stock-footage-like clips are collaged in between: a deer grazing in a field while "Spanish Dance" from *Swan Lake* plays, a nun reading, people on the street, images of World War II, clips from nature shows, a French guillotine, and a graveyard. The chaotic "behind-the-scenes" aesthetic of PKP-TV remains as, in this episode, a young woman reporting from the street ends her introduction with the cameras still roll, asking someone off camera, "More? Keeping going?"

78   Rogier van der Ploeg recalls that the last PKP episode was probably the 25th episode, which aired on Wednesday, November 4, 1981 and primarily covered their event in Paradiso on November 1, which was called "Nacht van de Zonde." He says that they had one more show later in 1981 that was broadcast via De Vrije Keyser TV.
79   Grootveld, interview by author.

Figure 13: Mike von Bibikov behind Liesbeth den Uyl at a PvDA meeting over the Lucky Luijk, October 19, 1982. Photo by Rob C. Croes. National Archive of the Netherlands.

During Rabotnik's time as an independent pirate TV channel, a large portion of their broadcasts were spent promoting De Reagering, an anarchic punk political party that incorporated performance and provocation on the streets of Amsterdam.[80] The figurehead of the party was the poet Mike von Bibikov [Fig.13]. Both on TV and out in public, he could be seen wildly ranting anarchist slogans and waving a toy pistol, wearing his trademark trench coat and fedora. The party was formed in June 1981 by Don Bierman—a former history student, freelance journalist, and photographer active in West-Amsterdam (which was synonymous with the squatters' movement at that time)—and his friends Frank Oorthuys and Rein Jansma. For these young men, it began as a thought experiment that reflected the ennui and disillusionment in youth culture of the time. The name, which Oorthuys came up with, was a pun combining the words for government (*regering*) and react (*reageren*).[81] They were soon joined by others in the punk, squatter, and art scene, including Bibikov, Hildo Krop, Nick Oosterbaan, Peter Giele,

80   Parts of this history plus a longer analysis of the postmodern politics and right-wing con-notations of the party can be found in Amanda Wasielewski, "'We Have Decided Not to Decide': The End of History and the Punk Politics of De Reagering," in *Aftermath: The Fall and the Rise after the Event*, ed. Robert Kusek, Beata Piątek, and Wojciech Szymański (Krakow: Jagiellonian University Press, 2019), 177–92.
81   Martijn Haas, *Bibikov for president: politiek, poëzie & performance 1981-1982* (Amsterdam: Lebowski Publishers, 2012), pp. 13, 22–25.

and Peter Klashorst. Ivar Vičs, aka graffiti artist Dr. Rat, came along for the first few meetings before his death from an overdose on June 21, 1981.[82] Their political position was encapsulated in the slogan: "We have agreed that we do not agree and we have decided not to decide."[83]

De Reagering, led by Bierman and his group, first announced their entry into the political scene in the Netherlands by appearing at the official opening of the cabinet on June 4, 1981 at the Palace on the Dam, wearing suits and posing for pictures. Their political manifesto was simple: they had "no interests, no standpoints, and did not have a single responsibility."[84] Bierman knew Bibikov from the alternative scene in Amsterdam. He was a full generation older than the founders of the party and came of age during Provo. In the '60s and '70s, he worked in advertising and tried to make a name for himself as poet, but he ultimately failed to gain any recognition for his poetry in his youth. He later became a heroin user and a fixture in the counterculture and drug scene of Amsterdam. By the late '70s and early '80s, he could be found haunting the artist cafés of the city and occasionally DJing on the radio. As a tall, angular man, who would show up at artist venues screaming and waving a toy pistol, he was hard to miss. His crazed, stream-of-consciousness rants were oddly funny and his sharp delivery was heightened by his distinctive Rotterdam accent. His performances parodied the excesses of dictators' speeches and could shock even the most blasé punks and squatters around him.[85] Bierman realized that Bibikov's wild rants and dictator-like persona might be harnessed in the service of De Reagering, so he began talking to Bibikov about the party when he would meet up with him at Peter Giele's hangout, the Shafthuis Royal in the NRC-Handelsblad complex.

Bibikov was quickly positioned as the leader of the party. According to writer Martijn Haas, "For him and for a growing group of people that agreed with him, De Reagering was primarily a ludic action, mindful of its own Blitzkrieg-performances that—apart from bringing a plastic pistol and studying a few readymades—required little to no preparation."[86] Bibikov had lived through Provo and the heyday of Robert Jasper Grootveld's performances at the Spui, and in some ways his relationship to De Reagering mirrored

82   Ibid., p. 27.
83   Ibid., p. 15.
84   Ibid., p. 29.
85   "Bibikov for President: Politiek, Poëzie & Performance 1981-1982," *OVT* (VPRO, March 4, 2012), https://www.nporadio1.nl/ovt/onderwerpen/47211-bibikov-for-president-politiek-poezie-performance-1981-1982.
86   Haas, *Bibikov for President*, p. 40.

Grootveld's relationship to Provo. Like Grootveld, Bibikov's background and interest in advertising entered into his performances. Although he came from the same generation as Grootveld, he found fame in in the center of the youth culture of the generation after him, which was more taken with Dadaistic absurdities, ennui, and heroin than mysticism and marijuana. He produced a variety of catchy slogans for De Reagering and elevated the intellectual exercise of the group, much to some of the participants' chagrin, to a level of absurdity that they had not envisioned in their first few meetings discussing classic political theory like Rousseau's *Social Contract*. He also honed his look: he wore a fedora and a long, black SS-style trench coat, and he typically carried a toy pistol or shouted into a megaphone.

In late 1981 Bierman registered the party for the Amsterdam municipal elections that would take place the following June. According to Rein Jansma, the party was "a sort of endless theater piece, the theater piece of De Reagering."[87] In a Rabotnik episode from the end of May, which aired just immediately prior to the elections on June 2, 1982, the majority of the program is devoted to Bibikov's speeches, De Reagering campaigning, and interviewing other parties' politicians at a local outdoor event ahead of the election. The broadcast ends with a slogan from De Reagering: *"Kiezen op elkaar"*—a pun on "clenched teeth" (*kiezen* are molars but also the verb for voting/choosing).

Led by Bibikov, the party had no shortage of witty, provocative taglines for the posters they produced. "Don't vote, choose yourself," one poster reads. [Fig.14] Under the slogan, the poster shows a row of riot Police whose shields have been replaced by white circles inside black squares, which Dutch voters would recognize as the symbol they use to fill in their choice on the ballot form. The juxtaposition of the slogan, the riot police, and the symbols equates the vote itself with the State violence of a militarized police force. Other De Reagering posters contain the phrase, "Get The Hague out of the Netherlands, beginning with Amsterdam". The Hague, which is the seat of the Dutch government, is used in this slogan as the embodiment of the parliamentary and bureaucratic apparatus of the state, which De Reagering rejected.

For a party founded on self-government and "agreeing to not agree," it is perhaps unsurprising that their meetings often dissolved into anarchy. The permissiveness at the core of the group meant that sometimes meetings would be overrun by skinheads and other undesirable right-wing extremist groups. Nevertheless, the majority of the party members agreed that it would

87   Ibid., p. 25.

Figure 14: *Stem niet, kies zelf*, 1981, poster, 32 × 43 cm. Internationaal Instituut voor Sociale Geschiedenis (IISG), Amsterdam.

be a betrayal of their grounding principles to formalize a more concrete and realizable political agenda.[88] Despite this, it seems that some of the members of the party, including Bierman, really did seem to want to get elected to the municipal government, if only to prove they could. Even if the aims of the participants shifted as the party grew in influence, the radical and nihilistic slogans and Bibikov's absurd performances were first and foremost a form of provocation, in the spirit of their Provo predecessors. The mixed messages were part of the game. Sometimes they stated that voters should not vote at all and, at other times, they proclaimed their ambition to take over the world with Bibikov as leader of the United States, the Soviet Union, and the Vatican. "Bibikov for President" was one often-repeated slogan.

De Reagering struck a nerve with the artists of Amsterdam and captured the zeitgeist of the artistic scene at the time. Young artists in Amsterdam were attracted to the radical slogans as well as the aesthetic and performative aspects of the party. As mentioned, De Reagering was featured on both PKP and Rabotnik cable television broadcasts, and Peter Giele worked with Bibikov and De Reagering as well, using the NRC-Handelsblad building as a base. They also held events held at W139, where they connected with artists

88   Ibid., pp. 40–41.

like Ad de Jong and Rob Scholte, and Bibikov frequently performed with Soviet Sex.[89] Bart Domburg, one of the founders of V2_, was also an active participant in De Reagering. In late January 1982, Domburg and his V2_ colleagues invited Bibikov to come rabble-rouse at their exhibition-turned-occupation at Nijmegen University, where they hung banners declaring "This is a coup" and "University occupied."[90] During the spring of 1982, artists in the squatter scene were active participants in De Reagering, making posters and attending the many demonstrations staged by Bibikov in the city. For the local elections in Amsterdam, each political party must register a list of candidates and, so, De Reagering went about collecting the names of local artists to fill out their list, including Klashorst, Giele, Scholte, and De Jong.[91]

During its short run, Bibikov was not only a subject of Rabotnik's broadcasts but was essentially a part of the editorial team, often orating during the program with his pistol or megaphone in hand. The ethos of Rabotnik and De Reagering were closely aligned: both sought to provoke the established order but had little interest in leaving the confines of their pirate utopias, the city within a city that the artist and squatter community had carved out. They were both forms of irritation and disruption, never serious attempts to join either the legal media or the national government. According to Menno Grootveld, "We wanted access to the media, but we also wanted freedom of the media. So, not politely doing what was allowed, that didn't interest us. We wanted to be able to watch our own television in our own space. To stand somewhere you are not allowed to and do something irritating."[92] While PKP and Rabotnik carved out a pirate utopia in the space of cable television broadcast, De Reagering tried to do the same thing in the realm of local politics.

So insular was their community at that point in time, that many among them truly believed they could secure over half the votes of Amsterdam (or at least one of the forty-five seats on the council). De Reagering only ended up getting 1,258 votes and no seat on the council.[93] It is easy to imagine that, in a close-knit youth culture scene that was permeated by De Reagering material, some of the young people began to feel as though their scene was the whole world, the whole of Amsterdam. But, like the pirate cable television of PKP, theirs was the underside or the reverse of the city at large and their

89   Ibid., pp. 118–19.
90   Ibid., pp. 128–29.
91   Ibid., p. 144.
92   Qtd. in ibid., p. 137.
93   The majority went to the Dutch Labor party, the PvdA [99,000 votes, 17 seats]. Ibid., pp. 176–77.

party, De Reagering, was a dark mirror image of a typical political party, replacing conviction with irony and idealism with cynical ennui.

While De Reagering was destined to fail as a political movement, it was a success as an aesthetic performance. It was a pastiche of the worst aspects of government: egotistical and power hungry urges disguised as benevolence and the threat of violence lingering in the air. Bibikov was a foreign invader—a Rotterdammer in Amsterdam—who embodied the childishness and menace of the worst authoritarians with his pistol-waving antics. Slogans were either nonsensical and absurd, like "Bibikov for President", or encouraged voters to boycott the system as a whole, like "Govern yourself".[94] Given the emphasis on aesthetics above practical politics, the artists involved in the party were relatively sanguine about the outcome of the election. Commenting on the disappointment of a few young fans who came into the party headquarters in tears after the election, Bart Domburg said, "I was also grumpy about it, but the feeling wasn't so deep. What we had created together had been, in my eyes, a beautiful performance. Tomorrow was another day."[95]

The success of De Reagering, the artists seemed to realize, was that it opened up another crack, another temporary autonomous zone to destabilize a different part of the system. Its impact as a brief political movement, however, was not negligible, particularly since this "beautiful performance" took the form of a real political party, no different in legal standing from any other on the ballot. Perhaps some of the high-flung ambition behind De Reagering came from the precedent set by the Provos/Kabouters, who had successfully entered local politics as a youth protest party just over a decade before. While the Provos are often remembered for the ludic actions they performed in the 1960s, they also managed to win one seat on the Amsterdam city council in 1966. Shortly thereafter, the Kabouters, the splinter political wing of the group, turned Provo's ideas into an actionable, concrete political platform, and won a total of five seats on the city council in 1970. Unlike De Reagering, however, both Provo and the Kabouters took their political ideas and activism quite seriously. However provocative their protests, they still participated in the earnest idealism of the Provo era. The layers of irony and cynicism found in De Reagering may have been alien to the youth movements of the '60s, but they were right at home in the 1980s.

94   Ibid., p. 120.
95   Qtd. in ibid., p. 178.

One of the key differences between these two moments of history was that the punk era broadly embraced fascist aesthetics, even if ironically. Their resistance to earnest politics complicates the reading of this aesthetic. At the time, the squatters' movement newspaper *Bluf!* went so far as to call the members of De Reagering "right-wingers disguised as leftists."[96] However, as noted, there were actual neo-Nazi skinheads in Amsterdam at the time, who often fought with the squatter-artists of the city during this period. So, it could be said that there was some difference between what De Reagering was doing and the agenda of local rightwing extremists.

Martijn Haas argues that Bibikov and De Reagering were more similar to the Italian Futurists than to Provo in the 1960s. However, De Reagering can be characterized as a pastiche of Fascist rhetoric, whereas Futurism developed fascist sympathies in earnest. The name itself, De Reagering, and the play on words it creates between government and react sets the party apart from the single-mindedness of Futurism. De Reagering realized that they were creating a temporary space of aesthetic and political freedom, a pirate utopia. The party was a crack in the fabric of the city, a fissure in the very idea of progress.

The PKP broadcast discussed above shows clips of the synth-punk/ industrial band Deutsch Amerikanische Freudschaft (DAF) playing their song "Der Mussolini" (1981), which, in the style of a square dance caller or a hype man, repetitively commands the listener to "Dance the Mussolini [...] Dance the Adolf Hitler / And again the Mussolini [...] Move your butt / Clap your hands / Dance the Jesus Christ [...] And dance the Communism." The irreverence with which serious political and religious figures/ideas are collapsed into a rotation of postures or dance moves in this song makes it an apt soundtrack for the political ennui of the era.

The continual progression of ideologies is delivered by a ruling class or government that commands the people to mindlessly follow a succession of political systems, like a DJ spinning a succession of records and watching the dance floor adapt to each new beat. Martijn Haas argues:

> Whoever listens to the music of Deutsch Amerikanische Freudschaft hears the singer Gabi Delgado-Lopez endlessly repeat the term *tanz der Mussolini!*, like a trainer at a pre-war youth camp. The implication of this musical aesthetic is that however well we tell ourselves who we are, we will not step out from under the shadow of our darker history. In industrial society, fascism is never totally disbanded because it was simply—to

96   Qtd in ibid., p. 156.

a certain degree—the perfect implementation of industrial society, given form without substantial input from the people (the workers), merely focused on productivity and efficiency, to the point of eliminating unwanted societal elements.[97]

I would argue, however, that music such as this is less a reminder that fascism always lurks in the wings of democracy than it is a call to cut the strings entirely (from the puppetry of being governed). The question then is: what happens when the puppeteers' strings are actually cut?

While practical political figures like Tycho Hillenius, a member of the squatters' movement who had briefly tried to shoehorn De Reagering into formulating an actionable housing agenda, were rejected by the group, the party found it more difficult to deal with right-wing interlopers. For example, when the rightwing populist André Vierling attended De Reagering meetings and stood up to give speeches against immigration and guest workers in the Netherlands, he was grudgingly tolerated although many in the group strongly opposed his views.[98] It would have been difficult for them to shut down unpopular opinions such as this, given their slogan, "We have agreed that we do not agree and we have decided not to decide". Likewise, when De Reagering parodied fascist marches by carrying homemade torches through the streets at night, they were joined by groups of neo-Nazis and other troublemakers who disrupted their disruption.[99]

When *Bluf!* published an article arguing that "De Reagering consists of ego-tripping politicians, and right-wingers disguised as leftists," the leftwing members of the party shrugged it off.[100] From their point of view, they were performing an experimental theatre piece, parodying and mocking the excesses of politics. They may well have asked themselves: how could something as overtly apolitical as De Reagering be construed as rightwing? Of course, De Reagering's brand of apolitical rhetoric is, of course, still a political position. The idea of "governing yourself" is a form of individual anarchism, which can veer easily both to the right and the left of the political spectrum.[101] As is the case in these sorts of postmodern games, the line between play and reality is never so easy to define. The resistance of illegal

97   Ibid., p. 44.
98   Ibid., p. 92.
99   Ibid., p. 148.
100   Qtd. in ibid., p. 156.
101   Interestingly, shortly before his death in 2004, Mike von Bibikov was again politically active, this time in the emerging populist, anti-immigration/anti-Islamic politics of Pim Fortuyn, who

pirate television and De Reagering as a political movement played on this line between the safe inner confines of the game and the real world outside it.

After the election, Mike von Bibikov was keen to continue his political career by running for mayor of Amsterdam, but his novelty had worn off and he never ended up running again. His popularity owed much to his constant presence on pirate cable television—he was always seen with a camera crew trailing him through the city. The end of pirate cable television in October 1982 was, therefore, the end of Bibikov as a public figure.[102] Although he was resurrected by Rabotnik in 1986 on SALTO, the public access channel that the municipal government established in 1984, he was no longer at the center of a movement. It is difficult to pinpoint the exact reason for the demise of pirate cable TV in 1982, but it was likely a combination of factors built around the increasing unrest in the city during that time. The flashpoint came in October 1982, with the city of Amsterdam's decision to evict the Lucky Luijk squat, located at Jan Luijkenstraat 3 around the corner from the Rijksmuseum. As officials moved in to start the eviction process on October 11, massive riots broke out, and militarized police units were called in. Barricades were erected on Van Baerlestraat, paving stones were ripped up, and—in the enduring image of the riot—a number 10 tram was set on fire right outside the Stedelijk Museum [Fig.4]. As Menno Grootveld describes it, "The fights between the police and the violent squatters became ever more violent by the week. [...] you just couldn't walk through town without seeing one or more riot cars speeding somewhere [...] it was impossible to shoot anything outdoors without noticing that."[103]

Grootveld claims that, in their final pirate broadcast, they filmed Bibikov at the Waterlooplein construction site as a column of riot police cars went driving by. Bibikov did a Nazi salute and began swearing and yelling at them as they drove past. Grootveld says

Of course, we broadcasted that, and that was the end of it. Next time we wanted to go on air, it was not possible anymore. And we were the only ones. [...] There seems to have been a special meeting by the cabinet of the mayor because of the crisis caused by the squatters and riots and some of his [the mayor's] associates watched [the] show and said, 'This is going too far. If people are going to watch this on TV, the night after it

was assassinated days before the 2002 election and succeeded by figures such as Geert Wilders in the Netherlands. See ibid., p. 198.
102 Ibid., p. 181.
103 Grootveld, interview by author.

happened, we will have an even bigger riot tomorrow. This has to stop.'
So they decided to block our entrance to the channel.[104]

First, broadcasts from Rabotnik-TV and De Vrije Keijser radio were blocked
but, the following week, by October 23, 1982, all illegal pirate broadcasting
was ended on KTA.[105]

As Van der Ploeg and Grootveld say, this may have been the last free media
of the West—at least in the realm of broadcast. Given this attitude, it is easy
to see why the emerging Internet garnered so much interest in the early '90s,
as it seemed to offer another chance to produce and distribute DIY content in
a free, open, and democratic manner. So, the legacy of pirate cable broadcast,
both conceptually and practically, can be found in computer and internet
technology in the following years. The mid-'80s in Amsterdam ushered in a
series of rapid changes to society and culture, initiated by the demise of the
funding structures detailed in chapter 2, that pushed organizations like V2_
more toward electronic media and media art festivals. At the same time,
another group of international artists involved with Time Based Arts were
broadening the scope of Dutch media critique both beyond the confines of
Amsterdam's squatter milieu and beyond its formal institutional apparatus.

104 Ibid.
105 "Kabelnet in Amsterdam Afgesloten Voor Piraten," *NRC Handelsblad*, October 23, 1982,
Dag edition; "Elektronisch Systeem Weert Signaal van Radio-Piraat Op Kabel," *De Volkskrant*,
October 16, 1982, Dag edition; "Burgemeester Polak Weert Televisiezender Kraak Beweging
A'dam," *Nederlands Dagblad*, October 20, 1982, Dag edition.

4. Passageways

Abstract

This chapter investigates the transitional period during which early '80s spatial and media practices developed into the emerging field of new media art in the Netherlands. This part of the book explores how the rhetoric of interactivity initially developed around television, starting with the 1985 media art festival Talking Back to the Media. By the end of the decade and in the first few years of the '90s, a series of "networked events"— events that utilized nascent internet technology—were staged, establishing a link between former squatters (and their tactics) and the radical leftwing media art platforms, practices, and theory of the '90s.

Keywords: squatting, pirate television, internet art, internet activism, tactical media, Netherlands

> *Our situations will be ephemeral, without a future. Passageways.*[1]
>
> – Guy Debord, 1957

In the heart of the old Jewish quarter of Amsterdam sits a half-hidden monument to the failures of 1960s urban planning: Mr. Visserplein. It is flanked by the historic Portuguese Synagogue to the east and the Moses and Aaron Catholic Church to the west, and, on its southeast corner is the Jewish Historical Museum, which has, since 1987, been located in a complex of four smaller seventeenth- and eighteenth-century synagogues. Although it is well-disguised today, Mr. Visserplein was once an integral part of the stymied 1967 urban renewal project that sought to "modernize" the center of the city with the construction of new highways and a new metro line to the Bijlmermeer housing

---

1   Ken Knabb, *Situationist International Anthology: Revised and Expanded Edition* (Berkeley: Bureau of Public Secrets, 2006), p. 41.

Wasielewski, A., *From City Space to Cyberspace: Art, Squatting, and Internet Culture in the Netherlands*. Amsterdam: Amsterdam University Press, 2021
DOI 10.5117/9789463725453_CH04

project southeast of the city.[2] At the time of its construction, Mr. Visserplein was more of an interchange than, as its name suggests, a public square (*plein*). It was designed to funnel car, tram, and pedestrian traffic through a series of overlapping concrete tunnels at the point where two proposed four-lane roadways, three smaller streets, and a tram line would converge. While the existing streets and buildings in the area were totally demolished in the construction of the square, the religious buildings were left untouched, attesting to the neighborhood's history as a refuge for non-Protestants.

Most of the other structures ringing the square are much newer, built on sites that have been razed and rebuilt multiple times in the last fifty years. Apart from the church and synagogues, the square's only other historical remnant is the complex of buildings housing the Academy of Architecture. Since 1946, the academy has been located in a seventeenth-century former almshouse and artillery storehouse, which, thanks to the demolitions in the '60s, is now at the south end of Mr. Visserplein. It is fitting, somehow, that the academy should be positioned here, where several generations of architecture students could closely observe the quagmire created by top-down urban planning vis-à-vis the demolition, construction, decay, and near-constant rebuilding(s) in the area.

As detailed in chapter 1, squatters and activists in the late '60s and '70s vociferously opposed the plan to build a highway along Sint Antoniesbreestraat, which would have cut through the Nieuwmarkt neighborhood and fed into Mr. Visserplein. In the face of long-term protests from a wide coalition of citizens, the city agreed to abandon the construction of the highway and build new social housing along the street in lieu of offices. Despite these setbacks, the construction of the other four-lane road passing through Mr. Visserplein went relatively smoothly. The plan was to build a road connecting the old city of Amsterdam to the northern part of the city via a tunnel across the IJ waterway. North Holland was, at the time, largely disconnected from the city of Amsterdam below the IJ and only accessible by ferry or the Hembrug railway bridge, which connected Amsterdam's industrial port in the far west of the city to Zaandam. Ultimately, the IJtunnel, the road, and Mr. Visserplein, were all completed as planned in 1968, but the city's decision to abandon its plan for a highway through the Nieuwmarkt made Mr. Visserplein's complex strategy for traffic separation largely redundant.[3]

2   Kees Schuyt and Ed Taverne, *1950: Prosperity and Welfare* (Assen: Royal Van Gorcum, 2004), pp. 123–95.
3   Tim Verlaan, "Stadsgezichten: Mr. Visserplein," *Het Parool*, March 10, 2010, https://www.parool.nl/kunst-en-media/stadsgezichten-mr-visserplein~a283230/.

Following the typical pattern of 1960s design, the junction was comprised of a series of raw concrete passageways that forced those on foot to walk a circuitous subterranean route to reach the other side of the square or the tram stop in the center. Not only did this serve as an inconvenience for pedestrians, but it also created a blind spot where illicit activities could occur. In the 1970s and '80s, junkies and graffiti artists were prominent among the transient denizens of the underpass, which was dirty, unkempt, and regularly stank of urine. As a result, those that used the passageway for more conventional purposes increasingly found it unsafe or unpleasant to walk through and, so, in many cases, preferred to brave the traffic above ground rather than descend into the underpass.[4] The square was, eventually, given the disparaging nickname the *Gierput* (manure pit), which had a double meaning: Anton de Gier was the name of the director of city development in the late '60s, who led the project, and the word *gier* also means manure in Dutch.[5] As the state of the underpass deteriorated after years of neglect, the city began to formulate a plan to permanently close it and reroute traffic elsewhere.

In 1983, amid ongoing discussions about the fate of the tunnel, Lous America, David Garcia, Henk Wijnen, and Annie Wright, a group of artists who had all attended the Jan van Eyck Academy in Maastricht, formulated a joint project at Mr. Visserplein that they called *The Underpass*. Inspired by the television pirates of Amsterdam, who had been shut down the previous autumn, they decided to make the underpass a television set for performances, which were largely spontaneous and totally open to the public. This project, like the pirate television initiatives PKP and Rabotnik before it, represents an attempt by artists to create a platform for art in urban space, open to the public and with the aim of allowing democratic participation in art-making and art consumption. The drive for autonomy in squatted urban space was, during the mid-1980s, translated into a drive for autonomy in media space, moving increasingly from television to the emerging "spaces" of network computing/early forms of the Internet. This "passageway" between urban space and media space (or cyberspace) was developed through a series of artist initiatives starting with *The Underpass* in 1983.

4   Theo Temmink, "Gangenstelsel Gaat Leven Onder Hand Videokunstenaars," *De Volkskrant*, May 7, 1983, Dag edition.
5   Remko Koopman, Hein Sonnemans, and Marcel van Tiggelen, *Amsterdam graffiti the battle of Waterloo: 25 jaar graffiti historie op het Waterlooplein/Mr. Visserplein* (Amsterdam: Stadsuitgeverij Amsterdam, 2004), p. 9.

Following this project, Garcia went on to create—with the help of a new constellation of collaborators—a media festival called Talking Back to the Media in 1985 that used not just one site as a platform but, rather, the entire city. In the late '80s, two artist initiatives that had operated in a squatter milieu earlier in the decade—Mediamatic and V2_—turned toward developing themselves into platforms for an emerging discourse on not just video/television art but other new media being developed with the aid of computers and computer networks. These institutional platforms, in turn, set the stage for the development of a series of "network events" in the late '80s and early '90s that were initiated by artists and sought to build both local and international connections through network media, harnessing the tight-knit nature of the alternative art and activist scene in the Netherlands while simultaneously fostering global connections.[6] These network events carried on the political project of squatting in that they aimed to create open, democratic, and autonomous communities like those that squatters built in the city, only, now, these communities would exist via computer networks rather than in physical space. The passageway between squatting the city and squatting virtual space was paved through the media platforms of the mid- to late '80s. These projects led directly to the creation, in 1993, of De Digitale Stad (DDS, The Digital City), a pioneering model of internet portal—designed by artists and anarchists rather than corporate entities—that created, in the digital realm, the ideal city they had long tried to create in physical space (i.e., an open, democratic, and autonomous city).

The Underpass

The Underpass took place over four consecutive Saturdays in May 1983—the 7th, 14th, 21st, and 28th—from 8:00pm to midnight. Lous America, David Garcia, Henk Wijnen, and Annie Wright, a group of artists who had all attended the Jan van Eyck Academy in Maastricht, invited participants to create art, music, or other types of performances in the Mr. Visserplein underpass during these times. The performances were then shot, edited, and broadcast on TV the following Wednesday evenings. Since pirate broadcasting was no longer an option, they made an arrangement with Kabeltelevisie

---

6   The Galactic Hacker Party (1989), 0+ ball (1990), The Wetware Convention (1991), The Next 5 Minutes (1993), Hacking at the End of the Universe (1993), and the Doors of Perception (1993). See Nevejan, interview by Lovink.

Amsterdam (KTA) to air the videos on the Nederland 2 channel, after the regularly scheduled programming had ended for the day (as the pirates had done illegally in years prior). Although the format was inspired by and similar to pirate television, the key difference was of course that *The Underpass* was not illegal. It was, in fact, fully sanctioned by the authorities and the artists received a grant of 24,000 guilders (worth approx. €20,000 today[7]) from the city of Amsterdam and the ministry for Welzijn, Volksgezondheid, and Cultuur (WVC, Welfare, Public Health, and Culture) for the project.[8]

Despite this essential difference in support structure, the aims of the Van Eyck artists were consistent with those of the erstwhile TV pirates. Both groups were interested in opening up broadcast television to a wider public by breaking into the closed and tightly-controlled medium. While the pirates of PKP-TV, discussed in chapter 3, made rough, low-budget DIY videos partly out of necessity and partly as an aesthetic choice, the Van Eyck artists were able to afford a higher level of production quality, which can be seen in their more polished camera work, sound design, interstitials, and graphics. Regardless, they were less concerned with the nature of the content that would appear on their program than with the notion of creating a platform for participation in television.

The Underpass turned out to be a coming-together of many familiar characters from the punk, music, and art scene in Amsterdam in the late '70s and early 1980s: graffiti artist Hugo Kaagman stenciled some of his trademark zebra stripes on the wall of the tunnel, poet Diana Ozon performed a passionate reading, Mike von Bibikov made an appearance with the band Casa Nostra, Maarten Ploeg and Rogier van der Ploeg performed with Blue Murder, and various other bands and street artists participated. In the video footage, the camera pans over the curves of the dimly-lit tunnel to a diverse crowd of onlookers, assembled among the graffiti-covered concrete slabs and stagnant puddles to watch the performances. Sometimes a presenter, Alexandra Zwaal, introduces the acts and, when speaking with the English designer Laurence Fitzwilliam, translates his explanation of "living concept," a utopian architectural maquette, into Dutch. There is even a catchy theme song for the program, created by a group called the Ron Zoutberg Ensemble (Zoutberg was also the sound designer), which contains the lyrics, "Going under the underpass / Not too slow and not too fast / Crazy graffiti and the

7   "Value of the Guilder / Euro," Institute of Social History, accessed May 23, 2018, http://www.iisg.nl/hpw/calculate.php.

8   Theo Temmink, "Gangenstelsel Gaat Leven Onder Hand Videokunstenaars," *De Volkskrant*, May 7, 1983, Dag edition.

smell of piss / It's a little bit scary in a place like this."[9] The tongue-in-cheek song is performed in the tunnel complete with air guitar and backup singers.

At the time *The Underpass* was staged, Mr. Visserplein was fast becoming the most important graffiti spot in the city. By 1983 it was a well-established pilgrimage site not only for graffiti artists from Amsterdam but for street artists from around the country. The style and culture of graffiti was also in a transitional period around that time: the anarchic punk era of street art, during which Ivar Vičs (Dr. Rat) and Hugo Kaagman (Amarillo) were two of the most visible artists, was ending and an American style of graffiti, which was more focused on individual aesthetic innovation rather than a particular "message," was just coming into fashion. Kaagman says:

> For us, Mr. Visserplein was the only real 'graffiti museum' of Amsterdam. We organized the Prix de Graffiti there twice (1978 and 1979). That was a graffiti competition. Dr. Rat won the first one and N-Power won the second. [...] In 1982, I got a commission from the Waterlooplein neighborhood committee to paint graffiti on the construction fence around the building site for the metro line. In 1983, after the fence had just been completed, the American graffiti movement swept in overnight.[10]

The Underpass, then, was staged at a time when a new interest in international graffiti styles was blossoming, and Mr. Visserplein was the most important site in the city for graffiti experimentation.

Although it was largely inspired by Amsterdam's television pirates and attempted to create a platform for anarchic, democratic participation in much the same way the pirates had, *The Underpass* represented more than just a reiteration of pirate television in a formalized context. It was an important juncture for media art in the Netherlands, as it connected international artists active in the video art circuit to the punk and squatter scene of the early 1980s. These artists were attracted to the do-it-yourself ethos of the squatters/punks and drew inspiration from their radical attempts to create and control media themselves. Figures like David Garcia were thus able to articulate the implications of cracking the media in ways that the punks or squatters themselves—given their antipathy toward intellectualization—had not yet done. Likewise, figures from the squatter media side, like Geert Lovink, who were already interested in the implications of

9   Lous America et al., *Underpass*, 1983, video, 51'25", 1983, LIMA, Netherlands, http://www.li-ma.nl/site/catalogue/art/lous-america-david-garcia-henk-wijnen-annie/underpass/2719.
10   Koopman, Sonnemans, and Tiggelen, *Amsterdam graffiti*, pp. 20, 22.

autonomous or independent media, were able to connect their political and activist praxis to the field of aesthetics.[11] Cracked media was, in this way, further entangled with and interconnected to aesthetics and artistic practice beginning in the mid-1980s.

The pedestrian underpass at Mr. Visserplein was finally closed to the public in March 1985, after which it was used exclusively by the graffiti artists and junkies who managed to get around the fences blocking off the entrance.[12] Ten years later, David Garcia revisited *The Underpass* with a new project titled *The Digital Underpass* (1995), which was hosted on De Digitale Stad. For the project, Garcia designed a digital graffiti wall and invited graffiti artists to participate in posting pictures and "tagging" it. In the browser-based project, the viewer could scroll right to left along the graffiti wall and insert digital images and text into the wall.[13] In the accompanying pamphlet for the exhibition, Garcia wrote:

> The real graffiti walls of the Underpass [sic] share many of the features of the Internet. No one controls the Net. No one is in charge. The Internet is often described as the world's largest functioning anarchy. An infinite web of continuously reconfiguring and interconnected conversations in texts and image.[14]

As was common in the early to mid-'90s, Garcia celebrates the anarchic potential of the internet, seeing it as a refuge for those who had formerly sought such spaces in the city. Noting that the physical underpass at Mr. Visserplein was closed to the public at that time but still operated as a free-for-all space for graffiti artists, Garcia argues that it should "remain an emblem of the city's unconscious." He writes, "That was the reason for creating the Digital Underpass Web site [sic]. It is a way of preserving and amplifying the site as a space for the imagination."[15] From the city to the *digital* city or the underpass to the *digital* underpass, the passageway from creating platforms for art on television to creating platforms in the wider

---

11   Lovink bases his theory of aesthetics in German media theory. He writes, "Media theory rejects the classical definition of aesthetics used by art historians (a set of rules to judge the artwork) and comes up with a new one, focusing on the technical determination of perception." Geert Lovink, *Dark Fiber: Tracking Critical Internet Culture* (Cambridge: MIT Press, 2002), p. 28.

12   Koopman, Sonnemans, and Tiggelen, *Amsterdam graffiti*, p. 5.

13   Karin Feenstra, "De Digitale Kamer van Blauwbaard," *Het Financieele Dagblad*, September 16, 1995.

14   David Garcia, "The Digital Underpass," *Stedelijk Museum Bureau Amsterdam* 16 (1995): p. 8.

15   Ibid., p. 9.

realm of networked computing and digital media was born in the cracks and the margins of the established order, harnessing the tactics used by squatters in urban space.

David Garcia, in particular, used *The Underpass* project as a starting point for further investigation into how media could be opened up and made more democratic. He sees the project as the first step in the development of what he and Geert Lovink would, in the '90s, call "tactical media," where art, activism, and politics overlap with the use of new media. He explains:

> Although I didn't think that *The Underpass* was a big, spectacular success, it did sow a seed in my mind of what the potential was of this situation. [...] you also had Rabotnik, you had PKP, Peter Klashorst who is now sort of a well-known painter, but, in those days, he was a mad-hat media artist with Maarten Ploeg [...] They were the ones who were making really interesting, wild stuff. And I thought, wow, this is great, this is amazing. And that's where I wanted to go. And I was really interested in that stuff. [...] people like Maarten Ploeg and Peter Klashorst, Rabotnik were more punk-squatters. And I was, if you like, the person who [...] was part of the story of connecting the punk/squatter thing to the art thing through tactical media.[16]

Garcia, therefore, became a bridge between institutionalized video art practice and the "wild" experiments of the punks and squatters of Amsterdam. He was not only interested in what open media meant for citizenship and political participation but also what it meant in the context of art practice. By opening up broadcast media, art could be sent directly into the homes of the viewing public, circumventing the exclusivity of art institutions. In a separate interview, Garcia reiterates this point, saying that *The Underpass* "was all about moving away from traditional video art in museums and galleries, and actually using the local TV infrastructure within Amsterdam to create autonomous zones, if you like, within the media landscape.[17] The project, therefore, widened the scope of squatter media criticism to include explicit critique of the structures and institutions of the art world.

As introduced in chapter 1, "tactical media" was coined during the first Next Five Minutes conference, a landmark event in Amsterdam in 1993 that sought to theorize and understand the emerging internet and how artistic

16   David Garcia, interview by author.
17   Angela Bartholomew and Steyn Bergs, "Tactics of Mischief: From Image to Infrastructure. Interview with David Garcia," *Kunstlicht* 38, no. 3 (2017): p. 87.

and activist projects could be realized in conjunction with new technology. The term was later clarified and defined by Garcia and Lovink as:

> ...what happens when the cheap 'do it yourself' media, made possible by the revolution in consumer electronics and expanded forms of distribution (from public access cable to the internet) are exploited by groups and individuals who feel aggrieved by or excluded from the wider culture. Tactical media do not just report events, as they are never impartial they always participate and it is this that more than anything separates them from mainstream media. [...] Tactical media are media of crisis, criticism and opposition.[18]

Lovink describes tactical media as an aesthetic practice, which combines art, activism, and new media tools.[19] The term tactical is borrowed from Michel de Certeau, who defines tactics as the type of action available to the weak that subverts or undermines the strategies of control implemented by those in positions of power. In *The Practice of Everyday Life*, first published in French in 1980, de Certeau bases his analysis of the everyday on what he defines as two contrasting terms: strategies and tactics. Tactics are improvised and spontaneous means of resistance, while strategies, on the other hand, are the systems of control implemented by powerful institutions or governments, such as those found in modern cities, that seek to order and rationalize the environment.

According to de Certeau, tactics are the "trickery" and "ruses" used to subvert, break into, or otherwise challenge the norms and proscribed behaviors imposed from above. He writes:

> The space of a tactic is the space of the other. Thus it must play on and with a terrain imposed on it and organized by the law of a foreign power. It does not have the means to *keep to itself*, at a distance, in a position of withdrawal, foresight, and self-collection: it is a maneuver 'within the enemy's field of vision,' [...] It does not, therefore, have the options of planning general strategy and viewing the adversary as a whole within a district, visible, and objectifiable space. It operates in isolated actions, blow by blow. It takes advantage of 'opportunities'

---

18   David Garcia and Geert Lovink, "The ABC of Tactical Media," <nettime> mailing list, May 16, 1997, http://www.nettime.org/Lists-Archives/nettime-l-9705/msg00096.html.
19   David Garcia and Geert Lovink, The GHI of Tactical Media, interview by Andreas Broeckmann, July 2001, https://art.ubiquitypress.com/articles/10.7238/a.v0i2.684/galley/3239/download/.

and depends on them, being without any base where it could stockpile
its winnings, build up its own position, and plan raids. What it wins
it cannot keep. This nowhere gives a tactic mobility, to be sure, but a
mobility that must accept the chance offerings of the moment, and seize
on the wing the possibilities that offer themselves at any given moment.
It must vigilantly make use of the cracks that particular conjunctions
open in the surveillance of the proprietary powers. It poaches in them.
It creates surprises in them. It can be where it is least expected. It is a
guileful ruse.[20]

Thus, de Certeau points to the tactic as a means by which cracks are
exploited. As defined in chapter 1, squatting and (later) media activism
in Amsterdam opened up cracks within the existing order that were used
both as spaces of potential—temporary autonomous zones—and ways by
which to destabilize (and effect change within) the established order of
the city space.[21]

Through their occupation of and use of existing city infrastructure, often
in new configurations and for new purposes, *krakers* (squatters) embodied
and enacted precisely the kind of spatial practice that de Certeau defines,
through the use of tactics. He writes:

> Innumerable ways of playing and foiling the other's game (*jouer / déjouer
> le jeu de l'autre*), that is, the space instituted by others, characterize the
> subtle, stubborn, resistant activity of groups which, since they lack their
> own space, have to get along in a network of already established forces
> and representations.[22]

It is worth reiterating de Certeau's point, here, that the use of tactics arises
where those that would resist *lack their own space*. This is precisely the
situation that squatters in Amsterdam found themselves in in the late '70s.
Having developed the tactics to operate in the empty or abandoned spaces
of the city, they were able to apply the same sorts of tactics to the closed
circuit of media, particularly television, in the early 1980s. In media, as in
the city, space had to be appropriated from the powerful.

20   Michel de Certeau, *The Practice of Everyday Life*, trans. Steven Rendall (Berkeley: Universiy
of California Press, 1984), p. 37.
21   Hakim Bey, *TAZ: The Temporary Autonomous Zone, Ontological Anarchy, Poetic Terrorism*
(Brooklyn: Autonomedia, 2003).
22   Certeau, *The Practice of Everyday Life*, p. 18.

In contrast to the trickery that characterizes tactics, de Certeau argues that strategies facilitate the implementation of the "proper," which is beholden to the proscriptions of rational/scientific thinking developed during the Enlightenment.[23] The proper is rational, organized, and designed with stability and permanence in mind. Tactics, on the other hand, are mobile and temporary/temporal (i.e., dependent on time), tied to bodies as they "narrate" through space, while strategies adopt a panopticism that is divorced from narrative. He writes:

> The child still scrawls and daubs on his schoolbooks; even if he is punished for this crime, he has made a space for himself and signs his existence as an author on it. The television viewer cannot write anything on the screen of his set. He has been dislodged from the product; he plays no role in its apparition. He loses his author's rights and becomes, or so it seems, a pure receiver, the mirror of a multiform and narcissistic actor. Pushed to the limit, he would be the image of appliances that no longer need him in order to produce themselves, the reproduction of a 'celibate machine.'[24]

For de Certeau, the inability of consumers to also "write" new media, such as television, creates a class of "readers" who can only receive what they are given and cannot make their own mark or interpretation on it. Television viewers are, thus, "'consumers' who cannot trace their own writing on the screen where the production of the Other—of 'culture'—appears."[25] Tactical media, therefore, allows access—even, temporary access—to these media spaces. It allows consumers to become producers (or, prosumers).[26]

In the latter half of the 1980s, as more people gained access to personal computers and were able to communicate in rudimentary networks such as BBSes (Bulletin Board Systems), a new space for tactics opened up. Artists and activists increasingly realized that digital tools, including early

23 Ibid., p. xix.
24 Ibid., p. 31.
25 Ibid., p. 169.
26 For origin of 'prosumer' see Alvin Toffler, *The Third Wave* (New York: Bantam Books, 1980). For critiques see Tiziana Terranova, *Network Culture Politics for the Information Age* (London: Pluto Press, 2004); David Beer and Roger Burrows, "Sociology and, of and in Web 2.0: Some Initial Considerations," *Sociological Research Online* 12, no. 5 (September 1, 2007): pp. 1–13; Ashlee Humphreys and Kent Grayson, "The Intersecting Roles of Consumer and Producer: A Critical Perspective on Co-Production, Co-Creation and Prosumption," *Sociology Compass* 2, no. 3 (May 1, 2008): pp. 963–80; George Ritzer and Nathan Jurgenson, "Production, Consumption, Prosumption: The Nature of Capitalism in the Age of the Digital," *Journal of Consumer Culture* 10, no. 1 (March 1, 2010): pp. 13–36.

networks, created the possibility for a kind of participation that could only be gained illegally in older broadcast media. As former squatters turned from TV and radio piracy to computer networks and interactive digital art, they envisioned a new space where "talking back" or participating in the creation of content was not illegal but integral.

Computer networks seemed, to many, to have the potential to become truly participatory platforms, the kind of platforms that artists working with television in the '70s and '80s dreamed about. Not everyone greeted the new technology with endless optimism, however. Acknowledging his debt to de Certeau, Garcia describes being simultaneously hopeful and wary of new media utopianism, saying:

> We felt that with the microelectronics revolution that gave rise to the camcorder and all those things, that suddenly, what had been invisible forms of practice were becoming visible. That would eventually become user generated content. But the interesting thing also, from my point of view, and remains interesting, is that, unlike the tech gurus of the early utopian phase of the internet, de Certeau wasn't starry-eyed about it. He knew that it was an asymmetrical relationship where the strategic media had all the power and the tacticians—the users—he was one of the first people to talk about cultural consumers as users, you know, before computers adopted that term—were always going to be at a disadvantage. Like natural organisms use camouflage and trickery, that's the way in which the weak turned the tables on the strong. [...] So the use of the term tactical in that way was a legacy of our reading of de Certeau.[27]

Thus, the utopian hopes for the emerging internet were often colored by a belief that the participatory nature of the technology finally held the solution to the media's power disparity but was nevertheless subject to cooptive strategies. While in the US, post-hippie, neoliberal/libertarian rhetoric—what Richard Barbrook and Andy Cameron called "the Californian ideology"—dominated this utopian impulse, in Europe, the internet was at first the repository for the hopes and dreams of leftwing theorists, activists, and artists rather than business entrepreneurs.[28]

27 Garcia, interview by author.
28 Richard Barbrook and Andy Cameron, "The Californian Ideology," in *Proud to Be Flesh: A Mute Magazine Anthology of Cultural Politics after the Net*, ed. Josephine Berry Slater and Pauline van Mourik Broekman (London: Mute, 2009), pp. 27–34.

Published in 1995, "The Californian Ideology" provided a seminal critique of the neoliberal ideology of internet pioneers in the United States,
particularly around the Bay Area, and dissected the ways in which "direct
democracy" becomes a euphemism for free market capitalism. Barbrook and
Cameron argue that the Californian Ideology is an odd mix of neoliberalism,
1960s counterculture, and technological determinism, which all feed off
the American myth of the frontier and the rugged individualism that was
necessary to "tame" it.[29] They contend that the social and technological
inequality between the "information-rich" and the "information-poor" is
embedded in this ideology.

In contrast to the US, Barbrook and Cameron cite the French government's
policy regarding the roll-out of the Minitel network approvingly. They write,
"Learning from the French experience, it would seem obvious that European
and national bodies should exercise more precisely targeted regulatory
control and state direction over the development of hypermedia." They
predict that, a combination of entrepreneurship, government regulation,
and DIY culture will create an instantiation of the internet where both large
corporations and small businesses will be able to thrive, where mainstream
and small-scale communities will all have their opportunity for political
participation.[30] Although Minitel was an early pioneer, it soon became an
outdated relic that ironically kept France out of the loop, tied to their own
antiquated national system, as the World Wide Web took off around the
world in the '90s. Needless to say, the solution offered by Barbrook and
Cameron—more government regulation—is not without its pitfalls. How
governments can successfully regulate internet corporations has become
an increasingly pressing question with no easily identifiable solutions.

In "The Holy Fools," a follow up to "The Californian Ideology" published in
1998, Barbrook turns his attention to the European context and the internet
pioneers on the continent, who he labels "deleuzoguattarians" due to the
influence that philosophers Gilles Deleuze and Félix Guattari had on them.
He writes, "Although these two philosophers were overt leftists during
their lifetimes, many of their contemporary followers support a form of
aristocratic anarchism which is eerily similar to Californian neoliberalism."[31]
Barbrook argues that Guattari was part of a New Left wave that thought

29   Ibid., p. 31.
30   Ibid., p. 33.
31   Richard Barbrook, "The Holy Fools," in *Proud to Be Flesh: A Mute Magazine Anthology of
Cultural Politics after the Net*, ed. Pauline van Mourik Broekman and Josephine Berry Slater
(London: Mute, 2009), p. 224.

"producing alternative media was the most effective and fun way of putting their revolutionary theory into practice."[32] According to Barbrook, Guattari championed pirate radio stations and, even, the early Minitel network in France as potential tools to implement his anarcho-communist theories.

As outlined in Deleuze and Guattari's influential theory tome, *Mille plateaux* (1980), the "arboreal" (hierarchical) structures—in society as well as in media—had to be overthrown in favor of "rhizomatic" (horizontal) distribution of power.[33] New computer network tools that arose in the 1980s, like the Minitel or BBSes and, eventually, the internet, seemed to present a practical realization of their theory. Barbrook argues, however, that the "revolutionary elitism" of the community radio station that Guattari set up in the early 1980s, which was meant to be open to the public, actually alienated potential allies and audience members and ended up being far more elitist and authoritarian than it set out to be.[34] Despite his useful critique of the utopian impulses of the "elite avant-garde," the European "techno-nomads" peddling "theory-art," Barbrook ends his essay by arguing for an alternative—but no less naïve—brand of internet utopianism: assuming that sharing and the open-source movement are organically "free" instantiations of "anarcho-communism," that they are naturally occurring gift economies that combat free market capitalism. As Florian Cramer points out in response to Barbrook, this was far from the case, even in the early '90s.[35] Twenty years on from Barbrook's essay, this is more evident than ever.

In addition to its primary critique of the elitist politics and posturing of deleuzoguattarians, Barbrook's essay also briefly hints at why and how the critique of urban space transitioned to the critical occupation of networked, digital "space." He argues that the New Left, the post-May '68 anarcho-communists who included Deleuze and Guattari, were increasingly calling for a "true libertarian revolution" with the goal of "destruction of the city" and the "'deterritorialization' of urban society."[36] This attitude led to the rise of back-to-the-land movements in the 1970s, in which the frustrated revolutionaries of the late '60s increasingly denounced city life as irredeemably colonized by capital. This in turn fed the desire to start over again on

32   Ibid., pp. 226–27.

33   Gilles Deleuze and Félix Guattari, *Mille plateaux: capitalisme et schizophrénie 2* (Paris: Éditions de minuit, 1980).

34   Barbrook, "The Holy Fools," p. 227.

35   Florian Cramer, "A Response to Richard Barbrook's Holy Fools," in *Proud to Be Flesh: A Mute Magazine Anthology of Cultural Politics after the Net*, ed. Pauline van Mourik Broekman and Josephine Berry Slater (London: Mute, 2009).

36   Barbrook, "The Holy Fools," p. 229.

a smaller, more autonomous scale. The revolutionary abandonment of the city, they believed, would result in horizontally connected nomadic tribes, where direct democracy and gift economies would supplant consumer capitalism. In certain ways, the pragmatic utopianism of the squatters in Amsterdam came closer than most post-'68 urban activists in transforming the city into a collection of horizontally connected yet autonomous tribes, decentralizing structures of urban control. Yet, the ultimate success of their activism—the government agreed to their demands that it provide more housing for young singles and couples—and the in-fighting among competing factions of squatters, as outlined in chapter 1, effectively reterritorialized the city space by the mid-'80s.

This development would not have come as a surprise, however, to anyone committed to the creation of temporary autonomous zones or the use of tactics, both of which require speed, adaptability, and mobility to be effective.[37] Many of the more adaptive squatters of Amsterdam saw that new opportunities to open cracks and TAZs were presenting themselves in the realm of new media. Arguing that, as it developed, internet criticism had to come from within rather than outside, Lovink writes, "The trick with net criticism [...] was to reverse the position of complaining outsider into one of an active, subversive production of discourse..."[38] The media art festival Talking Back to the Media,[39] which took place in Amsterdam in November 1985, was one of the first attempt to create a space of potential for the transition between urban tactics and tactical media.

Artists Talking Back to the Media

The Talking Back to the Media (TBTTM) festival was an important turning point for Dutch media art in a number of ways. On one hand, it encapsulated the extent to which ideas from squatting and the autonomous movements in the city had migrated into art discourse. On the other hand, it signaled a realignment of the alternative Dutch art circuit (namely, those who had been active in the In-Out Center and De Appel) toward forms of mass-media critique that intersected with the concerns of the squatters' movement. The

37 Bey, *TAZ*.
38 Lovink, *Dark Fiber*, 83.
39 The original title of the festival was "Artists Talking Back to the Media." One of the two originators of the festival, Raúl Marroquin, disclosed in an interview with the author that he was irritated that some of the other organizers decided to drop the "artists" part of the title without consulting him. For Marroquin the focus on the work of artists was essential.

festival, initiated by David Garcia and Raúl Marroquin and executed in collaboration with Time Based Arts (TBA) and De Appel, brought together local and international artists who were working with television, video, film, photography, sound art, posters, and theater for a month-long critical reflection on the mass media.

Although Garcia was part of the internationally-oriented De Appel/TBA circle, he was interested in creating work, including *The Underpass*, that was inspired by pirate television/squatter alternative media and its relationship to the city space. Frustrated by the lack of interest in media and video art from more mainstream institutions, the organizers of TBTTM, particularly Garcia, hoped to use the whole city of Amsterdam as an exhibition space, as a platform for interventions into the mass media. Garcia says:

> I would argue that what we were able to do by turning a city into a platform, not a museum, a whole city. We ignored the museums. [...] what was conscious was that the city was our platform. The mass media are our platform. Television, radio, cinema, poster. All the modalities of the mass media communication are our platform. No other project incapsulated that vision and succeeded in the way that we did in communicating that vision. [...] My slogan at that time was to be site-specific in the media landscape. Because you have site-specific artists, the Serras, you know all the artists who take the landscape and who do their installations in the landscape. Our vision was to do the same but for the media landscape. To treat the media communications as a landscape and to make something ambitious on that scale in the media landscape. To do Richard Long in the media landscape. That was what we set out to do.[40]

The venues that participated in TBTTM reflect a coming-together of various participants in this media landscape: squatted spaces, alternative art venues, and more established institutions. It was a combination of brick-and-mortar and broadcast spaces, including Peter Giele's Aorta art space in the squatted NRC-Handelsblad complex, De Appel, the student-led Kriterion cinema, Kabeltelevisie Amsterdam, the Art History Institute of the University of Amsterdam, the avant-garde independent Shaffy Theater, Stad Radio Amsterdam, VPRO-Radio, and the streets of the city (where the posters were exhibited).

---

40   David Garcia and Raúl Marroquin, Interview with David Garcia and Raúl Marroquin, interview by Camie Karstanje, November 19, 2013, Talking Back to the Media Research Document p.703-712, LIMA / De Appel.

Bringing art to a larger audience outside the confines of galleries and museums and into the city space was an important facet of TBTTM, just as it had been for *The Underpass*. The idea was to create a media festival that took place in the chaos and cacophony of the media-saturated urban environment, rather than in a sterile, white cube institutional space.[41] There was an openness, an inclusiveness, and a do-it-yourself universalist utopianism that attempted to draw "everyone" in the city in. Even those who were not inclined to visit an alternative art space, theater, or cinema would perhaps encounter the work on the radio or television. Garcia related this sentiment to Max Bruinsma, in an account from *Mediamatic* magazine, saying:

> I saw myself swimming in a stream of images, television images, post-ers, neon signs, glittering shop-windows. I thought: 'The media are all-pervasive and ubiquitous, they are there all the time.' This was what all our work was about, and wouldn't it be wonderful if it could be looked at in the context of a city, rather than a museum or a gallery?[42]

In addition to a program of videos that was shown on cable television throughout the month and the sound art that was broadcast over the radio, a series of posters commissioned from John Baldessari, Barbara Kruger, and Klaus Staeck were spread around the city.

The inclusion of many high-profile American artists in the festival created an opportunity for the public (as well as the participants) to compare European and American perspectives on the mass media. This was by design. According to Bruinsma's account, the idea for TBTTM came one evening while David Garcia and Raúl Marroquin were walking together on the Keizergracht talking about the work of Dara Birnbaum, which had recently been exhibited at the Stedelijk Museum. Garcia felt that techniques of appropriation in video and television art were being pitched as an American way of working and that European artists, who had been using such techniques for quite a while, were not getting adequate recognition for their efforts. Marroquin suggested that the reason for this might be that artists in the United States had more opportunities to show their work than

---

41   Angela M. Bartholomew argues that the Stedelijk "recuperat[ed]" this work into the institution two years later. See "Television's Feedback Loop: Talking Back to the Media (1985) and the Stedelijk Museum on TV." In *A Critical History of Media Art in the Netherlands*, edited by Sanneke Huisman and Marga van Mechelen. Prinsenbeek: Jap Sam Book, 2019: pp. 226-237.

42   Max Bruinsma, "Talks on Talking Back," *Mediamatic Magazine* 0, no. 0 (December 1985): p. 42.

artists in Europe. Consequently, the two artists began to formulate an idea for a festival that would showcase a European perspective on video and television art. According to Bruinsma, Garcia argued:

> Americans have got an entirely different approach to dealing with the mass media than the Europeans. [...] American and Canadian artists tend to be very literal about the media and present things much more as they are, without commentary and allow you to draw your own conclusions, while the work of [European artists] have got this sort of metaphorical approach to media. Now, wouldn't it be interesting to see the two different approaches together at a festival?[43]

Garcia and Annie Wright were, at that point, on the board of Time Based Arts, and Marroquin also had close ties to alternative art institutions in Amsterdam as well. Between them, they were able to connect and partner with a number of institutions in creating the festival.[44]

Time Based Arts took the lead intuitional role in organizing the program, artists, and venues that would participate. Beginning in 1983, Garcia and Marroquin gathered their core collaborators: artist Ulises Carrión; Rob Perée, who was then the chairman of TBA; Aart van Barneveld, who also worked with TBA; Saskia Bos, who was a curator at De Appel; Max Bruinsma, a music editor working in radio; Sabrina Kamstra, who was with De Appel at the time; and art historian Sebastián López, who worked at the Art Historical Institute at the University of Amsterdam. With the help of these collaborators, they were able to secure funding and organize the program of the event.[45] The aim of the festival, as the name suggests, was to showcase artworks

---

43   Ibid., p. 39.
44   Garcia, interview by author.
45   As noted in chapter 2, the mid-'80s saw changes to arts funding policy in the Netherlands that funneled government subsidies to foundations and institutions rather than individual artists. According to Perée, a lot of international artists had initially been drawn to the Netherlands due to the generous funding structures. For TBTTM, funding was sought as early as 1983, but the application was rejected, as all the allocated funds for the coming year were spoken for. They were advised that they should try again for the following year. Sabrina Kamstra took charge of the fund-raising operation and approached a broad range of both government and private sponsors for the event. In the end, the Ministerie van Welzijn, Volksgezondheid en Cultuur (WVC) [Ministry of Well-Being, Health and Culture], de Gemeente Amsterdam [the city of Amsterdam], and the Prins Bernhard Fonds [Prince Bernhard Fund] funded TBTTM. Despite it's "alternative" stance, the festival was, in the end, well-funded and supported by major government bodies. See Interview with Rob Perée, interview by Camie Karstanje, April 8, 2014, http://li-ma.nl/site/news/talking-back-media-project-update-0.

that critically addressed the mass media or "talked back" to the media in some way (i.e., works that formulated a model of participation in the media rather than passive reception). The organizers purposely left the festival's title open to wider interpretation by the participants in order to encourage discussion on the use of elements from the mass media in artistic practice. This produced a program that was, at times, celebratory of media culture and, in other cases, deeply critical of it. According to their press release, "The departure point for the festival is the fact that today many artists who work in video, film, photography, theater, sound, posters, and printwork translate and use elements of the mass media in their own work in order to subsequently present it via the media."[46] The scope for the festival was, therefore, very open-ended.

Although TBTTM ended up showing works in a wide range of media, Marroquin and Garcia, who both worked with video and television, conceptualized the festival as a riposte to the perceived disregard of local video art in the Dutch art scene. As noted, the Stedelijk Museum *did* show video art, but it was relegated to the "video stairs," a separate portion of the gallery space where the monitor or monitors were positioned at the bottom of a set of stairs. By the time the Stedelijk staged *Het Lumineuze Beeld* [The Luminous Image] in 1984, Talking Back to the Media was already in the works. According to Rob Perée:

> Both Time Based Arts and Montevideo were founded because video art wasn't accepted and exhibited. At the time, there was still a lot of discussion whether it was art, because of the fact that there was a camera between the artist and the art piece. Some people still have that conviction. Museums didn't know how to show it, they didn't have any specialised rooms for it. Actually, one of the only ones that had something like that was the Stedelijk Museum, with their video-stairs. The organisation of Time Based Arts and Montevideo but also TBTTM had a lot to do with the emancipation of the medium.[47]

For Garcia and Marroquin, however, TBTTM was not just about establishing video art as an "emancipated" medium. They hoped, in a larger sense, to start conversations around and show work that spoke to the emergence of a new Information Age, in which *television* (i.e., the network/broadcast) was more relevant than *video* (i.e., tapes).

46 "Talking Back to the Media – Inleiding" (Press release, 1985), Archief de Appel.
47 Perée, interview by Karstanje.

According to Bruinsma's reconstruction of their initial brainstorming session, Marroquin strongly advocated for the orientation of the festival towards the themes of information and media networks, saying, "It is important to see that we're not living in an industrial society anymore, we are living in an information society, and that this is affecting our work as artists too."[48] Bruinsma describes Marroquin's view of the contemporary culture as a "global network of information and media, which was only waiting for the appropriate impulse to become a global multimedia work of art."[49] According to Garcia and Ulises Carrión (who began collaborating with Garcia and Marroquin early on), the festival itself was a work of art, which would reflect the vast and complex web of visual and sonic experiences that was the hallmark of the new Information Age. Carrión, in particular, was interested in how the process of creating the festival would manifest itself as a work of art.[50]

The festival began with a press presentation on October 21st at Kriterion, and the opening night on November 1st was held at Aorta. For the opening, the American actor/artist Eric Bogosian performed a work titled *American Dream*, a theatrical monologue in which he reacts to audio recordings that contains snippets of television and radio broadcasts and also mimics the language of a television host. In general, the works in TBBTM fall roughly into one of two categories: they either appropriate mass media by mirroring and/or mimicking its forms, or they create their own narratives and mythologies that stand apart from the commercial norms of mass media content. Bogosian's monologue incorporated elements of both of these perspectives in that the piece was a reaction to the myths of Americana as perpetuated and amplified in the smooth commerciality of mass media.

In addition to the aforementioned works of Bogosian, Kruger, and Baldessari, a number of works by US-based artists were shown in the photography exhibition in Aorta. The artists shown, including Jenny Holzer, Sherrie Levine, Richard Prince, and Cindy Sherman,[51] were all working with representation, media messages, and appropriated imagery in one way or another. These artists are part of a generation that Douglas Crimp defined with his exhibition and subsequent essay "Pictures." In his estimation, the work of these artists reflects a critical postmodernism that digs beneath the

48 Bruinsma, "Talks on Talking Back," pp. 39, 41.
49 Ibid., p. 41.
50 It should be noted that Marroquin disagreed with this characterization. See Bruinsma, p. 41.
51 The other US-based artists included were Nan Goldin, Silvia Kolbowski, Dorit Cypis, Peter Nagy, Frank Majore, and Robert Heinecken.

surface signification of images to other layers of signification. In contrast to modernism's "topographic" formalism, where surface reveals structure, these artists' "radically new approach to mediums" are, according to Crimp, a "stratigraphic" formalism—a geological layering. He writes:

> Those processes of quotation, excerption, framing, and staging that constitute the strategies of the work I have been discussing necessitate uncovering strata of representation. Needless to say, we are not in search of sources or origins, but of structures of signification: underneath each picture there is always another picture.[52]

Crimp places these works in opposition to the idea of modernism popularized in the US by Clement Greenberg and Michael Fried, which was invested in the concept of medium specificity, though he acknowledges that this a very particular definition of modernist art.[53]

According to Crimp, the work of the artists he was writing about often appear as if they are fragments of a narrative. They suggest a narrative that does not exist—an incomplete narrative but a narrative nevertheless. They are floating signifiers, concocted to suggest an absent whole.[54] Narrative, for the Dutch and Amsterdam-based international artists, on the other hand, was generally less fragmented and more geared toward creating parables and fantasies that, as Garcia noted, often critique the media obliquely through metaphor rather than formal structure. A pair of Dutch art critics—Lucette ter Borg and Sacha Bronwasser—expressed precisely this point of view in an article published in *De Volkskrant* in 2001. Taking aim at "boring" video art, they use Anri Sala's work *Uomoduomo* (2000), which depicts a man falling asleep in a church, as a key example. They write, "You, as a viewer of Sala's *Uomodomo* [sic], might also nod off because the artist has not given his images any metaphorical added value."[55] This perspective was, to some degree, already present in the video program of the TBTTM festival.[56] During four broadcasts on November 10, 17, 24, and 29, a number of artists' videos were shown, including the work of organizers Garcia and

---

52 Douglas Crimp, "Pictures," *October* 8 (April 1, 1979): p. 87.
53 Ibid., p. 87.
54 Ibid., p. 80.
55 Lucette ter Borg and Sacha Bronwasser, "Ziende Blind," *De Volkskrant*, October 18, 2001. See also Anne van Driel, "The Entertainment Years," in *The Magnetic Era: Video Art in the Netherlands 1970-1985*, ed. Jeroen Boomgaard and Bart Rutten (Rotterdam: NAi Publishers, 2003), pp. 133–34.
56 The European-based artists included in the photography exhibition were Victor Burgin, Lydia Schouten, Katharina Sieverding, Henk Tas, Allan David Tu, and Julia Ventura.

Annie Wright, Carrión, and Marroquin. Dutch artists Lydia Schouten and Servaas, the German artist Klaus vom Bruch, as well as English artist Mark Wilcox were also included in the video program.

Schouten's work is a typical example of what could be termed, per Garcia, the metaphorical approach to media critique in Dutch video art. Her piece *Beauty Becomes the Beast* (1985), is a stylized mythological mash-up that follows the journey of a woman who has grown a devil's tail. The changes to her body alienate her from the world around her, so she goes out in search of other mythological creatures and encounters mermaids and magical crystals in a rocky seaside landscape. According to Karl Toepfer, the woman's bodily transformation acts as a metaphor for the grotesque, changing "real" human body that is confronted with the artificial and immortal beauty of the body captured and preserved in the media.[57] As Schouten says, "Artificial beauty is now the object of our desire. [...] The most important task of the media seems to be the destruction of chronological time. [...] Our lives are filled with these fantastic images from the media, which makes it difficult for us to accept death."[58] Appearing on a panel of participating artists for TBTTM's last television broadcast, Schouten discusses this piece and states that the motivation behind it was to create her *own* world, an autonomous world of sorts apart from the received images in the mass media. This technique contrasts the subversion of mythologies found in the work of the American artists—the veritable draining of signification identified by Crimp. Commenting on the work of Levine, he says, "These picture have no autonomous power of signification (pictures do not signify what they picture) [...] Levine steals them away from their usual place in our culture and subverts their mythologies."[59] On one side media mythologies are represented, analyzed through narrative and metaphor, while, on the other side, mythical significance is drained or subverted.

The difference between the work of the Americans and the Europeans, however, should not be overstated. Using myth as metaphor was not confined to the European context just as image subversion was not unique to the Americans. Despite the evidence that there were slight differences in strategy, both American and European artists in the mid-'80s took an active interest in classical mythology and legend and began to more explicitly

---

57   Karl Toepfer, "From Imitation to Quotation," *Journal of Dramatic Theory and Criticism* 4, no. 2 (Spring 1991): p. 134.
58   Qtd. ibid.
59   Crimp, "Pictures," p .85.

reference it in their work. Video art from the mid-'80s turned increasingly away from self-reflexive and un-edited work of the early '70s to deal with narrative, science fiction, and fantasy. Photography, too, turned toward elaborately constructed fantasies. For example, Cindy Sherman began a series of photographs that she called "fairy tales," and Joan Jonas began making work that dealt with mythology and science fiction. Dara Birnbaum's trilogy of films, *Damnation of Faust*, which was shown at TBTTM, also, of course, references German legend.

From the European point of view in TBTTM, the idea of creating one's own autonomous narrative within the media landscape was paramount. This did not mean that this was always a direct *counter*-narrative, however. As noted, the work featured in the festival was just as often celebratory as it was critical. David Garcia and Annie Wright's videos were some of the more ambiguously-situated works in the program. In *Callisto* (1984) and *Terra Incognita* (1985), they stage their own mythical narratives using characters and sets constructed with children's toys. *White Nights* (1985), which was shown in full on one of the TBTTM cable broadcasts, also operates in the realm of fantasy. In the group discussion that aired live for the *finissage* of the festival, Wright was asked whether *White Nights* was "fighting back" or "pushing back" against the media by mimicking the dialogue from classic films. She answers, "Quite the reverse! I wanted to integrate myself. [...] It was loving, talking back, rather than criticizing it."[60]

The lack of criticality in some aspects of the program is not only found in works, such as Wright's, that express a fascination for celebrity and classic Hollywood figures, but also in the optimism around do-it-yourself media in general. Rather than analyzing the way the media defines individual identity, the organizers were focused on the possibilities for access and participation presented by the alternative art circuit and the newly-established public television network SALTO. To illustrate this point, during the live broadcast at the end of the festival, a video feed was set-up that linked the stage and the café of the Shaffy Theater, so that the public could appear on camera and ask questions to the artists on the panel, who could see their questioner appear on a screen on stage. This represents an early attempt—which could easily be dismissed as a gimmick—to create an interactive platform. While the conceptual connection to the theme of the festival provides a clear motivation for creating such a set-up, the reason why a mediated interaction—to the adjacent café, of all places—would be meaningful is less apparent.

60   *Talking Back to the Media – November 29, 1985* (Amsterdam: Shaffy Theater, 1985).

Reflecting on the issue of criticality in the festival, Garcia says:

The worst of Talking Back to the Media was uncritical celebration for which I was partly responsible. Sometimes I was too [much] looking back to the Pop Art. [...] [The theme song based on "Walking Back to Happiness"] was my idea and I have some regrets, although it was catchy, it was pure celebration. For us the postmodern collapse of boundaries was a celebratory moment, we missed the darker implications of this collapse.[61]

In the realm of the media, postmodernism had opened up ideas and discourse to a greater plurality, which artists like Garcia celebrated in that it promised more democratic and inclusive participation in the media landscape. This plurality, however, also produced fractures in the leftist grand narratives that undergird the values of democratic participation. The ideological divide between European techno-utopianism and American identity politics would widen considerably in the following years as artists like Garcia embraced the emerging internet.

Dara Birnbaum's essay for the *Talking Back to the Media* publication speaks to this divide. Referencing both *Faust* and *Kiss the Girls: Make them Cry* (1979), she writes:

...in both 'characters' are the forms of restraint and near suffocation imposed through this current technological society; pressures which force a person to find the meaning of openly declaring, through communicated gestures, their own identity. [...] I consider it to be our responsibility to become increasingly aware of alternative perspectives which can be achievable through *our* use of media—and to consciously find the ability for expression of the 'individual voice.'[62]

Increasingly, in the American context, postmodern rhetoric and media critiques revolved around issues of individual identity and a refusal of the kind of universalism that Talking Back to the Media, to a certain extent, propagated. The artist's role, per Birnbaum, was to investigate individual voices not gather a broad, universally-defined public. For Garcia, however, the artist's role was to set up a platform that would be as accessible as possible.

---

61   Garcia and Marroquin, interview by Karstanje.
62   Dara Birnbaum, "Talking Back to the Media," in *Talking Back to the Media*, ed. Sabrina Kamstra, Sebastián Lopéz, and Rob Perrée (Amsterdam: Stichting Talking Back to the Media, 1985), pp. 48–49.

In the years following Talking Back to the Media, artists and activists in Amsterdam increasingly turned their attention to organizing events and conferences that, in the do-it-yourself spirit, attempted to create newer, better, more independent and inclusive platforms for participation that revolved around cutting-edge network technology.

Back to the Future

Talking Back to the Media marks the beginning of a shift in Dutch art/activist circles toward media art and theory, and V2_ and Mediamatic would soon emerge as leaders in this area. Both ex-squatter groups were clearly paying attention to what was going with TBTTM in Amsterdam. In Den Bosch, V2_ decided to hold their own event called V2 Media Week: Take the Media (November 1–9, 1985), riffing on the title of TBTTM and featuring a number of performances and artwork from industrial bands including Test Department. Mediamatic, on the other hand, launched the zero issue of their magazine during TBTTM, which aided its successful reception. In the years that followed, V2_ released its first manifesto, shifting its focus to "unstable" media, and Mediamatic created a forum for discussions on art and new technology. Both the alternative art circuit and the activists who had been busy in the squatters' movement increasingly turned to focus on the aesthetic aspects of networked technology as well as reaching out to others around the world who were similarly engaged.

In addition to their work with television during the latter half of the '80s, more and more artists were experimenting with making work on and with computers and connecting with one another via BBSes. This interest in network communication meant that artists were interacting with the nascent hacker scene of the Netherlands, who were mostly part of a younger generation eager to bring the alternative activist media tradition into the digital age. Cross-over initiatives and events began to percolate around 1988 and often included the participation of organizations like V2_ and Mediamatic.

After 1983, artists in the squatter milieu (as well as those in mainstream art circles) began to more explicitly orient themselves toward video and new media. In Amsterdam, despite the demise of pirate TV, the DIY attitude fostered by the pirates spread to a wider group of artists, who saw new media as a means to create more accessible, open, and participatory artworks. The club Mazzo, which had since 1980 pioneered audiovisual art in the club context, continued to promote the activities of early VJs (video jockeys), who montaged video and sound on the fly, and to participate in video and television experiments in the mid-1980s.[63] In 1984, the Stedelijk Museum, which had long been viewed as unreceptive to video and new media works, staged a large-scale video art exhibition titled *Het Lumineuze Beeld* [The Luminous Image] featuring twenty-two video installations.

The origin story of Dutch video art often begins with the 1971 exhibition "Sonsbeek buiten de perken" [Sonsbeek Beyond the Limits].[64] Organized by Wim Beeren in the city of Arnhem in the west of the Netherlands, the 1971 edition of the Sonsbeek series[65] prominently featured video art as part of the exhibition program and even allowed people to make videos on site, thanks to equipment provided by Philips.[66] Despite this promising "beginning," mainstream institutional support for video art was neither consistent nor widespread in the 1970s. In lieu of support from major art institutions, a number of competing alternative and independent organizations promoting and distributing video art were established in the intervening years.

Although the various parties interested in video were interconnected in the 1970s, a few separate factions developed by the end of the decade. In Maastricht in the far south of the Netherlands, where the Jan van Eyck Academy is located, Theo van der Aa and Ger van Dyck started Agora Studio. As noted in chapter 2, the Van Eyck academy had a wide array of equipment and video art flourished there. Raúl Marroquin was one of the earliest video artists in the Netherlands and collaborated with Van der Aa on his publication *Fandangos*. According to writer and curator Rob Perrée, "Van der Aa and Van Dyck no longer regarded art as tied to a location; the video tape, book, cable, satellite, telephone and magazine made it possible to transcend every boundary."[67] Around the time that Marroquin began creating video art, the American artist Jack Moore began building his video collection and distribution organization, Videoheads, in Amsterdam. Started in 1971, the organization accrued a huge collection of videos over the following decades—reportedly 72,000 hours of taped performances of avant-garde

63 Michiel van den Bergh and Maja van den Broecke, interview by Amanda Wasielewski, September 29, 2017.

64 Rob Perrée, "From Agora to Montevideo: Of Video Institutes, the Things That Pass," in *The Magnetic Era: Video Art in the Netherlands 1970-1985*, ed. Jeroen Boomgaard and Bart Rutten (Rotterdam: NAi Publishers, 2003), p. 52.

65 The exhibition series was established in 1949, after World War II, with a mandate similar to that of Documenta in Kassel (though predating it). It was initially intended to be a biennial but was held at irregular intervals in the intervening years. See "About Sonsbeek," Dutch Art Institute, accessed July 21, 2018, https://dutchartinstitute.eu/page/3908/about-sonsbeek.

66 Perrée, "From Agora to Montevideo," p. 52.

67 Ibid., p. 53.

art, music, and theater as well as independent films. This collection was, in many ways, Moore's personal collection, aimlessly assembled and largely based on Moore's own tastes (i.e., artists and musicians popular with the '60s counterculture).[68] According to Raúl Marroquin, Moore and his cohort did not ingratiate themselves to others interested in video within the art and activist scene in Amsterdam. He recalls, "It was one person surrounded by this bunch of misfits. [...] They were just too aggressive [...] Like, hey, we are the ones who know."[69] The Videoheads were not the last group to try to take ownership over the terrain of video in Amsterdam.

In 1978 René Coëlho, who had a background in commercial television, set up his own video art collection called Montevideo, which was focused on distribution of video art. Meanwhile, De Appel, which established itself as a cutting-edge alternative performance venue beginning in 1975, had—somewhat unintentionally—found themselves with a rather large collection of artists' videos by the early '80s. In 1980, De Appel founder Wies Smals began the process of setting up a separate video institute for this collection, which would become Time Based Arts (TBA) in 1983 shortly before her untimely death later in that year.[70] The shift in funding structures in the Netherlands in 1984 meant that TBA and Montevideo became rivals, both competing for the same limited funding. The artists of TBA tended to view Coëlho as a commercially-oriented opportunist who did not actually care about art, while those on the side of Montevideo saw the artists of TBA as pretentious elitists—coded gay and international—who had co-opted the Dutch scene for themselves.[71]

68   According to a report at the time of Moore's death, the collection consisted of 72,000 hours of footage including, "...rare performances by psychedelic practitioners the Grateful Dead and Pink Floyd and events such as Yoko Ono's 1966 performance at London's Jeanetta Cochrane Theatre and Ono and John Lennon's 'bagism' contribution to the fundraising Alchemical Wedding at the Royal Albert Hall in 1968." See "Jack Henry Moore – Obituary," *The Telegraph*, April 25, 2014, sec. News, https://www.telegraph.co.uk/news/obituaries/10788743/Jack-Henry-Moore-obituary. html; Perrée, "From Agora to Montevideo," p. 56.

69   Marroquin, interview by author.

70   Perrée, "From Agora to Montevideo," pp. 63, 69.

71   In an interview with the author, Garcia notes a divide in terms of sexual orientation (or perceived sexual orientation) and cultural differences. He says, "Time Based Arts was very much rooted in the art scene, the classical art scene, where you have performance which turned into video which... you have an absolute trajectory which related to the mainstream of the art world with ambitions to be in art museums or other kinds of galleries. René was more interested in, if you like, technology, and he didn't have the background or knowledge of the classical art scene. So you had this kind of almost class-like resentment between the *boefje*—the Dutch macho—and art, that was 'gay.' I think there was a bit of sexual politics as well going on, but again that's just me seeing it. This was like the macho Dutch boys and here was art with its internationals, its

As these conflicts between competing video art organizations in Amsterdam festered, two organizations outside of the city were formulating somewhat different perspectives on media art that took them beyond video and television. In the south of the Netherlands in Den Bosch, V2_, which had already been active as a squatter art venue in the preceding years, began focusing more on the industrial and experimental noise music scenes. This dovetailed with early media art installation and performance, and these activities led them to develop a series of manifestos on media art beginning in 1986. Mediamatic, meanwhile, was located in the north of the country in Groningen and began organizing their own media art initiatives around 1983. Their early exhibitions eventually led to the establishment of a media art magazine in 1985, which focused not just on video art but also on "electro media kunst" with the intention of theorizing and understanding emerging media.

In addition to V2_ and Mediamatic, there was also a third video and media art organization that arose outside of Amsterdam in the early '80s: the World Wide Video Festival (WWVF) at Het Kijkhuis in the Hague. Directed by Tom van Vliet, the WWVF ran a week-long festival every year for over twenty years between 1982 and 2004 that evolved out of the video art collection that Van Vliet and his collaborators had collected for, as he termed it, "a kind of postponed viewing."[72] Although WWVF, perhaps more than any other video or media art event in the Netherlands, exposed the Dutch public to the latest video works from around the world, the format of the event and the focus on distribution cleaved more to the structural apparatus of independent filmmaking rather than art-making, at least initially. Due to the WWVF's alignment with filmmaking and film festivals rather than squatting, alternative media, and art, this section will not cover their work in depth. Suffice it to say, their goal, though not explicitly stated, seemed to be to show international artists (i.e., non-Dutch artists) rather than locals, a fact that the locals inevitably resented.[73] The festival was devised as an add-on to the original distribution model that Van Vliet had devised for the collection, and the venue where the WWVF took place, Het Kijkhuis, eventually partnered with Electronic Art Intermix in New York to distribute video art from their collection in Europe.[74]

Latin Americans, and gay and part of the gay scene. So cultural, multi-cultural, gay—Dutch macho, we're here now, we're going to show you how it's done. Technology culture. And also, video art's only big enough for one."

72   "Archief," World Wide Video Festival, accessed June 13, 2018, http://www.wwvf.nl/; Tom van Vliet, World Wide Video, interview by Johan Pijnappel, 1993, http://www.wwvf.nl/.

73   Perrée, "From Agora to Montevideo," p. 67.

74   Vliet, interview by Pijnappel; Perrée, "From Agora to Montevideo," p. 66.

V2_ and Mediamatic, in contrast, were each, in their own way, oriented more to the squatter/DIY tradition in the Netherlands, setting them apart somewhat from the alternative institutions competing for prominence in the realm of video art collection and distribution. Both V2_ and Mediamatic were interested in creating platforms and charting a new frontier of media art beyond video. They sought to theorize the relationship between new technology and art as it developed. While both V2_ and Mediamatic were involved with exhibiting artwork, they were not only interested in getting this work in front of an audience but also in understanding the ways in which artists (and the public) could take control of production through the use of participatory media. The platform model, unlike a traditional exhibition model, is interactive. Like TBTTM, there is an element of talking back involved with each organization's program.

In 1986 V2_ published their first manifesto. Echoing the forceful and utopian tone of early twentieth-century artistic manifestos, they outlined a new theoretical direction for the organization and initiated a break with the early squatter phase of their operation. As detailed in chapter 1, V2_, which was named for their squat's original address at Vughtenstraat 234 in Den Bosch, was forced by the municipal government to move to another space at Muntelstraat 23/Aawal 2a in 1984. They remained at that space for the next ten years, positioning themselves at the forefront of the avant-garde of new media and experimental sound/music in Europe during that time. In 1994, as their relevance and status increased in the emerging internet age, they sought out a larger, more well-connected location in Rotterdam and continued to expand their media art program.

Although the founders of V2_ had directed its program toward new media projects—experimental sound, video, etc.—from its inception, they did not formalize this direction until late 1986. Their first manifesto, as a result, encapsulates a transitional moment for the former squatters and reflects a wider revival of progressive and avant-garde impulses in art at the time, defying the dictates of postmodern theory and leaving punk's proclamation of "no future" in the past. The excitement around new media technology, which peaked in the early '90s with the advent of the internet, created a new avant-gardism and utopianism in artistic practice in Europe, particularly in the Netherlands and Germany. This new optimism and progressive attitude is reflected in V2_'s manifestos, which retain elements of the DIY/punk era while simultaneously celebrating a new era of technological progress.

The first artist manifesto, the Futurist manifesto, was published on the front pages of both the *Gazzetta dell'Emilia* and *Le Figaro* newspapers in 1909. After the Futurists set this precedent—i.e., publishing their manifestos in major newspapers—subsequent generations of artists followed suit. With this history undoubtedly in their mind, V2_ decided to publish their first manifesto in the *Volkskrant* newspaper on New Year's Eve 1986 as an advertisement at the bottom of page 3. Its placement was, perhaps, not as dramatic as that of the Futurists, but it was, nevertheless, an important signal that the squatter-artists of V2_ had embarked on a serious change of direction. With new media, particularly computer and networked media increasingly at their disposal, artists were once again beginning to imagine a future writ large. The manifesto reads, in part:

> OUR GOAL IS TO STRIVE FOR CONTINUOUS CHANGE. WE WANT TO PROPAGATE THE CONTINUOUS REVOLUTION [...] WE MUST GIVE FORM TO THE NEW [...] ART MUST BE A REVOLUTIONARY POWER IN SOCIETY [...] WE LOVE UNCERTAINTY AND CHAOS. [...] WE FOCUS ON THE NOW AND NOT ON THE FUTURE.

However, this change in direction does not completely dispense with the attitude of the late '70s and early '80s. Although V2_ are still attached to the notions of anarchy, uncertainty and chaos that dominated the punk era and speak of living in the "now," their stated goals are progressive and forward-looking. This is a serious turn away from the rhetoric of autonomy within both the squatter milieu and amongst expressionist painting in the early '80s, signaling a return to the virtue of social engagement in art. The overt celebration of the new also heralds a revival of an avant-garde posture and is inseparable from the excitement that new media fostered during this time.

The first manifesto was written in connection with an exhibition, *Manifest[o]*, at V2_ from January 3–17, 1987, which showcased the ways in which an interest in avant-garde music at V2_ overlapped with other electronic and digital art forms. The opening night of the show featured industrial and experimental noise bands The Haters, Strafe für Rebellion, Selektion, and Iron Brotherhood, as well as a telephone interview with San Francisco-based electronic musician Kim Cascone. The exhibition, similarly, featured the work of groups and individuals, including Selektion Optik, Die Tödliche Doris, Annemie van Kerckhoven, Bernd Kastner, G.X. Jupitter-Larsen, Vivenza, V2_ themselves, and Sigi Sinyuga, who were active in the avant-garde of industrial/noise music and its attendant performance and media art experimentation.[75]

75   V2_, "V2 Archive: Manifest[o] Exhibition," V2_ Lab for Unstable Media, accessed June 3, 2018, http://v2.nl/events/manifest-voor-de-instabiele-media/.

For V2_, the transition from a squatted alternative art space to a new media art institute began with their focus, from the mid-80s, on not only the music but, concurrently, the films, performances, and electronic art installations of industrial bands. In the early '80s, they had operated on a smaller, more ad-hoc level, showing mostly local Dutch and Belgian artists, but, by the mid-'80s, their program was broadening to include artists from further afield. In 1985 they hosted concerts by legendary industrial groups Einstürzende Neubauten (Germany), Laibach (Slovenia), and Test Department (UK). They also hosted Sonic Youth (US), who were in their early noise rock phase, as well as several other noise and industrial groups. Their program at the time consisted of concerts as well as accompanying exhibitions and film screenings from many of the same individuals who were in the bands that performed.

Michael Goddard, who argues that the cultural significance of industrial music goes well beyond its present designation as merely one genre of music among many, writes that groups like Laibach, a Slovenian band who helped found the Neue Slowenische Kunst (NSK) movement in 1984, "should not be understood as a simple rock band but rather as a multimedia art collective using rock and pop music as a medium; an arena for investigating the relations between art, ideology, popular culture and totalitarianism."[76] V2_, then, with their focus on industrial music, were adherents to an emerging multimedia art scene in Europe that critically remixed the aesthetics of early twentieth-century political movements—including nationalist, fascist, and communist totalitarianisms—through the use of new technological tools. This type of remixing is reflected in V2_'s urge, in the mid- to late '80s, to commence writing manifestos. To borrow a term from Marina Gržinić, V2_'s manifestos could be considered "retro-avant-garde."[77]

Writing about the emergence of a new avant-gardist impulse in former-Yugoslavian Slovenia after the death of Tito in 1980, Gržinić argues that use of new media and technology created a "soft revolution" which "allows one to question the visible and the political."[78] She writes that while the West typically cites the fall of the Berlin Wall in 1989 as the point at which a "New World Order" came into existence, ex-Yugoslavians artists began

76   Michael Goddard, "We Are Time: Laibach/NSK, Retro-Avant-Gardism and Machinic Repetition," *Angelaki* 11, no. 1 (April 1, 2006): p. 45.
77   Peter Weibel used the term "retro-avant-garde" to describe the work of Slovenian artists in the '80s and early '90s and the term was, in turn, taken up as the title of an exhibition in Ljubljana in 1994. Marina Gržinić, *Fiction Reconstructed: Eastern Europe, Post-Socialism & the Retro-Avant-Garde* (Vienna: Edition Selene, 2000), p. 41.
78   Ibid., pp. 9–10.

conceptualizing "post-Socialist" work after the death of Tito.[79] Gržinić argues that: "Thanks to its Socialist heritage, NSK was able to appear on purely ideological foundations. Laibach (and eventually other NSK members) used all the classic methods of the avant-garde: manifestos, collective performances, public provocation and intervention in politics."[80] The artists of V2_ were undoubtedly inspired by these activities, due to their close contact with Laibach. In their own context, as a new order of sorts was forming in the Dutch art world with the dissolution of the Beeldende Kunstenaars Regeling (BKR, see chapter 2) and the government crackdown on squatting, V2_ was propelled to formulate their own avant-gardism around new media and the "virtual" realm. This reconfiguration of government subsidy and dismantling of the welfare state can perhaps be characterized as post-Socialist on a smaller scale. For V2_ as well as their Eastern European counterparts, the end of Socialism precipitated reflections on the "visible and non-visible, between the imaginable and un-imaginable" and how competing political and ideological positions could be presented and represented in the new media landscape.[81]

In October 1987, ahead of another exhibition featuring interactive media installations and a concert by Test Department, V2_ refined the ideas in their first manifesto to create a "Manifesto for Unstable Media." The concept of instability and the ideas laid out in the manifesto have, to this day, remained important to the organization, which calls itself an "institute" or a "lab" for unstable media. The manifesto text reads, in part:

> WE STRIVE FOR CONSTANT CHANGE; FOR MOBILITY. [...] WE MAKE USE OF THE UNSTABLE MEDIA, THAT IS, ALL MEDIA WHICH MAKE USE OF ELECTRONIC WAVES AND FREQUENCIES [...] THE UNSTABLE MEDIA ARE THE MEDIA OF OUR TIME. [...] WE LOVE INSTABILITY AND CHAOS, BECAUSE THEY STAND FOR PROGRESS.[82]

In this revised manifesto, V2_'s optimism around "progress," achieved through the use of new technology and science, is even more explicitly stated than it had been in their first manifesto.

Although it may seem counterintuitive, given the breakdown of grand narratives and criticism of Enlightenment thinking that permeated continental

79   Ibid., p. 37.
80   Ibid., p. 102.
81   Ibid., p. 38.
82   This is the official translation from V2_'s archive.

philosophy and critical theory in the '70s and early '80s, the anarcho-communism favored by groups of squatters in the Netherlands, like those of V2_, was always based on the idea of internal progress—both on the local level and, as the movement internationalized, within networks of solidarity throughout Europe. This form of progressive politics was not contingent on a technocratic view of society, like that of the utopian progressives of the '60s, but, rather, it was reflected in de Certeauian "tactics," the *bricolage* or DIY that arose in tandem with and was empowered by new technologies. Although the Netherlands was never part of the socialist bloc, the Dutch art world was, in the '70s and '80s, connected to a network in Germany, Eastern Europe, and, even, Latin America, who were more concerned with resisting government intrusion than battling the illusory spectacle of consumption. Punks and squatters did not dream of a fully automated utopian city, as utopianists in the '60s had done, but of the small-scale DIY utopia that a photocopier and rudimentary computer or typewriter could facilitate. Do-it-yourself initiatives were a grassroots—a "rhizomatic"—form of progress that was mobile and temporary. The new media that was emerging in the '80s felt different than the old "closed" media—it put production power in the hands of the poor and the weak in unprecedented ways.

Squatters' occupations of urban space formed temporary autonomous zones or cracks in the system that had, despite their temporariness, effected real change in the structure of the city and government policies in the realm of housing. Likewise, pirate media led to more inclusivity in the media and the beginnings of government-sponsored public-access/community television like SALTO [Stichting Amsterdamse Lokale Televisie Omroep] in Amsterdam, which was initiated in 1984. Thus, former squatters increasingly turned to digital media and computer networks, not only because they offered the promise of the kind of autonomy that had been, largely, lost in the realm of squatting, but also because they provided new tactical avenues for progress, not only in society but with regard to artistic expression. The postmodern feeling of avant-garde déjà vu, that the idea of progress in art was no longer relevant, was evaporating in the face of so many new tools. While "media" artists of the '70s and early '80s—notably Nam June Paik, who had maintained a sense of optimism around new technology throughout his long career—were perhaps always wedded to the idea of progress, even as their peers demurred, organizations like V2_ were somehow able to fuse the ennui of the "no future" era—an era of uncertainty, instability, and chaos—with the optimism promised by emerging technology. This combination created a potent mixture of politics and aesthetics and fostered a unique critical discourse around new media in the Netherlands.

While V2_ emerged from the squatter-artist milieu in the south of the Netherlands, another media art initiative formed in the north of the country, in Groningen: Mediamatic. In 1983, artists Willem Velthoven, Jan Wijle, Frits Maats, Barbara Pyle, Marieken Verheyen, and Willem Mulder decided to funnel their interests in video and new media into screenings and exhibitions in the city. Although Groningen is the largest city in the north of the country and home to a major university as well as a historic art academy, Minerva Academy, its art scene is relatively small and provincial. According to Velthoven, "Groningen was not very active. And we were the people doing things. You could organize your own shit. The vacuum also that you could feel around you in such a place makes the urgency to do something yourself."[83] Velthoven went to Minerva to study design but found the lack of intellectualism at the school disheartening. At the time, his friend Max Bruinsma was studying art history at the university, and, hearing that Velthoven was looking for a degree course with more critical engagement, convinced him to join the art history program.

At the time, there was a contingent of lecturers and professors at the university, including Lon de Vries Robbé and Sabrina Kamstra, who were deeply engaged with contemporary art writing and curation and became instrumental in introducing Velthoven to the wider art world. Velthoven also cites Leendert van Lagestein, who ran an art center in the town called Corps de Garde, as a means by which he came in contact with the work of contemporary artists and critical engagement with their work. According to Velthoven, "[Van Lagestein] brought a lot of very interesting people through the Netherlands. Very inspirational work. [De Vries Robbé] was teaching me contemporary art. She was teaching us about how artists use film and video, and stuff like that. It was like, 'Wow... Wow, this is cool.'"[84] As part of the art history program, the students were organized into groups and tasked with designing their own exhibitions in town, which gave Velthoven and his peers a taste for curating. Additionally, Velthoven secured access to the video department at the university and was able to offer local artists access to equipment that would have been prohibitively expensive had they rented it privately. This experience and his connections to art historians, curators, and technicians in the city all contributed to the formation of Mediamatic.

Once Velthoven and the other artists he was working with had decided to organize events together, they needed a name. According to Velthoven, it was something he came up with as a joke. He recalls:

83   Willem Velthoven, interview by Amanda Wasielewski, April 27, 2018.
84   Ibid.

We were seated in a café called the Brasserie in Groningen [...] having a meeting on how we are going to organize ourselves and we needed a name. And we were just brainstorming, and I made a joke because I had this ironic habit — if something was really plastic-y crappy I would call it plastomatic, because [...] this trailing word '-matic' was used in the '50s to signify modernity. [...] So I joked like, 'Let's call it Mediamatic,' and Barbara Pyle said, 'Oh, wow, that's a great name, that's a fantastic name, let's do Mediamatic.' And I said, 'No, no, no, let's not do that that. It was a joke. It's not serious. That was irony.' And she goes, 'No, that's a great name. Let's call it Mediamatic.' And she convinced all the others.[85]

In 1983, once Mediamatic was born, they staged their first screening events in a squatted local theater—the Grand Theatre on the Grote Markt—in the center of Groningen. They put on four of these events, screening the work of a selection of international video artists. They were able to access this work by tapping into the already-established networks of video art distribution in the Netherlands and, in the process, joined the growing circuit of video art venues around the country.[86]

Following their success in organizing these initial screenings, Mediamatic decided to stage a more ambitious exhibition of video art at the end of 1983. On December 16, they hosted the event *Ooghoogte* (Eye-height) at the Artotheek in Groningen, which was located in the De Faun building at Zuiderdiep 35. This location became their regular venue until they moved to Amsterdam permanently in 1986. The program for *Ooghoogte* featured multimedia/video installations and performance works and included two members of the Mediamatic collective (Barbara Pyle and Frits Maats) as well as four other local artists (Jannie Pranger, Cristie van Proosdij, Klaas Koetje, and Christine Chiffron). The response from the public was largely positive and the exhibition was well-attended. Emboldened, the group made their video exhibitions at De Faun a regular occurrence and held three more events in Groningen the following year.

In 1985 Leendert van Lagestein, who ran Corps de Garde, failed to secure additional funding to keep it running and had to close. He decided to move down to Amsterdam to a large squatted complex on Conradstraat in the

85 Ibid.
86 Pauline Terreehorst, "Opkomst En Ondergang van Videokunst in Nederland," in *Kunst En Beleid in Nederland 5*, ed. Fenna van den Burg et al. (Amsterdam: Boekmanstichting/Van Gennep, 1991), p. 54; Velthoven, interview by author.

islands east of the central station and encouraged Velthoven and his then-partner Jans Possel—who continues to direct Mediamatic with Velthoven today—to stake out a space there as well. In addition to planning six more video art events in Groningen, showing work by a variety of international artists, Velthoven and Possel were frequently travelling back and forth between Groningen and Amsterdam. According to Velthoven:

> Then we have a pied-à-terre in Amsterdam, it's handy. [...] There were artists and junkies and mentally disordered and freedom fighters... and it was all a big, big mess. There were also some people doing art projects inside the squats [...] I kept my studio in Groningen. I had this equipment like a dark room and things like that.[87]

While in Amsterdam, Velthoven and Possel were able to solidify their connections to the video art scene outside of Groningen, working with both Montevideo and Time Based Arts on different occasions, which put them on the map of media and video art organizations around the country.

While Mediamatic's video art exhibitions in Groningen were ambitious, Velthoven soon felt that their ambition had outgrown the audience in the small northern city. Their next move was to start a media art magazine. Velthoven describes the motivation for starting the magazine as something that was born "out of necessity," due to the isolation they felt in Groningen and their desire to connect to others interested in new media and video. He says:

> We were in the car, driving to Amsterdam, in the Polder. We were just talking we were like, 'What are we going to do?' You know, we were sitting there in Groningen. Then we thought maybe we should start a magazine, a communication platform to exchange with others. Now you would just start a blog. Since I had graphic design skills, I was then a graduated graphic designer, making my living by designing exhibitions and books and stuff. [...] we had all the skills. I was studying still art history, so we had all of the people that did the thinking and the writing, the library and we had artist friends and I knew how to make a graphic product and how to get a discount at the printers. [...] So we got a bit of initial funding to make a zero issue and that came out in '85.[88]

87   Velthoven, interview by author.
88   Ibid.

With the help of Jan Wijle, who was familiar with arts funding applications, Mediamatic secured 5000 guilders (approx. €4000 today[89]) in funding to produce a zero issue of the magazine in 1985.

The main aim of the magazine was international exchange, so it was published bilingually in both English and Dutch from the beginning. Mediamatic was already an international collective, as one of the founders, Barbara Pyle, was American, and the art scene in Netherlands was extremely international at that point thanks in part to post-graduate institutions like the Jan van Eyck Academy and the international participants they attracted. In addition to these internal connections, Velthoven and Possel also frequently travelled to see shows in neighboring countries and were interested in connecting to an audience outside the Netherlands. According to Velthoven, "The goal was to have an exchange. We can't do that in a funny local language. But, also, the scene was quite international, then that's why you want to connect."[90] The magazine represented a definitive shift away from the cut-and-paste aesthetics of the punk era. Using their photography, graphic design and early computer skills, the Mediamatic collective was able to produce a high-quality professional publication right from the start.

Given his background in design and publishing, Velthoven already had a certain amount of equipment at his disposal—both on his own and through his ties to the university—and had spent some time learning computer programming and creating computer-generated sound and graphics compilations in the summer of 1983. This was not his first experience with computers, though; his father had worked as Head of Records at the university hospital and used a big mainframe computer, so Velthoven had early experience of "very big, very noisy, very inconvenient computers."[91] This interest in and knowledge of rudimentary programming proved to be beneficial to the publication, as they were then able to secure professional typesetting via modem. Velthoven explains:

> I discovered something, namely that the national newspapers, [...] *Volkskrant* and *Trouw* and *Parool*, had a shared printing facility and a typesetting facility. Because they are daily newspapers, they had a backup typesetting system. [...] When one breaks down, you still have to produce three newspapers. They were actually selling downtime use of their spare

---

89   "Value of the Guilder / Euro," Institute of Social History, accessed May 23, 2018, http://www.iisg.nl/hpw/calculate.php.
90   Velthoven, interview by author.
91   Ibid.

typesetting system for very little money... if you knew how to use it, because they would not do the typesetting. You'd send the digital version of your text via a modem directly to the typesetting system. Already in '85. They published a protocol, like, how can you do extra codes in your text, this is a headline, etc. It is a bit like HTML kind of markup. [...] Of course, to have that quality, also attracted more people like, 'Oh wow, this is real. I want to be published here.'[92]

In addition to the use of computers for typesetting and sending their material to the printers, Velthoven and his Mediamatic colleagues were active BBS users as well. Velthoven describes being part of the Fidonet system, a world-wide network of BBSes created in 1984 that was an early precursor to the World Wide Web.[93]

Unlike V2_, Mediamatic never released a retro-avant-garde manifesto or any baldly utopian statements of purpose. To the extent that V2_'s manifestos were abstract and poetic, Mediamatic's magazine was, in contrast, relatively pragmatic. Their clear, practical approach to defining the emerging field of media art was, however, no less optimistic than V2_ and similarly reflected the enthusiasm and excitement around new technological tools in the Netherlands at the time. The magazine ran from 1985 until 1999, during which the publication reflected the zeitgeist of the early internet era and commented on many of the important issues in European media art scene at the time. Beginning in 1989, they also produced and distributed CD-ROMs along with the print magazine, which contained artworks and multimedia material.[94] Over the years, they covered a diverse range of theoretical perspectives on media art, published essays on media art history, and reported on festivals and exhibitions such as Ars Electronica and Documenta. Beginning in 1988, BILWET (see chapter 1), via Geert Lovink, were frequent contributors to *Mediamatic*. Lovink himself is credited as part of the editorial team starting in that year.

The zero issue of the magazine was produced in late 1985. The subheading of the title reads, simply, "Dutch Magazine on Media Art and Hardware Design," and their first editorial statement at the beginning of the issue outlines a clear, practical ambition for the publication: to reflect on and

92   Ibid.
93   Mediamatic's first e-mail address, published in their Winter 1992 issue (v.7#1), was media@ neabbs.nl (NEABBS stood for Nederlands Eerste Algemene Bulletin Board System, First General Dutch BBS).
94   The first CD-ROM player/drive for a PC, the CM-100, was, incidentally, developed and released by the Dutch electronics company Philips in 1985.

legitimize emerging media art practices. The statement is notable in that it makes pains to cover media art in general, rather than just video art. Naming Nam June Paik as its founding figure, the short statement declares that, "In the Netherlands [...] a large number of artists use audio, video, and computers."[95] Incidentally, in later issues, the subheading was simplified to "Media Art and Hardware Design" (October 1986, v.1#2) and then "European Media-Art Magazine" (September 1987, v.2#1). The logo for the magazine, which can be seen on the cover of the zero issue, is an hourglass and a lightning bolt, time and electricity being the essential elements of their field of interest.

The contents of *Mediamatic*'s zero issue certainly reflected the open-ended editorial perspective of the magazine. In the issue, the editorial statement is followed by drawings and a short statement by media and installation artist Servaas Schoone on "emotional TV for the future" and an essay by Marie-Adèle Rajandream on preserving the work of Livinius van de Bundt, who is characterized as "the first artist in our country who utilized video techniques."[96] These texts are followed by an essay by artist Jouke Kleerebezem, who provides perhaps the most theoretically-oriented statement on media art in the issue. Referencing the segregation of video art in a stairwell at the Stedelijk Museum, Kleerebezem argues that media art has an important role deconstructing power structures in contemporary culture. Using language similar to that used by V2_ in their manifestos, he writes:

We must adapt ourselves to complexity. In order to get used to a state of chaos, we must, first, increase chaos as much as possible. Right now, fragmentation controls the means as well as the application of technology and media. It threatens commonly accepted significations as well as the validity of the term *significance* itself.[97]

In addition to these articles, the issue also includes an essay by Jans Possel on Italian designer Ugo La Pietra, imagery by Kleerebezem, Frits Maats,

95   Willem Velthoven and Jans Possel, "Redactioneel," trans. Fokke Sluiter, *Mediamatic Magazine* 0, no. 0 (December 1985): p. 3.

96   Servaas Schoone, "De Nieuwe TV: Emotionele Televisie Voor de Toekomst," *Mediamatic Magazine* 0, no. 0 (December 1985): pp. 6–9; Marie-Adèle Rajandream, "Livinius En Het Licht," *Mediamatic Magazine* 0, no. 0 (December 1985): pp. 10–15. (Trans. Fokke Sluiter, Marten Gerritsen resp.)

97   Jouke Kleerebezem, "More Tales from the Beauty Farm," *Mediamatic Magazine* 0, no. 0 (December 1985): p. 16.

and Beatrijs Hulskes, and a review of Bruce Naumen's piece *Good Boy, Bad Boy* (1985) that had recently been screened as part of the World Wide Video Festival.[98]

Serendipitously, the launch of *Mediamatic Magazine* coincided with the organization of Talking Back to the Media (TBTTM). The zero issue, therefore, also includes an article on the genesis of the TBTTM project. Due to the close-knit nature of the media and video art scene in the Netherlands in the mid-'80s, Mediamatic already had strong ties to the organizers of the festival, including Sabrina Kamstra, and the participating artists, including Max Bruinsma, who wrote up the article on TBTTM in *Mediamatic*.[99] They were, thus, able to sell the magazine in conjunction with the festival and attract an enthusiastic audience that was already critically engaged with and interested in the development of new media art.

Networked Events

> *How you left the space, days or year later, varied [...] Some drifted on in other circuits, from Alpine meadows to cyberspace. Others just stayed. No one who has been inside the space can ever leave again; at night in your dreams you go back.*[100]
> — BILWET

In the late '80s, Caroline Nevejan emerged as a key figure in the organization of "networked events," which were designed around and facilitated by the use of computer networks. She helped to bring Amsterdam into the internet era by coordinating The Galactic Hacker Party in 1989 and the Seropositive ball [o+ ball] in 1990, and she went on to play a supporting role in subsequent networked events.[101] The success of these events and the conversations they started around network technology at the intersection of art, politics, computer hacking, and journalism meant that others soon followed: The Wetware Convention (1991), The Next 5 Minutes (1993), Hacking at the End of the Universe (1993), and the Doors of Perception (1993). Prior to her work with network events, Nevejan had been active in squatter circles and

---

98   Jans Possel, "Media/Ritual/Design," *Mediamatic Magazine* 0, no. 0 (December 1985): pp. 26–32; Lidewijn Reckman, "Good Boy/Bad Boy," *Mediamatic Magazine* 0, no. 0 (December 1985): pp. 33–35.
99   Bruinsma, "Talks on Talking Back."
100 ADILKNO, *Cracking the Movement: Squatting Beyond the Media* (Brooklyn: Autonomedia, 1994), pp. 32–33.
101 Caroline Nevejan, "Presence and the Design of Trust" (Amsterdam, University of Amsterdam, 2007), p. 11.

was one of the initial contributors to the squatter newspaper *Bluf!* in 1981. From 1988 until 1999, she was the events producer at the formerly-squatted music and culture venue Paradiso, where she was instrumental in planning events that combined the political concerns of the squatter milieu—namely issues around anarchism, autonomy, and democracy—with the use of new technological tools. As exemplified by these events, media theory, as it developed in the Netherlands, walked a line between two extremes: pragmatic optimism on one hand and wariness of the ways new media might be exploited by the powerful on the other.

Dutch artists and activists were excited about exploring the potential for democratic exchange that network technology presented, and, indeed, it promised (and facilitated) a level of participation they could only ever dream about before. They took up working with network computing systems with the goal of using them to connect with like-minded people elsewhere in the world. Despite their enthusiastic and often-utopian outlook, critical thinking and critical analysis were still central to their engagement with new technology; they wanted to understand possible points of control within the system and how computer code can be altered or manipulated. Nevejan, in an interview with Geert Lovink, explains:

> In the 1980s networks like Peacenet and Greennet provided us with news, which could travel beyond the censorship rules from countries like South Africa. So the Internet provided ways to get around not to be trusted formal news reports and it generated 'trust' because the witnesses themselves could speak up and testify unedited. When I started to make shows in Paradiso I collaborated with hackers and through them I found out how the technology itself is easily manipulated, how any code can be broken and how the business propaganda of delivering 'safe' environments was (and is) a fairy tale. At the time I could not have formulated it in these terms, but in hindsight I can see that we were dealing with multidimensional designs and were struggling how all these related and contextualized each other and in this process trust appeared to be fundamental to be able to understand what was happening.[102]

In a way, these networked events, which centered around a core community of tight-knit local artists/activists in Amsterdam, served as foil to the wild, untamed world that the internet had opened up. They were in-person

102 Caroline Nevejan, interview by Geert Lovink, accessed June 17, 2018, http://networkcultures.org/geert/interview-with-caroline-nevejan/.

meetings that operated in the context of Amsterdam's art and activist scene—organized within a local tradition of activism with a local point of view on the issues discussed—that could support exploration into the wider world via technological mediation.

For Nevejan, there was always an aesthetic component to these meetings.[103] Just as Talking Back to the Media had been positioned by Garcia and Carrión as an artwork in itself, the conferences that Nevejan helped organize were discussed as aesthetic performances that centered around public debate. Nevejan says:

> In conjunction with De Balie, the cultural centre next door [to Paradiso], an Amsterdam style was developed in which a lot of emphasis was put to create an 'aesthetics of public debating'. Discussion was more than a disagreement between key actors. It had theatrical elements in which the producer took up the role of director. It was in this context that new communication technology such as telephone, fax, video conferencing, bulletin board systems and the Internet started to play a role. Why limit a dialogue to those who were able to gather in a particular time and space when you can also involve others remotely?[104]

Thus, communication technology was, first and foremost, seen as a way for a small community in the Netherlands to open up their political debate to a wider public.[105] For European artists and activists, in-person meetings in "meatspace" (or, as Geert Lovink puns, "meetspace") maintained a delicate balance between the development of network practice in the local community and the unwieldy outside world. Conferences and meetings, therefore, became a crucial component in the development of both theory and practice around emerging network technologies in the early 1990s and another manifestation of the temporary autonomous zone.[106]

103 Ibid.

104 Ibid.

105 The idea of public debate as an aesthetic "object" or work is an idea that has also been developed by Lovink. He has characterized the <nettime> email list he created with Pit Schultz as "a meta-visual process art" and "a text-only social sculpture," referencing artist Joesph Beuys's concept of "social sculpture." See Lovink, *Dark Fiber*, p. 99.

106 Lovink writes, "Conferences are known and respected as effective accumulators and accelerators. They offer ideal opportunities to recharge the inner batteries in the age of short-lived concepts. Temporary media labs are even more effective in this respect: they focus, speed up, intensify, and exert a longer-term effect on local initiatives and trans-local groups. Meetings in real space are becoming more and more a precious good for the way they add a crucial stage to almost any networked media project, whether in arts, culture, or politics." Lovink, *Dark Fiber*, p. 249.

In 1989 Nevejan, Rop Gonggrijp, Patrice Riemens, and Marieke Nelissen organized one of the first critical technology conferences in the Netherlands that dealt with the intersections of hacking, activism, and art.[107] They called it the Galactic Hacker Party, a name inspired by Douglas Adams's *The Hitchhiker's Guide to the Galaxy* (1979), but it was also, more formally, known as the International Conference on the Alternative Use of Technology Amsterdam (ICATA '89).[108] Taking inspiration from squatter activist publications like *Bluf!* as well as other hacker publications such as *Datenschleuder* (produced by the Chaos Computer Club in Germany) and the *2600 The Hacker Quarterly* (from the US hacker scene), twenty-year-old Rop Gonggrijp and a group of other young hackers started the zine *Hack-tic*, which released its first issue in January 1989. The title was a portmanteau of hack and tactic, and the subheading of the magazine, which sums up its founding principle, was "a magazine for techno-anarchists."[109] This new generation of young anarchists updated the autonomist and anarchist politics from their punk predecessors by shifting their focus from the city to internet. The cyberpunks had arrived on the scene.

In 1988 Nevejan invited a group from Chaos Computer Club (CCC), the pioneering German hacker collective founded in 1981, to Amsterdam, where they could meet and exchange ideas.[110] The CCC had made headlines around the world in 1984 by hacking a security flaw at a Hamburg savings bank that enabled them to transfer 135,000 Deutschmark out of the bank's accounts. The hackers immediately returned the money, and the stunt was praised for exposing the vulnerabilities of the new electronic systems being used in Germany. The CCC also set the precedent for in-person hacker meetings in Europe when they staged their first Chaos Communication Congress in Germany in that same year. Inspired by the activities of the CCC, the newly founded Hack-tic group in Amsterdam, working with Nevejan, decided to organize their own hacking event in 1989. On March 29th of that year, they posted an announcement for the festival on the NEABBS (Nederlands Eerste Algemene Bulletin Board System) followed by a press release from Paradiso, more explicitly stating that the event would foster "demystification of modern, and especially computer-technology" in order to prevent the technology being "restricted to a limited elite of professional and/or business

107 Nevejan, "Presence," p. 109.
108 Ibid., p. 106.
109 "Hack-Tic," accessed June 19, 2018, http://www.hacktic.nl.
110 Caroline Nevejan and Alexander Badenoch, "How Amsterdam Invented the Internet: European Networks of Significance 1980-1995," in *Hacking Europe: From Computer Cultures to Demoscenes*, ed. Gerard Alberts and Ruth Oldenziel (London: Springer, 2014), p. 199.

people."[111] According to Nevejan, "Apart from a few artists, the formal art world, the funding bodies and the business world would not support artists who were involved in art and technology."[112] And so, she argues, the media organizations and collectives had self-organized to help facilitate artist's experiments with new technology and that infrastructure, in turn, made organizing GHP and future events possible.

The event consisted of a "cockpit" hacking area in the main hall of the venue as well as smaller workshops and presentations that took place in the balconies, dressing rooms, and other small areas of the space.[113] Members of the CCC, including founder Wau Holland, were invited to Amsterdam to attend and participate in the event. Geert Lovink, Geke van Dijk, and Gert de Bruyne were in charge of reporting the proceedings online to remote audiences as they happened as well as producing an edited publication of the activities at GHP. The organizers were eager to make connections outside of western Europe and the US and to give the topics of the event a more global perspective. Groups in New Zealand, Kenya, and Russia participated remotely using the text-based network connections that had been set up in the venue (although the Kenyan group ended up having technical difficulties participating live).[114] The venue was also able to connect to nodes in the US, Germany, France, South Africa, Brazil, and Uruguay.[115] A videophone link was established with Russia, where those on the Russian side were able wave hello from behind the Iron Curtain, which Nevejan cites as a momentous occasion for those present, akin to witnessing the moon landing.[116]

The follow-up to GHP (and also known as ICATA '90) was the Seropositive Ball, an event centering around AIDS/HIV activism and network culture. The 69-hour program, between 5pm June 21 and 2pm June 24, 1990, was again held at Paradiso and coordinated by Nevejan and Riemens together with artist David Garcia. The work of AIDS activists in the US in the late '80s, particularly ACT-UP, Gran Fury, and Gay Men's Health cable programs, had made a strong impression on Garcia, who was keen to investigate how he and his fellow artists in Europe could similarly respond to the AIDS crisis. He saw the activist artwork being made in the US as a powerful implementation of the kind of artistic practice that he would later categorize as tactical media.

111 Nevejan, "Presence," p. 110.
112 Ibid., p. 95.
113 Ibid., p. 111.
114 Ibid., pp. 112–13.
115 Hack-Tic and Paradiso, "GHP/ICATA '89 Proceedings" (Paradiso, Amsterdam, 1989), Instituut voor Sociale Geschiedenis, Amsterdam.
116 Nevejan, "Presence," p. 114.

In line with the idea of the "aesthetics of debating," Garcia saw the role of tactical media in art as a way to bring a discourse or a conversation about, rather than force a dogmatic political position on the public. He says:

> ...something like silence equals death for me was the perfect emblem of something which uses art's ability to live with ambiguity. And, therefore, an invitation to discourse rather than an answer to a question. And yet it's deployed within the context of a campaign, so it's kind of intimate media and mass media simultaneously. And does things that no other form of politics, to my knowledge, had done before. So not agitprop. And so, those were the differences and that's what engaged me. That sense that it was changing the nature of art and the nature of politics so that those two entities were no longer big enough... That's why we wanted a term like tactical media because art or politics didn't quite encapsulate what exactly we wanted to communicate about both of those discourses.[117]

For Garcia, whose friend and collaborator Ulises Carrión had died from AIDS the previous year, the beginnings of his involvement with planning network events started from the feeling that artists in Europe needed to act on behalf of those in their community dying from the disease.

The event was planned to coincide with the 6th International Conference on AIDS in June 1990, which many AIDS activists were boycotting due to the US policy to restrict travel into the country for people with HIV and AIDS. Since the Seropostive ball was taking place without any break throughout the night, network connections were established that would facilitate interaction with boycotters in other time zones, including San Francisco and Rio de Janeiro.[118] Although the program included talks by AIDS professionals and researchers as well as opportunities to share information, the relationship between art and AIDS activism was both the inspiration for the event and its core conceit. There was an exhibition of photographs, posters, film, and video, as well as a performance program put together by Wil van der Meer with over two hundred artists performing.[119]

Several Americans artists involved in AIDS activism travelled to Amsterdam for the event. Gran Fury members Mark Simpson and Robert Vasquez were on hand to speak about their work, and one of their banners, "ALL

117 Garcia, interview by author.
118 Heleen Riper, David Garcia, and Patrice Riemens, eds., *The Seropositive Ball* (Amsterdam: Paradiso / Time Based Arts, 1990), p. 5.
119 Ibid., p. 6.

PEOPLE WITH AIDS ARE INNOCENT," was hung over the entrance to the venue. ACT-UP members Gregg Bordowitz and Alexis Danzig were present, and filmmaker Marlon Riggs also spoke at the event. Towards the end of the program, pieces of the AIDS Memorial Quilt were unfurled over the balconies.[120] A number of Netherlands-based artists showed work as well. Jaap de Jonge installed a "video-chandelier." Floris Vos created various private spaces inside the hall that were separated by velvet curtains, which Nevejan argued, "gave the debates the intimacy needed to encourage public participation."[121] A balcony of the event contained a photo exhibition by Frits de Ridder, who was living with AIDS himself and made the lives of AIDS patients the subject of his work. Additionally, Nan Hoover, an American artist who had long been based in Amsterdam, showed her video installation *Walking in Any Direction* (1984).

The 0+network, a computer network developed by Rolf Pixley, was used during the event to post information and reports and hosted an art gallery that was created by David Garcia, Peter Mertens, and Joel Ryan. It was designed so that it would be easy for those with no computer experience to use.[122] They also established network links to AIDS hospital wards, bookstores, and the home of someone with AIDS who was too ill to leave his house to participate in the event.[123] The principle aim, as expressed by Heleen Riper and David Garcia was to allow people, "to speak for themselves" and "to look at it from a variety of perspectives and not simply from the medical point of view."[124] The technology they used was HyperCard, a piece of software and programming tool released by Apple in 1987 that predated much of the functionality of the World Wide Web and early web browsers. HyperCard allowed the organizers of the Seropositive ball to create a graphical user interface in a series of digital "cards" that users could dial into and navigate through. Pixley configured the system in this way so that users would not have to contend with terminals or command line inputs to read messages on the network. The idea was that all the material would be accessible with a mouse click.[125]

---

120 Ibid., p. 121.
121 Ibid., p. 5.
122 Ibid., p. 6.
123 It should be noted that the use of network technology did not go over well with the Americans in attendance, who felt that their European colleagues were using "technology for technology's sake" and ignoring the experiences of those most affected by the disease. Ibid., pp. 6–7; Garcia, interview by author.
124 Riper, Garcia, and Riemens, *The Seropositive Ball*, p. 11.
125 Ibid., p. 65.

The next important networked event was the Wetware Convention on August 2, 1991, which was organized by Geert Lovink and artist Franz Fiegl, with Menno Grootveld doing live TV broadcasts of the event. Marleen Stikker, who would become a leading figure in the media art scene of the '90s, was also involved in organizing the event in her capacity as director of the Summer Festival program at De Balie, a theater and center for public debate on arts and culture that was established in Leidseplein in 1982. Later, Stikker would become one of the founders of both De Digitale Stad (she was the first mayor of the Digital City) and De Waag, a media arts organization founded in 1996. For Wetware, De Balie helped facilitate the planning of the event as well as a publication of theoretical essays on the theme of the conference, but the event actually took place nearby at the Melkweg, a music venue at Leidseplein (nearby both Paradiso and De Balie) that had, like Paradiso, been established as a music venue during the counterculture era.[126]

Some of the participants, like Lovink, were a consistent presence at all the network events of the '80s and early '90s, but each event was organized by a slightly different constellation of people. Unlike the GHP and Seropositive ball, Wetware was oriented toward the media art scene within industrial music. Alongside software and hardware, the organizers were interested in speaking about and addressing "wetware," a term to describe water-based "bio-machines" like the human brain or the cyborg body. The term had been around since the 1950s but became a popular buzzword during the late '80s within cyberpunk circles. The event was, by all accounts, a chaotic day with performances by artists, experiments with equipment, and theoretical reflections on the human technological apparatus, all capped off by an enormous party. Little documentation remains from the event, but, according to Grootveld, it included performances by industrial bands like Minus Delta T and Laibach, video DJing, a contingent of theoreticians around Lovink, and a group of artists from Fiegl's circle. Grootveld says, "It was a very strange but also fruitful, productive combination of theoretical people and people from the art world and from the musical scene and also from the world of technology."[127]

The event, like the other conferences/events related to network technology during the era, brought together artists, theorists, and experts in computing. According to Grootveld:

The Wetware Convention, in my opinion, is one of the most underestimated and crucial events of the — well, let's not exaggerate — the last

---

126 Geert Lovink and Rik Delhaas, eds., *Wetware* (Amsterdam: De Balie, 1991).
127 Grootveld, interview.

30 years. That is really true because it was, it came at this very specific moment in time and lots of things that happened later on, you can more or less trace back to that event. [...] you have hardware, you have software and there is also wetware. And we should already now pay attention to what is happening to the wetware with all these emerging technologies, which is still a valuable proposition as far as I'm concerned. I think that was a crucial event.[128]

The event established a discourse about the relationship between the human body and computing systems, which was an extension of the investigation of the man-machine relationship in experimental industrial music in the '80s.

According to Stikker's introductory statement in the publication for the event, Wetware was attempting, at least in some ways, to bridge the gap between techno-utopianism and criticality, neither backing away from an optimistic outlook on new technology nor falling victim to blind enthusiasm for it. Her text strikes a defiant note against those that might wholesale reject the adoption of emerging digital technologies: "The phenomenon of technology is not treated here with distrust, but held upside down in a consciously naive way, shaken back and forth and taken apart, in order that its power can be examined."[129] The critical thrust of the convention highlighted the tension between the "mental space" of virtual reality versus the human body versus the human as cyborg. The theoretical essays in the resultant publication delve heavily into the spiritual implications of such man-machine hybrids, and many of the essays attempt to understand not just the implications of digital technology but how the human body and human life are affected by the use of this technology.

Following this, in 1992, the first Next 5 Minutes (N5M) conference, organized by Geert Lovink and David Garcia, began percolating. The organizers released a packet of "working papers" setting out their goals and theoretical perspectives ahead of the conference. Initially, they discussed the conference in terms of "tactical television" and the booklet they produced was labelled a "zapbook" because readers could flip "channels" or "zap through different kinds of material on tv" in the context of the book.[130] In this booklet, Bas

128 Ibid.
129 Marleen Stikker, "The Human Remnant," in *Wetware*, ed. Geert Lovink and Rik Delhaas (Amsterdam: De Balie, 1991), p. 6.
130 Jeroen van Bergelijk et al., eds., *The Next Five Minutes (N5M) Zapbook* (Amsterdam: Paradiso, 1992), p.5.

Raijmakers wrote, "As always, tv-tacticians are lurking, ready to move in the cracks as they appear. Ready to exploit and even enlarge these cracks. The N5M wants to give a platform to these efforts."[131] Although the conference was originally organized around the concept of tactical television, over the course of the event itself, which took place from the 8th to the 10th of January 1993, the term was broadened to tactical media.

The stated aim of N5M was "to leave behind the rigid dichotomy between the mainstream, commercial, and national tv on one hand and the marginal and independent tv on the other."[132] Tactical television would find a way between the mass-market style universalism of mainstream television and the introspection and atomization of independent television. Likewise, tactical media in general would work within the cracks of the mainstream rather than stay in a segregated realm. The three-day conference was divided into five main topics: the Camcorder Revolution, the South, Wartime, Eastern Europe, and the Visual Arts.

Coming at a time when the former-Yugoslav countries were enmeshed in an on-going war and, given Dutch ties to Slovenian art and music via NSK, conversations about tactical television in Eastern Europe led by Geert Lovink featured heavily in the program. The first day of event, January 8, featured panels and screenings on the theme of the Camcorder Revolution, looking at how the availability of personal camcorders had fostered independent television projects. Starting from the point of view of local alternative TV, the program featured talks by, among others, Menno Grootveld and Raúl Marroquin. In another panel, the discussion was opened up to an international selection of television producers from Austria, Zimbabwe, Romania, the US, and the Netherlands. Other media—such as network computing and satellite television—were also featured at certain points over the three days of the conference, and Rop Gonggrijp spoke on alternative networks and computer hacking as a source for journalists.

The second day of N5M featured more discussion on the role of tactical television in times of war, particularly with regard to the Yugoslav conflict. The day also featured an event on tactical television projects in the global South with the aim of exposing "Northern" tactical TV producers to the activities outside of the US and northwestern Europe. Finally, the last day of the event focused more on the role of art and visual artists in tactical

131 Bas Raijmakers, "Introduction," in *The Next Five Minutes (N5M) Zapbook*, ed. Jeroen van Bergelijk et al. (Amsterdam: Paradiso, 1992), p.8.
132 Ibid., p.7.

television production. For Garcia, the role of the visual arts was a central concern. In the working papers, he writes:

> Many who once would have called themselves artists have now adopted this title ["media activist"]. As television is created by teams these inter-disciplinary groups may prove in the long term to have more impact than those who insist on the more individualistic models of artist's television.[133]

N5M raised questions around not only the role of individual artists but the role of medium-specificity in the context of video and television. In this document, Garcia includes an article by John Wyvers from 1992 that argues that the term video art should be "done away with." Wyvers writes that, because digital culture makes the boundaries of medium indistinct and their uses pluralistic, video must be free to mix and mingle with other media—"from digital imaging, from film, from interactive and other technologies, from television [...]"[134] The change in terminology from tactical television to tactical media is a product of this shift in the thinking beyond medium.

Two additional events/exhibitions in 1993 continued the conversations initiated at the start of the year by N5M. Again, what was unique about these meetings was the way in which they united aesthetics, computing, and activism under one umbrella, one platform of exchange. The questions that were emerging around the internet and computing were seen as part and parcel of both aesthetics and politics.

Positioned as a sequel to the Galactic Hacker Party and organized through Hack-tic, Hacking at the End of the Universe (HEU) took place from August 4–6 on the Flevopolder, a piece of reclaimed land that had been built in the 1950s and '60s to the east of Amsterdam on a former lake. For three days, participants camped out at Larserbos campground outside of Lelystad, installing artworks, demonstrating hacks, and taking part in discussions on the use of network technology by activists. According to Gonggrijp:

> What was especially important for that event was that the image of hackers and computer freaks had to be adjusted. The image of a hacker was someone who sits behind a computer in a dusty attic room, but now people

---

133 David Garcia, "Visual Arts: Introduction," in *The Next Five Minutes (N5M) Zapbook*, ed. Jeroen van Bergelijk et al. (Amsterdam: Paradiso, 1992), p. 61.

134 Bergelijk et al., *The Next Five Minutes (N5M) Zapbook*, p. 68.

suddenly saw young people with cables between their teeth climbing trees.[135]

The idea was to consider the relationship between technology and the environment and to combine computing with the DIY spirit of camping or surviving in nature.

The opening discussion of HEU was titled, "Networking for the masses," and was designed to pick up where the Galactic Hack Party had left off, taking time to reflect on how attitudes toward new technology had changed in the previous four years. The program states:

> One of the main discussions at the 1989 Galactic Hacker Party focused on whether or not the alternative community should use computer networking. Many people felt a resentment against using a 'tool of oppression' for their own purposes. Computer technology was, in the eyes of many, something to be smashed rather than used. Times have changed. Many who were violently opposed to using computers in 1989 have since discovered word-processing and desktop publishing. [...] Not all is well: many obstacles stand in the way of the 'free flow of information.' Groups with access to information pay such high prices for it that they are forced to sell information they'd prefer to pass on for free. Some low-cost alternative networks have completely lost their democratic structure. Is this the era of the digital dictator, or are we moving towards digital democracy?[136]

Like the networked events before it, the organizers of HEU emphasized discussion, public debate, and critical reflection on how participation and democratic principles could be enacted on computer networks.

The event, which attracted over one thousand participants, also featured a number of demos on the use of technology, hacking techniques, and how artists make work with the use of computers.[137] One artwork on display at HEU was the *Stone-Age Computer* (1993) by Mathilde µP.[138] The piece, a working computer keyboard made from rocks and surrounded by soil, was installed in the campsite in a patch of moss and greenery, completely

---

135 Qtd. Leonor Jonker, *No future nu: punk in Nederland 1977–2012* (Amsterdam: Lebowski Publishers, 2012), p. 240.

136 Rop Gonggrijp, "Hacking at the End of the Universe," *Alt.Hackers*, July 27, 1993, https://groups.google.com/forum/#!topic/alt.hackers/li5VeGWgVmGw.

137 Joost Flint, *Handleiding voor: De Digitale Stad XS4ALL internet* (Amsterdam: Hack-tic / De Balie, 1994), pp. IV–3.

138 Jonker, *No future nu*, p. 240.

embedded in natural surroundings. Somewhat echoing the concerns of the
Wetware convention, the piece was designed to bring the computer (and
the computer user) back in touch with nature and reflect on how the sterile
beige boxes of delicate electronic equipment could be integrated into the
organic workings of the natural world.

In addition to the art, hacking, and partying that took place on the polder
that week, the idea to create the a widely accessible public internet service,
De Digitale Stad, was born.[139] According to Geert Lovink, the organizers of
HEU used the event to attract press attention to the government's "harsh"
computer crime laws passed in that year and the restrictions on freedom that
these laws represented. Lovink writes, "The idea being that programmers,
artists, and other interested parties, can, if they are moving early enough,
shape, or at least influence, the architecture of the networks."[140] The next
step would be to take control over how the internet was implemented in
the Netherlands before the government could hobble it with legislation.

A few months after HEU, from October 30-31, another network event,
the Doors of Perception, took place in Amsterdam. Like the GHP/HEU and
N5M, it was the first in a series of (mostly) biannual events. It was named
after Aldus Huxley's 1954 account of his experiences taking mescaline—a
hippie classic in the 1960s. Initiated by British writer John Thackara and
co-organized Willem Velthoven, the event focused on the future of design
in the digital era and its ecological and social impact. The event came about
as part of an ongoing, international conversation on the topic of digital
design between the organizers and many of the participants. For example,
Velthoven and Thackara were introduced to one another through mutual
connections to Kayoko Ota, a designer and architect in Tokyo that Velthoven
had collaborated with through Mediamatic. The Doors of Perception website
explains the reasoning for organizing the first event, saying:

> We did the first conference in 1993 to find out what the Internet meant for
> design – and vice versa. There was a lot of talk in the US about teleshop-
> ping, and video-on-demand. This sounded boring, so we organised Doors
> to consider more exciting and useful alternatives. The result was more
> excitement than answers, but at least we added a critical note to the
> debate about the role of ICTs.[141]

139 Ibid., p. 242.
140 Lovink, *Dark Fiber*, p. 46.
141 "Conference Archive," Doors of Perception, accessed July 2, 2018, http://old.doorsofperception.
com/_conference_archive.html#doors1.

Originally planned to take place at the Stedelijk museum, the turn-out was so good—650 people attended—that they were forced to move the event to the large conference center at the RAI in the south of the city.[142] Topics covered included interactive architecture and art, the relationship between nature and cyberspace, video games, and the shift from printed work to electronic text.[143]

This event, like the others that came before it, continued to foster debate and open up new lines of inquiry into the meaning of the emerging culture of computer networks. Geert Lovink, however, criticized the event, writing that Mediamatic had the potential to be "a sophisticated European counterpart of *Wired*," but instead allied itself with "business-geared design conferences Doors of Perception."[144] Lovink also criticized Mediamatic for focusing on CD-ROMs instead of developing a larger online presence in the early to mid-'90s. Despite Lovink's criticism, however, each of the networked events that took place in 1993—including Doors of Perception –added something different to the discourse around internet culture that was flourishing in Amsterdam at the time. While Doors of Perception focused more on design, HEU focused on the tension between the environment and computing, and N5M developed the concept of tactical media. All of these events worked at the intersection of aesthetics, politics, and media. The platforms that they created for meditation on the meaning of emerging media technology placed thinkers in Amsterdam at the forefront of net theory during the 1990s.

142 "About Doors of Perception 1 (1993)," Doors of Perception, accessed July 2, 2018, http:// museum.doorsofperception.com/doors1/about.html.
143 "Content Doors of Perception 1 (1993)," Doors of Perception, accessed July 2, 2018, http:// museum.doorsofperception.com/doors1/content.html.
144 Lovink, *Dark Fiber*, p. 111 nt. 22.

Conclusion: The Digital City

We live in a single constricted space resonant with tribal drums.[1]
– Marshall McLuhan

With the advent of the internet, McLuhan's concept of the "global village" became a popular metaphor (a cliché, really) to describe the increasingly interconnected planet. McLuhan envisioned a future where people would be free to experience and live among many cultures at once, slipping out of the confines of geography and borders on a stream of electrons. A small country like the Netherlands had a role to play, not as individuals surfing global cultures but as a tribe with jointly-developed ideas about how culture on the network and networked culture should operate. Thanks to Provo and the squatters' movement, Amsterdam had long contained a city within a city (or, a village within a village)—a tight-knit community of artists and activists who were staunch believers in autonomy and personal freedom *within* a cooperative community.

Squatters had developed ways to crack into the urban fabric and carve out new spaces—new temporary autonomous zones—within the established order. As these squatters, together with artists and activists, moved into a virtual space (i.e., a media space), urban tactics became media tactics. The playing field had changed but the values of openness, democracy, participation, interaction, and autonomy survived. So, when it came time to enter the "global village," these artists and activists (and hackers) entered as a tribe, not as individuals. In 2001 David Garcia described the Next 5 Minutes as a "tribal gathering of indymedia," and, indeed, networked events, including N5M, helped guide the tribe through the transition from city space to cyberspace by creating platforms that fostered both local tribal unity as well as a utopian hope of connecting to like-minded people around

---

1   Marshall McLuhan, *The Gutenberg Galaxy: The Making of Typographic Man* (Toronto: University of Toronto Press, 1962), p. 31.

Wasielewski, A., *From City Space to Cyberspace: Art, Squatting, and Internet Culture in the Netherlands*. Amsterdam: Amsterdam University Press, 2021
DOI 10.5117/9789463725453_CONCL

the globe.² As networked culture developed in Amsterdam, the concerns of the local—and the tribe—were always balanced against the ways that tribe reached out to the wider world.

The internet art that developed in Europe in the mid-1990s, particularly the work associated with the Net.art movement, united old tribe members and new ones. The artists of Jodi (Joan Heemskerk and Dirk Paesmans), for example, who met at the Jan van Eyck Academy in 1990, joined the ranks of veterans of the squatter art and alternative media scene like Franz Feigl, Geert Lovink, Erik Hobijn, Walter van der Cruijsen, and Dick Verdult in both virtual spaces like the <nettime> mailing list and brick-and-mortar computer labs like Desk.nl, located in a canal house in the center of Amsterdam.³ They, in turn, met up on- and offline with artists/theorists/writers from Germany like Pit Schulz and Tilman Baumgärtel, artists from Slovenia like Luka Frelih and Vuk Cosic—who had their own version of the Desk. nl computer art lab called Ljudmila, Russians like Olia Lialina and Alexei Shulgin, and the English artist Heath Bunting, to name a few key figures. The development of online, virtual artwork—accessible to anyone with an internet connection and a web browser—was, however, still a few years away. If the story of squatting and media art that I have outlined in the preceding chapters can be viewed as a pre-history of internet art in the Netherlands, it would be fitting for it to end at the point where most histories of internet art begin: with the invention of the internet. Or, rather, with the invention of the *Dutch* internet.

The Dutch role in shaping an alternative internet culture, one that did not revolve around internet start-ups or Silicon Valley entrepreneurship, has been explored by some of the figures who helped shape it, including Caroline Nevejan. Riffing on an often-misquoted statement from former Vice President Al Gore regarding his role in promoting the development of the early internet, the title of Caroline Nevejan and Alexander Badenoch's essay "How Amsterdam Invented the Internet" is meant as a humorous legerdemain.⁴ The essay does not actually claim that Amsterdam invented

2   David Garcia and Geert Lovink, The GHI of Tactical Media, interview by Andreas Broeckmann, July 2001, 5, https://art.ubiquitypress.com/articles/10.7238/a.v0i2.684/galley/3239/download/.

3   Geert Lovink, *Dark Fiber: Tracking Critical Internet Culture* (Cambridge: MIT Press, 2002) p. 85; Josephine Bosma, *Nettitudes: Let's Talk Net Art* (Amsterdam: Institute of Network Cultures, 2011), p. 137.

4   Caroline Nevejan and Alexander Badenoch, "How Amsterdam Invented the Internet: European Networks of Significance 1980–1995," in *Hacking Europe: From Computer Cultures to Demoscenes*, ed. Gerard Alberts and Ruth Oldenziel (London: Springer, 2014), pp. 189–217.

the internet any more than Gore did. Instead, Nevejan and Badenoch detail the role that grassroots politics and activism played in bringing the internet to the Dutch public, mirroring Gore's actual (if awkwardly-worded) statement from 1999 that he "created" the internet by pushing for legislation that would enable its implementation. In the case of Amsterdam, as I have outlined in depth in this book, artists in the Netherlands played a leading role in developing a critical, leftwing, anti-capitalist politics around new media and—eventually—network technology, via autonomist/anarchist ideals in the squatters' movement and the practice of creating DIY, pirate, and alternative media.

The development of De Digitale Stad (DDS)—the Digital City—is the product of artists' and activists' decade-long obsession with creating autonomous platforms, cracks in the established order or temporary autonomous zones (TAZs) where citizens can direct the destiny of their own open, free, and fair communities.[5] As the possibility of squatting the physical city was increasingly foreclosed, the virtual realm seemed to offer the tantalizing opportunity to create a new crack, a new TAZ, to occupy for a time. It is fitting, then, that this first public internet portal—free and open to the public—would be developed using the metaphor of the city.

Born ten years after the squatters' movement in Amsterdam began to decline, De Digitale Stad allowed members of the alternative culture scene in Amsterdam to once again reinvent the notion of "home." It was a new opportunity to realize a temporary autonomous city, albeit now in a dematerialized realm. Douglas Murphy argues that the displacement of utopian aspirations from physical home to homepage effectively quashed the experimentalism prevalent in 1960s architecture and urbanism. He writes:

> Gone were pretensions towards large-scale physical change; from then on utopia was within cyberspace, in the frontier lands of the Internet. [...] In this severance, something important was lost. Abandoning genuinely spatial terrain in favour of conducting battles in the frontier of cyberspace meant also that the fight over the ideas that had been so vital—over how people should be housed, over what rights they had to the spaces of the city, over notions such as dwelling itself—were completely forfeited.[6]

5   Geert Lovink, addressing the uptake of Hakim Bey's TAZ within early '90s internet culture, writes, "TAZ, as it was understood within the first phase of the hypes (1993–1996), became attached to a (cyber) libertarian agenda, a geek culture to which the anarchist author of TAZ had only loose ties." See *Dark Fiber*, pp. 234–239.

6   Douglas Murphy, *Last Futures: Nature, Technology and the End of Architecture* (London: Verso, 2016) p. 135.

Housing activism did not, however, simply decline with the advent of postmodern architecture and the invention of the internet, as Murphy argues. Even as professional architectural production made a conservative turn in the late '70s and '80s, radical utopian housing strategies were being advanced by squatters' movements like that in Amsterdam. Many of the values that were applied to housing in the '60s and '70s were not so much forfeited as adapted to the changing technological landscape in the years that followed. As the potential for freedom, flexibility, creative expression, and autonomy were whittled away in urban space in the late '80s, cyberspace arose as the "place" where the values developed in the squatters' movement could be advanced further. Just as the utopian architecture of the '60s began to seem dystopian to many in the decades that followed,[7] the utopian hope for cyberspace in the '90s now seems naive. For artists and activists in the squatter milieu of the late '80s, however, a move to cyberspace was not intended as a retreat but, instead, a bold move forward into a new autonomous zone. Like others before it, it was destined to be temporary.

De Digitale Stad was launched on January 15, 1994, as a joint project of De Balie and Hack-tic, having been developed over the course of the previous year. As detailed in chapter 4, 1993 was an important year for artists and activists in Amsterdam to deepen their understanding—over the course of three networked events (the Next 5 Minutes, Hacking at the End of the Universe, and the Doors of Perception)—of their role in and relationship to emerging network technology. Shortly after Hacking at the End of the Universe, in the summer of 1993, Marleen Stikker, on behalf of De Balie, approached Rop Gonggrijp of Hack-tic about doing an internet project together.

Eager to drum up more political engagement before an upcoming municipal election in the city, local politicians were looking to facilitate and fund projects that encouraged public dialogue. Stikker, in her capacity organizing events at De Balie, jumped at the opportunity. The name "the Digital City" was inspired by a suggestion from David Garcia, who proposed that the network be called "the Invisible City," in reference to the Italo Calvino novel *Invisible Cities* (1974). Although Stikker felt that "invisible" was not quite the right adjective, she was enthusiastic about using the metaphor of the city for the project and, so, settled on the name the Digital City. She says, "I was intrigued by the city concept, not in order to build a bridge to the

---

7   Murphy cites Reyner Banham's critique in *Megastructure: Urban Futures of the Recent Past* (1976) as a theoretical basis for the rejection of megastructure architecture as outdated, inhuman, and inflexible. See ibid., pp. 88, 102.

geographic reality, as to metaphorically use the dynamics and diversity of a city [...] the way different cultures and domains meet."[8] In the tradition of ex-squatter media art organizations as well as the conferences organized in the early '90s, discussed in chapter 4, the DDS was set up as an artistic, cultural and political project rather than a business venture.

Hack-tic provided the technical knowledge necessary to realize the project. Since May 1993, they had been running a machine that was connected to the nascent internet twenty-four hours a day. They called it XS4ALL (access for all) and used it to run their subscription-based Hack-tic Network.[9] XS4ALL later developed into the first internet service provider in the Netherlands—after Hack-tic broke away from DDS in 1995—which, at least initially, stayed true to the group's radical roots.[10] Reflecting the anarchist and autonomist politics of its instigators, DDS was designed to be a digital temporary autonomous zone, where public debate and democratic participation could flourish with little oversight. Although it was government funded, the system was independently controlled: autonomy and freedom were its core founding values. Because it was initially an experiment to increase public participation in politics ahead of the Amsterdam municipal elections in March of 1994, the DDS was only meant to last for ten weeks. The experiment was so successful, however, that the platform survived until 2001.[11] As more mainstream internet access became profitable in the Netherlands, DDS lost its relevance and was eventually sold off.[12]

According to social scientist Manuel Castells, who featured Amsterdam in his book *The Internet Galaxy* as a key site for the development of "citizen networks," the DDS "epitomized the origins of European citizen networks in the countercultural movements and in the hacker culture [...]."[13] The DDS was a "freenet," which meant that it was a type of platform developed in the late '80s that was set up and run independently by citizens and free for

8   Qtd. Lovink, *Dark Fiber*, p. 48.
9   Joost Flint, *Handleiding voor: De Digitale Stad XS4ALL internet* (Amsterdam: Hack-tic / De Balie, 1994), pp. IV-3–4.
10   Manuel Castells, *The Internet Galaxy: Reflections on the Internet, Business, and Society* (Oxford: Oxford University Press, 2001), p. 149.
11   Lovink, *Dark Fiber*, p. 47.
12   In order to execute the DDS, the City of Amsterdam awarded the organizers €45,000 worth of funding and they received an addition €110,000 from other government agencies. Peter van den Besselaar and Dennis Beckers, "The Life and Death of the Great Amsterdam Digital City," in *Digital Cities III. Information Technologies for Social Capital: Cross-Cultural Perspectives*, Lecture Notes in Computer Science (International Digital Cities Workshop, Springer, Berlin, Heidelberg, 2003), pp. 67–68.
13   Castells, *The Internet Galaxy*, p. 149.

Figure 15: De Digitale Stad [The Digital City] interface, 1994. De Waag Society.

public use. Its interface [Fig.15], unsurprisingly, was constructed around the metaphor of the city with its own city square, post office, red light district, bars, and more. These city features were not, however, depicted as exact skeuomorphic representations but had their own abstract navigational forms.[14] Users also had the option to connect to the wider internet via the DDS system.

Even though the network was conceptualized, on some level as a local community forum, the organizers made it clear that the city limits should extend beyond Amsterdam and beyond the Netherlands. The user manual states:

> The Digital City is, nonetheless, set up as an international city, an open city connected with the greatest and most important computer network in the world: the internet. The computer of the Digital City has a permanent connection with 1.8 million other internet-computers in 137 countries.[15]

14   Lovink, *Dark Fiber*, p. 51.
15   Flint, *Handleiding*, pp. II–1.

Ultimately, the creation of DDS was tactical. The experienced band of ex-squatters, media artists and activists were well aware that agency in foreclosed spaces must be carved out and held fast. They knew that soon the experimental networks they had been playing with at alternative media events would be commercialized and they could be suddenly excluded from the conversation in a system that did not conform to the ethics and values they believed in. As Geert Lovink says,

> What had to be prevented, in the eyes of the Digital City founders was a 1:1 copy-paste from the 'old' days of mass democracy [...] the group decided not to write manifestoes [sic] or reports with recommendations but to take the avant-garde stand and move into the terrain as soon as possible: establish a beachhead, land as many troops as possible and occupy the entire territory.[16]

From the city to the digital city, a coalition of squatters, artists, and activists were able to direct the conversation around networked culture and digital life in the Netherlands in ways that still echo today.

From browser-based artworks and critical internet theory in the '90s to the emerging resistance to contemporary social media and platform economics today, the lessons of squatting and tactical media remain relevant to computing and network technology and its role in society. The history of new media art in Amsterdam has shown that artists can play a central role in understanding these shifts and occupying the cracks, creating something new in the margins of the established order.

The idea of media as an aesthetic category—of television or digital art as new domains that would manifest particular medium specificity—was never the main focus for those working with new technological tools. This can be seen in the way that the use of television and digital media in Amsterdam—including pirate TV—was often not (and is still not) explicitly categorized as fine art, even if it was the work of artists. The main reason for this disconnect is that the politics of autonomy that had been cultivated during the height of the squatters' movement, which in turn owe much to the radical politics of Provo, laid the foundation for many of these projects. This political base, which operated outside the mainstream art world, was largely unconcerned with individual authorship/ownership and market forces.

In the Netherlands, the focus on and tradition of forming alternative and autonomous spaces and initiatives only strengthen over time and had created

16   Lovink, *Dark Fiber*, p. 49.

a situation where, by the late '80s, there was a powerful infrastructure for extra-institutional art and activism already in place. Autonomous art spaces were heavily invested and involved with other autonomous spaces that were not specifically focused on art. This solidarity network between alternative art and other forms of activism meant that "non-artists" were uniquely focused on aesthetics while artists were uniquely involved with politics, without labelling or certifying their activities as any kind of institutionally-recognized social praxis. It seems that no one was overly concerned with policing the boundaries of art, activism, politics, journalism, or computer science, and, so, the networked events that were organized between 1989 and 1993 were fluid between all of these disciplines.[17] At the center of these activities was a concern for how network technology could facilitate democratic participation on both the local and global scale and how alternative media could be used tactically to check the power of governments and capitalist enterprise alike.

In January 1994, this series of networked events culminated in the creation of the first freenet in the Netherlands, De Digitale Stad (DDS, The Digital City). DDS was, unlike the internet service providers we know today, not created by business entrepreneurs, nor was it created by the government or academia. It was an independent platform dreamed up by a group of cyberpunk hackers and veterans of the squatters' movement, who saw the emerging internet as an opportunity to organize, communicate, and create. The crack that had opened in urban space during the squatters' movement in Amsterdam in the early '80s had been a space of freedom and autonomy, but the decline of squatting was not the end of the tactical politics undergirding it. As the crack in the city closed, another crack was opening in the digital realm.

17   Nevejan, interview by Lovink.

Primary and Archival Sources

"Aktiegroep nieuwmarkt 1968–1973," 1973 1968. SAVRZ028 Doos 001B Map 1. Instituut voor Sociale Geschiedenis, Amsterdam – Staatsarchief.

"Bart Domburg, Alex Adriaansens, Joke Brouwer, Roeland Rutten," 1981. R1997/0532 26 E23. Stedelijk Museum Library.

Bélanger, Brigitte, and Camie Karstanje. Interview met Sebastian Lopez, December 9, 2013. LIMA/De Appel Talking Back to the Media Research Document.

Bergh, Michiel van den, and Maja van den Broecke. Interview by Amanda Wasielewski, September 29, 2017.

Boersma, Auke. "Witte kippenplan." *Provo*, no. 9 (May 12, 1966): 12–13. Instituut voor Sociale Geschiedenis, Amsterdam – Provoarchief.

Brummelen, Peter van. "Kunstenaar met een doe-het-zelf-mentaliteit." *Het Parool*, February 21, 2004. Maarten Ploeg Knipselmap 16305. Stedelijk Museum Library.

Christiaans, Pim. "Video-art: de kunst van de toekomst." *Zero*, November 1982. Maarten Ploeg Knipselmap 16305. Stedelijk Museum Library.

Duppen, Leo. "De implosieve schilderkunst van Maarten Ploeg." *Kunstbeeld*, April 1985. Maarten Ploeg Knipselmap 16305. Stedelijk Museum Library.

Evel and Geert. "Bluf Aan de gang! Skriptie over de kraakbeweging & Bluf," February 22, 1984. Instituut voor Sociale Geschiedenis, Amsterdam Staatsarchief.

David Garcia. "The Digital Underpass." *Stedelijk Museum Bureau Amsterdam* 16 (1995): 7–9. David Garcia Knipselmap 06594. Stedelijk Museum Library.

———. Interview by Amanda Wasielewski, April 13, 2017.

Garcia, David, Lous America, Henk Wijnen, and Annie Wright. *Posterama*, 1980. http://www.li-ma.nl/site/catalogue/art/lous-america-david-garcia-henk-wijnen-annie/posterama/396.

Garcia, David and Raúl Marroquin. Interview by Camie Karstanje, November 19, 2013. LIMA / De Appel Talking Back to the Media Research Document.

Groot, Paul. "Rob Scholte en Sandra Derks." *NRC Handelsblad*, August 20, 1982. Sandra Derks Knipselmap 04672. Stedelijk Museum Library.

Hack-tic, and Paradiso. "GHP/ICATA '89 Proceedings." Paradiso, Amsterdam, 1989. Instituut voor Sociale Geschiedenis, Amsterdam.

Houts, Cathérine van, and Pietje Tegenbosch. "Waar blijven de vrouwen?" *Het Parool*, December 31, 1993, sec. Kunst. Sandra Derks Knipselmap 04672. Stedelijk Museum Library.

Imanse, Geurt. "Kunstenaarsinitiatieven," April 6, 1984. Folder 1984. V2_ Archive.

"Interview met Peter Klashorst en Maarten Ploeg." Gerrit Schoolkrant van de Rietveld Akademie Extra Editie no. 4, June 1984. Maarten Ploeg Knipselmap 16305. Stederlijk Museum Library.

Kagie, Rudie. "Klashorst en Ploeg." *VPRO Gids*, August 11, 1984. Maarten Ploeg Knipselmap 16305. Stedelijk Museum Library.

Lennarts, Joep. "V2: het Bossche kunstlab," 1984. Folder 1984-Press. V2_ Archive.

Lovink, Geert. Interview by Amanda Wasielewski, April 5, 2017.

"Maarten Ploeg (1958–2004): veelzijdig kunstenaar." *NRC Handelsblad*, February 20, 2004. Maarten Ploeg Knipselmap 16305. Stedelijk Museum Library.

Marroquin, Raúl. Interview by Camie Karstanje and Brigitte Bélanger, November 23, 2013. LIMA/De Appel Talking Back to the Media Research Document.

——.Interview by Amanda Wasielewski, September 21, 2017.

Niemöller, Joost. "Een wild gevoel." *Plug*, April 1982. Maarten Ploeg Knipselmap 16305. Stedelijk Museum Library.

Piët, Susanne. "Televisie-piraten wapenen zich tegen invallen van opsporingsdienst." *NRC Handelsblad*. July 25, 1981, Dag edition. Maarten Ploeg Knipselmap 16305. Stedelijk Museum Library.

Ploeg, Rogier van der. "PKP-TV Text." Email, February 9, 2018.

——. Interview by Amanda Wasielewski, November 30, 2017.

Provo. "Witte kinderenplan," September 10, 1967. Box 02, Folder 13, No. 162. Internationaal Instituut voor Sociale Geschiedenis – Provoarchief.

Roegholt, Mart. "Nee, geen porno Meneer," n.d. Maarten Ploeg Knipselmap 16305. Stedelijk Museum Library.

"Schilderijen wandelen door museum." *Het Parool*, August 20, 1982. Maarten Ploeg Knipselmap 16305. Stedelijk Museum Library.

"Soviet Sex." *Vinyl*, June 1981. Maarten Ploeg Knipselmap 16305. Stedelijk Museum Library.

"Talking Back to the Media – Inleiding." Press release, 1985. LIMA/De Appel Talking Back to the Media Research Document.

Tuinder, Dick. "De Michelangelo van de Amiga." *De Groene Amsterdammer*, February 28, 2004. Maarten Ploeg Knipselmap 16305. Stedelijk Museum Library.

Velthoven, Willem. Interview by Amanda Wasielewski, April 27, 2018.

"Witte huizenplan," April 1966. Box 01, Folder 12, No. 59a. Internationaal Instituut voor Sociale Geschiedenis – Provoarchief.

"Witte kinderenplan." *Provo*, no. 15 (March 30, 1967): 3. Internationaal Instituut voor Sociale Geschiedenis – Provoarchief.

Zwetsloot, Rob. "Maarten Ploeg: 'Je moet zorgen dat je je eigen stroming wordt.'" *De Waarheid*, January 26, 1985, sec. Kunst. Maarten Ploeg Knipselmap 16305. Stedelijk Museum Library.

Bibliography

Abbing, Hans. *Why Are Artists Poor? The Exceptional Economy of the Arts.* Amsterdam: Amsterdam University Press, 2008.

"About Doors of Perception 1 (1993)." Doors of Perception. Accessed July 2, 2018. http://museum.doorsofperception.com/doors1/about.html.

Acconci, Vito. "10-Point Plan for Video." In *Video Art: An Anthology*, edited by Ira Schneider and Beryl Korot, 8–9. New York: Harcourt Brace Jovanovich, 1976.

ADILKNO. *Cracking the Movement: Squatting Beyond the Media.* Brooklyn: Autonomedia, 1994.

Adler, David, Neil Brenner, Bradley L. Garrett, Andrea Gibbons, Huw Lemmey, David Madden, Peter Marcuse, et al. *The Right to the City: A Verso Report.* Edited by Verso Books. London: Verso, 2017.

Aerden, Monica, Dominic van den Boogerd, Esther Darley, Ton Geerts, Han Schuil, Dirk van Weelden, and Gerrit Willems. *Stop making sense: Nederlandse schilderkunst uit de jaren '80.* Edited by Emine Kara and Loes Vlsch. Wezep: Uitgeverij de Kunst, 2013.

America, Lous, David Garcia, Henk Wijnens, and Annie Wright. *Underpass.* 1983. Video, 51'25". LIMA, Netherlands. http://www.li-ma.nl/site/catalogue/art/lous-america-david-garcia-henk-wijnen-annie/underpass/2719.

"Amsterdam begint in januari met kabel-TV." *NRC Handelsblad.* December 18, 1976, Dag edition.

"Amsterdam gaat kabel-TV verkopen." *De Volkskrant.* June 30, 1994, Dag edition.

"Antennes verdwijnen voor aanleg kabel-TV." *De Waarheid.* March 22, 1977, Dag edition.

"Aorta Beeldstroom: de enige stijl is een dynamische." *De Waarheid*, August 31, 1982, sec. kunst.

"Archief." World Wide Video Festival. Accessed June 13, 2018. http://www.wwvf.nl/.

Austin, Joe. *Taking the Train: How Graffiti Art Became an Urban Crisis in New York City.* New York: Columbia University Press, 2002.

Barbrook, Richard. "The Holy Fools." In *Proud to Be Flesh: A Mute Magazine Anthology of Cultural Politics after the Net*, edited by Pauline van Mourik Broekman and Josephine Berry Slater, 223–36. London: Mute, 2009.

Barbrook, Richard, and Andy Cameron. "The Californian Ideology." In *Proud to Be Flesh: A Mute Magazine Anthology of Cultural Politics after the Net*, edited by Josephine Berry Slater and Pauline van Mourik Broekman, 27–34. London: Mute, 2009.

Bartholomew, Angela M. "Television's Feedback Loop: Talking Back to the Media (1985) and the Stedelijk Museum on TV." In *A Critical History of Media Art in the*

Netherlands, edited by Sanneke Huisman and Marga van Mechelen. Prinsenbeek: Jap Sam Book, 2019: 226-237.

Bartholomew, Angela, and Steyn Bergs. "Tactics of Mischief: From Image to Infrastructure. Interview with David Garcia." *Kunstlicht* 38, no. 3 (2017): 86–94.

Barzyk, Fred, Charles Johnson, Barbara London, Brian O'Doherty, and Nam June Paik. *Fred Barzyk: The Search for a Personal Vision in Broadcast Television*. Milwaukee: Patrick and Beatrice Haggerty Museum of Art, 2001.

Baudrillard, Jean. *For a Critique of the Political Economy of the Sign*. Translated by Charles Levin. St. Louis: Telos Press, 1981.

———. *Simulacra and Simulation*. Translated by Sheila Faria Glaser. Ann Arbor: University of Michigan Press, 2014.

Baumgärtel, Tilman. *Net.art: Materialien zur Netzkunst*. Nürnberg: Verlag für Moderne Kunst, 1999.

———. *Net.art 2.0: New Materials Towards Net Art*. Nürnberg: Verlag für Moderne Kunst, 2001.

Beer, David, and Roger Burrows. "Sociology and, of and in Web 2.0: Some Initial Considerations." *Sociological Research Online* 12, no. 5 (September 1, 2007): 1–13.

Beeren, Wim A. L. *Actie, werkelijkheid en fictie in de kunst van de jaren '60 in Nederland*. 's-Gravenhage: Staatsuitgeverij, 1979.

"Bellissima Makers." Bellissima. Accessed July 1, 2018. http://www.bellissima.net/index.cfm?page=detail_maker&makerid=1505&title=Makers.

Bergelijk, Jeroen van, Geke van Dijk, Karel Koch, and Bas Raijmakers, eds. *The Next Five Minutes (N5M) Zapbook*. Amsterdam: Paradiso, 1992.

Besselaar, Peter van den, and Dennis Beckers. "The Life and Death of the Great Amsterdam Digital City." In *Digital Cities III. Information Technologies for Social Capital: Cross-Cultural Perspectives*, 66–96. Lecture Notes in Computer Science. Springer, Berlin, Heidelberg, 2003.

Bey, Hakim. *TAZ.: The Temporary Autonomous Zone, Ontological Anarchy, Poetic Terrorism*. Brooklyn: Autonomedia, 2003.

"Bibikov for President: politiek, poëzie & performance 1981–1982." *OVT*. VPRO, March 4, 2012. https://www.nporadio1.nl/ovt/onderwerpen/47211-bibikov-for-president-politiek-poezie-performance-1981-1982.

"Bij kabel-TV vergoeding aan het buitenland." *Het Parool*. September 5, 1975, Dag edition.

BILWET. *Bewegingsleer: kraken aan gene zijde van de media*. Amsterdam: Ravijn, 1990.

Birnbaum, Dara. "Talking Back to the Media." In *Talking Back to the Media*, edited by Sabrina Kamstra, Sebastián Lopéz, and Rob Perrée, 46–49. Amsterdam: Stichting Talking Back to the Media, 1985.

Bishop, Claire. "Antagonism and Relational Aesthetics." *October* 110 (October 1, 2004): 51–79.

———. *Artificial Hells: Participatory Art and the Politics of Spectatorship*. London: Verso, 2014.

———. "Digital Divide." *Artforum International* 51, no. 1 (2012): 434–441.

Blokker, Bas. "'Ik voer actie tot de dood.'" *NRC-Handelsblad*, June 20, 2016. https://www.nrc.nl/nieuws/2016/06/20/ik-voer-actie-tot-de-dood-1627236-a1506139.

Bogaarts, René. "KPN en Philips stevenen af op fusie in kabel-TV." *De Volkskrant*. September 30, 1995, Dag edition.

Boomgaard, Jeroen, and Bart Rutten. "Early Days: Dutch Video Art in the 1970s." In *The Magnetic Era: Video Art in the Netherlands 1970–1985*, edited by Jeroen Boomgaard and Bart Rutten. Rotterdam: NAi Publishers, 2003.

Borg, Lucette ter, and Sacha Bronwasser. "Ziende blind." *De Volkskrant*, October 18, 2001.

Bosma, Josephine. *Nettitudes: Let's Talk Net Art*. Amsterdam: Institute of Network Cultures, 2011.

Bosma, Marja. "WEG met de steriele kultuurkathedralen! WEG met het ambtelijk kutkunstbeleid! op straat is onze strijd. de ESKAGEE leeft met u mee!" In *Peter L.M. Giele: verzamelde werken*, edited by Harry Heyink and Anna Tilroe, 145–50. Amsterdam: Aksant, 2003.

Bosma, Martin. "De een bepaalt, wat de ander ziet." *Trouw*. April 30, 1994, Dag edition.

Bourriaud, Nicolas. *Relational aesthetics*. Dijon: Les Presses du réel, 2002.

Boyle, Deirdre. *Subject to Change: Guerrilla Television Revisited*. New York: Oxford University Press, 1997.

Bracken, Len. *Guy Debord: Revolutionary*. Venice, CA: Feral House, 1997.

Brems, Hugo. *Altijd weer vogels die nesten beginnen: geschiedenis van de Nederlandse literatuur 1945–2005*. Amsterdam: Bert Bakker, 2013.

Bruinsma, Max. "Talks on Talking Back." *Mediamatic Magazine* 0, no. 0 (December 1985): 38–42.

Buchloh, Benjamin H. D. "From Gadget Video to Agit Video: Some Notes on Four Recent Video Works." *Art Journal* 45, no. 3 (1985): 217–27.

Buikhuisen, Wouter. "Achtergronden van de nozemgedrag." Utrecht University, 1965.

"Burgemeester Polak Weert Televisiezender Kraak Beweging A'dam." *Nederlands Dagblad*. October 20, 1982, Dag edition.

Cain, Nancy. *Video Days: How Street Video Went from a Deep Underground Phenom to a Zillion Dollar Business. From Pirate TV to YouTube, What Was Gained and Lost along the Way and What We Saw through the Viewfinder*. Palm Springs, CA: Event Horizon Press, 2011.

Calleja, Gordon. "Erasing the Magic Circle." In *The Philosophy of Computer Games*, 77–91. Philosophy of Engineering and Technology. Springer, Dordrecht, 2012.

Calvino, Italo. *Invisible Cities*. Translated by William Weaver. San Diego: Harcourt Brace & Company, 1974.

Cardona, José Ramón, and Antoni Serra Cantallops. "Historia social del desarrollo turístico en Ibiza (décadas de 1960 y 1970): análisis desde perspectivas historiográficas." *Investigaciones Turísticas* 5 (June 2013): 86–109.

Castells, Manuel. *The Internet Galaxy: Reflections on the Internet, Business, and Society*. Oxford: Oxford University Press, 2001.

Cattaneo, Claudio, Miguel A Martínez, and Thomas Aguilera, eds. *The Squatters' Movement in Europe Commons and Autonomy as Alternatives to Capitalism*. London: Pluto Press, 2014.

Certeau, Michel de. *The Practice of Everyday Life*. Translated by Steven Rendall. Berkeley: University of California Press, 1984.

Cherix, Christophe. *In & Out of Amsterdam*. Edited by Jennifer Liese. New York: Museum of Modern Art, 2009.

Clay, Melvin. "Een happening op Ibiza." *Randstad* 11–12 (1966): 238–40.

Colomb, Claire. "Pushing the Urban Frontier: Temporary Use of Space, City Marketing, and the Creative City Discourse in the 2000s in Berlin." *Journal of Urban Affairs* 34, no. 2 (May 1, 2012): 131–52.

"Conference Archive." Doors of Perception. Accessed July 2, 2018. http://old.doorsofperception.com/_conference_archive.html#doors1.

Constant. "Een nieuwe stad voor een nieuwe leven, 1959." In *Constant New Babylon: aan ons de vrijheid*, edited by Laura Stamps, 206–9. Veurne: Hannibal, 2016.

———. "New Babylon na tien jaren. Lezing gehouden aan de afdeling Bouwkunde van de TH Delft, 23 mei 1980." In *Constant New Babylon: aan ons de vrijheid*, edited by Laura Stamps, 206–9. Veurne: Hannibal, 2016.

"Content Doors of Perception 1 (1993)." Doors of Perception. Accessed July 2, 2018. http://museum.doorsofperception.com/doors1/content.html.

Cramer, Florian. "A Response to Richard Barbrook's Holy Fools." In *Proud to Be Flesh: A Mute Magazine Anthology of Cultural Politics after the Net*, edited by Pauline van Mourik Broekman and Josephine Berry Slater. London: Mute, 2009.

Cresswell, T. "The Crucial 'Where' of Graffiti: A Geographical Analysis of Reactions to Graffiti in New York." *Environment and Planning D: Society and Space* 10, no. 3 (June 1, 1992): 329–44.

Crimp, Douglas. "Pictures." *October* 8 (April 1, 1979): 75–88.

Crombez, Thomas. "Waarin de mens niet pretendeert te Spelen: Carlos Tindemans en de receptie van Het Living Theatre in de jaren '60." *Etcetera*, no. 135 (January 2013): 9–13.

Daalder, Hans. "The Netherlands: Political Opposition in a Segmented Society." In *Political Oppositions in Western Democracies*, edited by Robert A Dahl, 188–236. New Haven; London: Yale University Press, 1966.

Daniels, Dieter. "Television—Art or Anti-Art?," February 15, 2007. http://www.medienkunstnetz.de/themes/overview_of_media_art/massmedia/.

De Appel. "In-Out Center." presented at the De Appel Arts Center, Amsterdam, December 15, 2016. https://deappel.nl/en/exhibitions/in-out-center.

Debord, Guy. *Comments on the Society of the Spectacle*. Translated by Malcolm Imrie. London: Verso, 2011.

———. *Panegyric*. Translated by James Brook. London: Verso, 2009.

———. "The Game of War." In *Guy Debord: Revolutionary*, translated by Len Bracken, 240–51. Venice, CA: Feral House, 1997.

Dekker, Angela. "Nuis geeft de laatste resten BKR-kunst weg." *Vrij Nederland*, September 27, 1997.

Deleuze, Gilles, and Félix Guattari. *Mille plateaux: capitalisme et schizophrénie 2*. Paris: Éditions de minuit, 1980.

Dickens, Luke. "Placing Post-Graffiti: The Journey of the Peckham Rock." *Cultural Geographies* 15, no. 4 (October 1, 2008): 471–96.

Diedrichsen, Diedrich. "Intensity, Negation, Plain Language: Wilde Maler, Punk, and Theory in Germany in the '80s." In *Sympathy for the Devil: Art and Rock and Roll Since 1967*. Chicago: Museum of Contemporary Art Chicago, 2007: 142–153.

———. "Geniuses and Their Noise: German Punk and the Neue Welle 1978-1982." In *Geniale Dilletanten: Subkultur der 1980er-Jahre in Deutschland*. Ostfilden: Hatje Cantz Verlag, 2015: 10–22.

Dietz, Harry, and Wim Coster. *Het Dorp van binnen en buiten, 1962–1997: ontstaan en ontwikkeling van een woonvorm voor mensen met een lichamelijke handicap in maatschappelijk perspectief*. Arnhem: Stichting Het Dorp, 1997.

Dovey, Jon, and Helen Kennedy. *Games Cultures: Computer Games as New Media*. Maidenhead, UK: Open University Press, 2005.

Dreyfuss, Henry. *Symbol Sourcebook: An Authoritative Guide to International Graphic Symbols*. New York: McGraw-Hill Companies, 1972.

Driel, Anne van. "The Entertainment Years." In *The Magnetic Era: Video Art in the Netherlands 1970–1985*, edited by Jeroen Boomgaard and Bart Rutten, 133–56. Rotterdam: NAi Publishers, 2003.

Duivenvoorden, Eric. *Een voet tussen de deur: geschiedenis van de kraakbeweging (1964–1999)*. Amsterdam: De Arbeiderspers, 2000.

———. *Het kroningsoproer: 30 april 1980, reconstructie van een historisch keerpunt*. Amsterdam: De Arbeiderspers, 2005.

———. *Magiër van een nieuwe tijd: het leven van Robert Jasper Grootveld*. Amsterdam: Arbeiderspers, 2009.

———. *Rebelse jeugd: hoe nozems en provo's Nederland veranderden*. Amsterdam: Nieuw Amsterdam Uitg., 2015.

"Een eiland van anarchie: Galerie Aorta in het oude Handelsbladgebouw." *NRC Handelsblad*, October 9, 1982, sec. Cultureel supplement.

Eijk, Cees van der. "The Netherlands: Media and Politics between Segmented
    Pluralism and Market Forces." In *Democracy and the Media: A Comparative Per-
    spective*, edited by Richard Gunther and Anthony Mughan, 303–42. Cambridge:
    Cambridge University Press, 2008.

"Elektronisch systeem weert signaal van radio-piraat op kabel." *De Volkskrant*,
    October 16, 1982, Dag edition.

Enzensberger, Hans Magnus. *The Consciousness Industry: On Literature, Politics
    and the Media*. Edited and translated by Michael Roloff. New York: Seabury
    Press, 1976.

Ex, Sjarel, and Sandra Derks. Interview by Maarten Westerveen. VPRO Radio,
    March 2, 2012. https://www.vpro.nl/speel~POMS_VPRO_186673~rom-87~.html.

Farrell, Robyn. "Network(Ed) TV: Collaboration and Intervention at Fernsehgalerie
    Gerry Schum and Videogalerie Schum." *Afterimage* 43, no. 3 (December 11,
    2015): 12.

Feenstra, Karin. "De digitale kamer van blauwbaard." *Het Financieele Dagblad*,
    September 16, 1995.

Flanagan, Mary. *Critical Play: Radical Game Design*. Cambridge, MA: MIT Press, 2013.

Flint, Joost. *Handleiding voor: De Digitale Stad XS4ALL internet*. Amsterdam:
    Hack-tic / De Balie, 1994.

"Fluxus." *De Waarheid*. June 29, 1963, Dag edition.

Foster, Hal. *The Anti-Aesthetic: Essays on Postmodern Culture*, 1983.

———. *Bad New Days: Art, Criticism, Emergency*. London: Verso, 2015.

Foster, Richard. "'Afwijkende Mensen': Understanding the Dutch Ultra Scene." In
    Postgraduate Voices in Punk Studies: Your Wisdom, Our Youth., edited by Laura
    Way and Mike Dines, 55–66. Cambridge: Cambridge Scholars Publishing, 2017.

Foster, Richard James. "'Afwijkende Mensen.' Formulating Perspectives on the
    Dutch ULTRA Scene." Master thesis, Leiden University, 2014.

Freeman, Joshua B. *Behemoth: A History of the Factory and the Making of the Modern
    World*. New York: W.W. Norton, 2018.

Friedman, Yona, and Martin van Schaik. "In the Air: Interview with Yona Fried-
    man – 28 October 2001." In *Exit Utopia: Architectural Provocations 1956–76*,
    edited by Martin van Schaik and Otakar Máčel, 30–35. Munich: Prestel, 2005.

Frieling, Gijs. "Desire and Relevance: Curating for the Many at W139." *Manifesta
    Journal*, no. 10 (2010 2009): 27–37.

Garcia, David. "A Pirate Utopia for Tactical Television." Tactical Media Files, May 5,
    1996. http://www.tacticalmediafiles.net/articles/3568/A-Pirate-Utopia-for-
    Tactical-Television.

———. "Visual Arts: Introduction." In *The Next Five Minutes (N5M) Zapbook*, edited
    by Jeroen van Bergelijk, Geke van Dijk, Karel Koch, and Bas Raijmakers, 61–62.
    Amsterdam: Paradiso, 1992.

Garcia, David, and Geert Lovink. "The ABC of Tactical Media." <nettime> mailing list, May 16, 1997. http://www.nettime.org/Lists-Archives/nettime-l-9705/msg00096.html.

"Geheime zender buurtwapen tegen slopers." *De Volkskrant.* April 10, 1971, Dag edition.

Gemeentemuseum The Hague. *Constant New Babylon: aan ons de vrijheid.* Edited by Laura Stamps. Veurne: Hannibal, 2016.

Gielen, Pascal. "Performing the Common City: On the Crossroads of Art, Politics, and Public Life." In *Constant New Babylon: To us, Liberty,* edited by Laura Stamps, 50–63. Veurne: Hannibal, 2016.

———. "Voorbij de creatieve stad: over de relatie tussen kunst, politiek en publiek leven in het stedelijk gemeen." In *Constant New Babylon: aan ons de vrijheid,* edited by Laura Stamps, 50–63. Veurne: Hannibal, 2016.

Gladdish, Ken. "Opposition in the Netherlands." In *Opposition in Western Europe,* edited by Eva Kolinsky, 195–214. London: Croom Helm, 1987.

Goddard, Michael. *Guerrilla Networks: An Anarchaeology of 1970s Radical Media Ecologies.* Amsterdam: University of Amsterdam Press, 2018.

———. "We Are Time: Laibach/NSK, Retro-Avant-Gardism and Machinic Repetition." *Angelaki* 11, no. 1 (April 1, 2006): 45–53.

Golden, Thelma, Judith Wilson, and Shamim Momin. *Bob Thompson.* New York: Whitney Museum of American Art, 1998.

Gonggrijp, Rop. "Hacking at the End of the Universe." *Alt.Hackers,* July 27, 1993. https://groups.google.com/forum/#!topic/alt.hackers/h5VeGWgVmGw.

Greenberg, Clement. "Post Painterly Abstraction." *Art International* 8, no. 5–6 (1964): 63.

Greene, Rachel. *Internet Art.* New York: Thames & Hudson, 2004.

Groen, Adriënne. "De weg naar Rome." *De Groene Amsterdammer,* March 1, 2012. https://www.groene.nl/artikel/de-weg-naar-rome.

Groos, Ulrike, Barbara Hess, and Ursula Wevers. *Ready to Shoot: Fernsehgalerie Gerry Schum, Videogalerie Schum.* Köln: Snoeck, 2004.

Grootheest, Tijmen van, and Frank Lubbers, eds. *Amsterdam 60/80: twintig jaar beeldende kunst.* Amsterdam: Museum Fodor, 1982.

Grootveld, Menno. Interview by Amanda Wasielewski, November 7, 2017.

Gržinić, Marina. *Fiction Reconstructed: Eastern Europe, Post-Socialism & the Retro-Avant-Garde.* Vienna: Edition Selene, 2000.

Haas, Martijn. *Bibikov for President: politiek, poëzie & performance 1981–1982.* Amsterdam: Lebowski Publishers, 2012.

———. *SKG.* Amsterdam: Lebowski Publishers, 2010.

"Hack-tic." Accessed June 19, 2018. http://www.hacktic.nl.

Halleck, Deedee. "Paper Tiger Television: Smashing the Myths of the Information Industry Every Week on Public Access Cable." *Media, Culture & Society* 6, no. 3 (July 1, 1984): 313–18.

Halsey, Mark, and Alison Young. "'Our Desires Are Ungovernable': Writing Graffiti in Urban Space." *Theoretical Criminology* 10, no. 3 (August 1, 2006): 275–306.

Hardt, Michael, and Antonio Negri. *Empire*. Cambridge, MA: Harvard University Press, 2000.

Harvey, David. *Rebel Cities: From the Right to the City to the Urban Revolution*. London: Verso, 2012.

Heide, Anno van der. "W139 – Container Art." Accessed October 24, 2017. http://w139.nl/en/article/17404/container-art/.

Heintz, John. "New Babylon – A Persistent Provocation." In *Exit Utopia: Architectural Provocations 1956–76*, edited by Martin van Schaik and Otakar Máčel, 212–19. Munich: Prestel, 2005.

"Helft Amsterdam aangesloten op kabeltelevisienet." *Nieuwsblad van Het Noorden*. March 24, 1979, Dag edition.

"Heli eist snelle ontruiming V2." *Brabants Dagblad*, June 30, 1984. Folder 1984-Press. V2_ Archive.

Heuvel, Hans van den, and Gerard Mulder. *Het vrije woord: de illegale pers in Nederland 1940–1945*. 's-Gravenhage: SDU-Uitg., 1990.

Heyink, Harry, and Anna Tilroe, eds. *Peter L.M. Giele: verzamelde werken*. Amsterdam: Aksant, 2003.

Higgins, Dick. "The Origin of Happening." *American Speech* 51, no. 3/4 (1976): 268–71.

Hobijn, Erik. Pionieren in het buitenland: interview met Erik Hobijn. Interview by Marianne Vollmer. De Nieuwe: kunstmagazine van Arti et Aemicitiae, June 2004. https://www.denieuwe.nl/Initiatief/artikelen/MarianneVollmer.html.

Hofland, H.J.A. "Van Zazou tot Provo." *De Gids* 129, no. 1 (1966): 3–8.

Hofland, H.J.A., Ronald Hoeben, and Steye Raviez. *De Stadsoorlog: Amsterdam '80*. Alphen aan den Rijn: AW Sijthoff, 1981.

Hollenberg, Sarah. "Art on Television: 1967–1976." Ph.D., University of Southern California, 2012.

Houts, Cathérine van, and Jan Bart Klaster. "De Nieuwe Wilden!?" *Het Parool*, May 16, 1981, sec. PS Kunst.

Huijboom, Suwanne. "ADM Logo," September 16, 2017.

Huizinga, Johan. *Homo Ludens: A Study of the Play-Element in Culture*. Kettering, OH: Angelico Press, 2016.

———. *Homo Ludens: proeve eener bepaling van het spel-element der cultuur*. Amsterdam: Amsterdam University Press, 2010.

Humphreys, Ashlee, and Kent Grayson. "The Intersecting Roles of Consumer and Producer: A Critical Perspective on Co-Production, Co-Creation and Prosumption." *Sociology Compass* 2, no. 3 (May 1, 2008): 963–80.

Hussey, Andrew. *The Game of War: The Life and Death of Guy Debord*. London: Jonathan Cape, 2001.

IJdens, Teunis. "Van kunstenaarsverzet tot politieke vakband: over de ontwikkeling van de BBK in de periode 1945–1973." *Bulletin Nederlandse Arbeidersbeweging*, 1994, 81–95.

"'Ik ben de pornopiraat': illegaal zenden is altijd mijn hobby geweest." *De Telegraaf.* December 30, 1978, Dag edition.

"Illegale 'Sirene' bewaakt Nieuwmarkt." *Het Parool.* April 10, 1971, Dag edition.

"Interesse Philips voor KTA." *Het Parool.* January 12, 1995, Dag edition.

Jameson, Fredric. *Postmodernism or, The Cultural Logic of Late Capitalism.* Durham: Duke University Press, 2001.

Jankowska, Małgorzata. *Wideo, wideo instalacja, wideo performance w Polsce w latach 1973–1994: historia, artyści, dzieła.* Warsaw: Wydawn. Neriton, 2004.

Jankowski, Nicholas Warren. "Community Television in Amsterdam: Access to, Participation in and Use of the 'Lokale Omroep Bijlmermeer.'" University of Amsterdam, 1988.

Jansen, Bert. "Ploegs aandacht voor de vorm." *Metropolis M*, April 1985.

Jencks, Charles. *What Is Post-Modernism?* London: Academy Editions, 1986.

Jongh, Aad de. *Provo. een jaar Provo-activiteiten.* Rotterdam: Kerco, 1966.

Jonker, Leonor. *No Future nu. punk in Nederland 1977–2012.* Amsterdam: Lebowski Publishers, 2012.

Joselit, David. *Feedback: Television against Democracy.* Cambridge, MA: MIT Press, 2007.

Juul, Jesper. *Half-Real: Video Games between Real Rules and Fictional Worlds.* Cambridge, MA: MIT Press, 2005.

"Kabelnet in Amsterdam afgesloten voor piraten." *NRC Handelsblad*, October 23, 1982, Dag edition.

"Kabel-TV in hoofdstad." *Het Vrije Volk: Democratisch-Socialistisch Dagblad.* September 4, 1975, Dag edition.

Kennedy, James. "Building New Babylon: Cultural Change in the Netherlands during the 1960s." Ph.D., The University of Iowa, 1995.

KK Dubio. "Verklaring bij het eindexamen," October 1979. http://rondos.nl/kunst_kollektief_dubio/index.php?id=abk.

Klashorst, Peter. *Kunstkannibaal: memoires van een beruchte kunstenaar.* Amsterdam: Prometheus, 2012.

Klaver, F, J. Joppe, W.F.G. Meurs, Th. M. Oremus, M.L. Snijders, and J.J. Taks. *Visie op kabeltelevisie.* Amsterdam: Stichting Moderne Media, 1973.

Klaver, Fransje, and A. van der Meer. *Kabel en satelliet: een onderzoekscollege.* Amsterdam: Universiteit van Amsterdam, Vakgroep Massacommunicatie, 1984.

Kleerebezem, Jouke. "More Tales from the Beauty Farm." *Mediamatic Magazine* 0, no. 0 (December 1985): 16–23.

Klein, Sami. "Everybody Will Be On Television." *Rolling Stone*, March 18, 1971.

Klemek, Christopher. *The Transatlantic Collapse of Urban Renewal: Postwar Urbanism from New York to Berlin*. Chicago: University of Chicago Press, 2012.

Knabb, Ken, ed. *Situationist International Anthology*. Berkeley, Calif.: Bureau of Public Secrets, 1981.

———. *Situationist International Anthology: Revised and Expanded Edition*. Berkeley: Bureau of Public Secrets, 2006.

Koopman, Remko, Hein Sonnemans, and Marcel van Tiggelen. *Amsterdam graffiti the battle of Waterloo: 25 jaar graffiti historie op het Waterlooplein/Mr. Visserplein*. Amsterdam: Stadsuitgeverij Amsterdam, 2004.

Koops, Peter. "Yoghurt en pop, met excuses." *De Volkskrant*, April 6, 1985, sec. Vervolgens.

Krauss, Rosalind. "Video: The Aesthetics of Narcissism." *October* 1 (1976): 51–64.

Kruijt, Jakob Pieter. *Verzuiling: een Nederlands probleem al of niet voorzichtig benaderd*. Zaandijk: Heijnis, 1959.

Lefebvre, Henri. *Le droit à la ville: suivi de espace et politique*. Paris: Anthropos, 1968.

Lefebvre, Henri. *The Production of Space*. Translated by Donald Nicholson-Smith. Malden, MA: Blackwell, 1991.

Lefebvre, Henri. "The Right to the City." In *Writings of Cities*, translated by Eleonore Kofman and Elizabeth Lebas, 147–59. Cambridge, MA: Blackwell, 1996.

Lefebvre, Henri. *The Urban Revolution*. Translated by Robert Bononno. Minneapolis: Minnesota Press, 2003.

Lehner, Ernst. *Symbols, Signs and Signets*. Newburyport: Dover Publications, 2012.

Lente, Dick van. "Huizinga's Children: Play and Technology in Twentieth Century Dutch Cultural Criticism (From the 1930s to the 1960s)." *Icon* 19 (2013): 52–74.

Leuzzi, Laura. "Interventions, Productions and Collaborations: The Relationship between RAI and Visual Artists." *Journal of Italian Cinema & Media Studies* 3, no. 1–2 (March 1, 2015): 155–70.

Liebermann, Wanda Katja. "Humanizing Modernism?: Jaap Bakema's Het Dorp, a Village for Disabled Citizens." *Journal of the Society of Architectural Historians* 75, no. 2 (June 1, 2016): 158–81.

Lijfering, J.H.W. *Illegale recreatie: Nederlandse radiopiraten en hun publiek*. Wageningen: Landbouwuniversiteit, 1988.

Lijphart, Arend. *The Politics of Accomodation: Pluralism and Democracy in the Netherlands*. Berkeley, Calif: University of California Press, 1968.

Lochner, J.L. *New Babylon*. The Hague: Haags Gemeentemuseum, 1974.

López, Sebastián, ed. *A Short History of Dutch Video Art*. Amsterdam: Gate Foundation, 2005.

Lorber, Richard. "Epistemological TV." *Art Journal* 34, no. 2 (1974): 132–34.

Lorwin, Val R. "Segmented Pluralism: Ideological Cleavages and Political Cohesion in the Smaller European Democracies." *Comparative Politics* 3, no. 2 (1971): 141–75.

Lovink, Geert. *Dark Fiber: Tracking Critical Internet Culture.* Cambridge: MIT Press, 2002.

———. Interview met Erik Hobijn. Accessed May 2, 2018. http://thing.desk.nl/bilwet/Geert/HOBIJN2.txt.

———. *Zero Comments: Blogging and Critical Internet Culture.* New York: Routledge, 2008.

Lovink, Geert, and Rik Delhaas, eds. *Wetware.* Amsterdam: De Balie, 1991.

"Lucky Strike Art Showcase," May 23, 1983. Maarten Ploeg Knipselmap 16305. Stedelijk Museum Library.

Lütticken, Sven. "Guy Debord and the Cultural Revolution." *Grey Room*, no. 52 (Summer 2013): 108–27.

———. "Playtimes." *New Left Review*, II, no. 66 (2010): 125–40.

Lyotard, Jean-Francois. *La condition postmoderne: rapport sur le savoir.* Paris: Minuit, 1979.

Macdonald, Nancy. *The Graffiti Subculture: Youth, Masculinity, and Identity in London and New York.* New York: Palgrave Macmillan, 2006.

Mailer, Norman. *The White Negro.* San Francisco: City Lights Books, 1957.

Malaby, Thomas M. "Beyond Play: A New Approach to Games." *Games and Culture* 2, no. 2 (April 1, 2007): 95–113.

Mamadouh, Virginie. *De stad in eigen hand: Provo's, Kabouters en krakers als stedelijke sociale beweging.* Amsterdam: SUA, 1992.

Marcus, Greil. *Lipstick Traces: A Secret History of the Twentieth Century.* Cambridge, MA: Belknap Press of Harvard University Press, 1989.

Marcuse, Peter. "From Critical Urban Theory to the Right to the City." *City* 13, no. 2–3 (June 1, 2009): 185–97.

McDonough, Tom, ed. *Boredom.* London: Whitechapel Gallery, 2017.

McLuhan, Marshall. *The Gutenberg Galaxy: The Making of Typographic Man.* Toronto: University of Toronto Press, 1962.

———. *Understanding Media: The Extensions of Man.* Cambridge, MA: MIT Press, 2013.

Mechelen, Marga van. *De Appel: Performances, Installations, Video, Projects, 1975–1983.* Amsterdam: De Appel, 2006.

Medosch, Armin. "Good Bye Reality! How Media Art Died But Nobody Noticed." *Post.Thing.Net*, February 7, 2006. https://post.thing.net/node/742.

Mellen, Joe. "Bart Huges." *The Transatlantic Review*, no. 23 (1966): 31–39.

Merrill, Samuel. "Keeping It Real? Subcultural Graffiti, Street Art, Heritage and Authenticity." *International Journal of Heritage Studies* 21, no. 4 (April 21, 2015): 369–89.

"Met 26 tegen 17 stemmen Amsterdam krijgt kabeltelevisie." *De Volkskrant.* September 4, 1975, Dag edition.

Mignot, Dorine, and Ursula Wevers. *Gerry Schum*. Amsterdam: Stedelijk Museum, 1979.

Mubi Brighenti, Andrea. "At the Wall: Graffiti Writers, Urban Territoriality, and the Public Domain." *Space and Culture* 13, no. 3 (August 1, 2010): 315–32.

Mulder, Arjen, and Maaike Post. *Boek voor de elektronische kunst*. Amsterdam: De Balie, 2000.

Murphy, Douglas. *Last Futures: Nature, Technology and the End of Architecture*. London: Verso, 2016.

Muskens, George. *Beeldende kunstenaars, beeldende kunstenaarsregeling: eindverslag van het onderzoek naar het functioneren van de BKR*. 's-Gravenhage; Tilburg: Ministerie van Sociale Zaken en Werkgelegenheid; IVA-Instituut voor Sociaal-Wetenschappelijk Onderzoek, 1983.

Muskens, George, and J.M.A.G. Maas. *Materiele afhankelijkheid, beroepsmatigheid, autonomie: de leefsituatie van Nederlandse beeldende kunstenaars*. Tilburg: Katholieke Hogeschool Tilburg, IVA, Instituut voor Sociaal-Wetenschappelijk Onderzoek, 1983.

Nealon, Jon, and Jenny Raskin. *Here Come the Videofreex*, 2015.

Negri, Antonio. *The Savage Anomaly: The Power of Spinoza's Metaphysics and Politics*. Translated by Michael Hardt. Minneapolis: University of Minnesota Press, 1991.

Nevejan, Caroline. Interview by Geert Lovink. Accessed June 17, 2018. http://networkcultures.org/geert/interview-with-caroline-nevejan/.

———. "Presence and the Design of Trust." University of Amsterdam, 2007.

Nevejan, Caroline, and Alexander Badenoch. "How Amsterdam Invented the Internet: European Networks of Significance 1980–1995." In *Hacking Europe: From Computer Cultures to Demoscenes*, edited by Gerard Alberts and Ruth Oldenziel, 189–217. London: Springer, 2014.

Nieuwenhuys, Constant. "Manifest." *Reflex: orgaan van de experimentele groep in Holland* 1 (October 1948): 2–13.

"Nog eit jaar twee Engelse zenders erbij." *De Waarheid*. June 20, 1978, Dag edition.

Oele, Anneke. "Jonge kunst in Amsterdam: Aorta en The Living Room." *Ons Erfdeel* 29, no. 1 (February 1986): 349–54.

Owens, Lynn. *Cracking Under Pressure: Narrating the Decline of the Amsterdam Squatters' Movement*. Amsterdam: Amsterdam University Press, 2009.

Paradiso. "Terroristencongres door Stads Kunst Guerilla." Accessed May 6, 2018. https://www.paradiso.nl/nl/programma/terroristencongres-door-stads-kunst-guerilla/30417/.

"Park 4DTV." PARK 4DTV, August 2017. https://www.park.nl/.

Pas, Niek. *Imaazje! De verbeelding van Provo, 1965–1967*. Amsterdam: Wereldbibliotheek, 2003.

———. *Provo!: mediafenomeen 1965–1967*. Amsterdam: Wereldbibliotheek, 2015.

Perée, Rob. Interview by Camie Karstanje, April 8, 2014. http://li-ma.nl/site/news/talking-back-media-project-update-0.

Perrée, Rob. "From Agora to Montevideo: Of Video Institutes, the Things That Pass." In *The Magnetic Era: Video Art in the Netherlands 1970–1985*, edited by Jeroen Boomgaard and Bart Rutten, 51–75. Rotterdam: NAi Publishers, 2003.

Petten, Edith, and Robertus Dettingmeijer. *Beeldende kunstenaars en televisie: de aktiviteiten van Gerry Schum*. Utrecht: Utrechtse Kring, 1972.

Pontzen, Rutger. "De verleden toekomst van de No Future-generatie." *Vrij Nederland*, January 18, 1997.

"Porno-piraat uur op TV." *Het Vrije Volk: Democratisch-Socialistisch Dagblad*. December 14, 1978, Dag edition.

Possel, Jans. "Media/Ritual/Design." *Mediamatic Magazine* 0, no. 0 (December 1985): 26–32.

Pots, Roel. *De BKR: kunst- of sociaal beleid? ontstaan, groei en resultaten van de contraprestatieregelingen*. 's-Gravenhage: VUGA, 1981.

———. "De Nederlandse overheid en de beeldende kunsten in historisch perspectief." In *Second opinion: over beeldende kunstsubsidie in Nederland*, edited by Lex ter Braak, Taco de Neef, Gitta Luiten, and Steven van Teeseling, 238–48. Rotterdam: NAi Uitgevers, 2007.

Prevots, Naima. "Zurich Dada and Dance: Formative Ferment." *Dance Research Journal* 17, no. 1 (1985): 3–8.

"Raad besluit tot project van f 127 miljoen Amsterdam krijgt kabel-televisie." *Nieuwsblad van Het Noorden*. September 4, 1975, Dag edition.

Raijmakers, Bas. "Introduction." In *The Next Five Minutes (N5M) Zapbook*, edited by Jeroen van Bergelijk, Geke van Dijk, Karel Koch, and Bas Raijmakers, 7–8. Amsterdam: Paradiso, 1992.

Rajandream, Marie-Adèle. "Livinius en het licht." *Mediamatic Magazine* 0, no. 0 (December 1985): 10–15.

Reckman, Lidewijn. "Good Boy/Bad Boy." *Mediamatic Magazine* 0, no. 0 (December 1985): 33–35.

Reijnders, Tineke. "Adressen van de autonome geest: kunstenaarsinitiatieven in de jaren tachtig en negentig." In *Peter L.M. Giele: verzamelde werken*, edited by Harry Heyink and Anna Tilroe, 177–83. Amsterdam: Aksant, 2003.

———. "De toekomst tonen: 'non-genrekunstenaar' Gerald Van Der Kaap." *Ons Erfdeel* 47, no. 1 (February 2004): 687–97.

"Review of *Die graphischen Gaunerzinken* by Hubert Streicher." *Journal of the American Institute of Criminal Law and Criminology* 20, no. 1 (1929): 157–157.

Righart, Hans. *De eindeloze jaren zestig: geschiedenis van een generatieconflict*. Amsterdam; Antwerpen: De Arbeiderspers, 1995.

Riper, Heleen, David Garcia, and Patrice Riemens, eds. *The Seropositive Ball.* Amsterdam: Paradiso / Time Based Arts, 1990.

Ritzer, George, and Nathan Jurgenson. "Production, Consumption, Prosumption: The Nature of Capitalism in the Age of the Digital." *Journal of Consumer Culture* 10, no. 1 (March 1, 2010): 13–36.

Ronduda, Łukasz. *Polish Art of the 70s.* Warsaw: Centrum Sztuki Wspoczesnej Zamek Ujazdowski, 2009.

Ross, Kristin, and Henri Lefebvre. "Lefebvre on the Situationists: An Interview." *October* 79 (1997): 69–83.

Sadler, Simon. "New Babylon versus Plug-in City." In *Exit Utopia: Architectural Provocations 1956–76,* edited by Martin van Schaik and Otakar Máčel, 57–67. Munich: Prestel, 2005.

Salen, Katie, and Eric Zimmerman. *Rules of Play: Game Design Fundamentals.* Cambridge, MA: MIT Press, 2003.

"Saturday 18 September." V2_. Accessed October 19, 2017. http://v2.nl/events/zat-18-sept.

Schaik, Martin van. "Psychogeogram: An Artist's Utopia." In *Exit Utopia: Architectural Provocations 1956–76,* edited by Martin van Schaik and Otakar Máčel, 36–54, 104–24, 220–35. Munich: Prestel, 2005.

Schellinx, Harold. *Ultra.* Amsterdam: Lebowski, 2012.

Schiller, Friedrich. *On the Aesthetic Education of Man.* Translated by Reginald Snell. Mineola, NY: Dover Publ., 2004.

Schimmelpennink, Luud. "Provo fietsenplan." *Provo,* no. 2 (August 17, 1965): 1–5.

———. "Provo's witte schoorstenen plan." *Provo,* no. 6 (January 24, 1966): 1–6.

Schoenberger, Janna. "Ludic Conceptualism: Art and Play in the Netherlands from 1959 to 1975." Graduate Center, CUNY, 2017.

Scholte, Rob. Digging Up Dutch Undergrounds – An Interview with Rob Scholte – artist – and of The Young Lions and Suspect. Interview by Richard Foster, May 4, 2014. http://luifabriek.com/2014/05/digging-dutch-undergrounds-interview-rob-scholte-artist-young-lions-suspect/.

Schoone, Servaas. "De nieuwe TV: emotionele televisie voor de toekomst." *Mediamatic Magazine* 0, no. 0 (December 1985): 6–9.

Schouten, Martin. "De wereld is een kraakpand." *NRC Handelsblad,* March 3, 1979, Zaterdag edition.

Schrijver, F. J. *De invoering van kabeltelevisie in Nederland.* 's-Gravenhage: Staatsuitgeverij, 1983.

Schuyt, Kees, and Ed Taverne. *1950: Prosperity and Welfare.* Assen: Royal Van Gorcum, 2004.

Seelen, Joost. *De stad was van ons.* Documentary, 1996.

"Sirene." *NRC Handelsblad.* May 1, 1971, Dag edition.

Smolik, Noemi. "Very Funny: Wim T. Schippers on His Long and Diverse Career." *Frieze*, February 2017.

Spielmann, Yvonne. *Video: The Reflexive Medium*. Cambridge, MA: MIT Press, 2008.

Stallabrass, Julian. *Internet Art: The Online Clash of Culture and Commerce*. London: Tate Publishing, 2003.

Stamps, Laura. "Constant's New Babylon: Pushing the Zeitgeist to its limits." In *Constant New Babylon: aan ons de vrijheid*, edited by Laura Stamps, 12–27. Veurne: Hannibal, 2016.

Steen, Bart van der, Ask Katzeff, and Leendert van Hoogenhuijze, eds. *The City Is Ours: Squatting and Autonomous Movements in Europe from the 1970s to the Present*. Oakland: PM Press, 2014.

Stenros, Jaakko. "In Defence of a Magic Circle: The Social, Mental and Cultural Boundaries of Play." *Transactions of the Digital Games Research Association* 1, no. 2 (February 1, 2014). http://todigra.org/index.php/todigra/article/view/10.

Stikker, Marleen. "The Human Remnant." In *Wetware*, edited by Geert Lovink and Rik Delhaas, 5–6. Amsterdam: De Balie, 1991.

Stiles, Kristine. "Between Water and Stone: Fluxus Performance: A Metaphysics of Acts." In *In the Spirit of Fluxus*, edited by Elizabeth Armstrong, Joan Rothfuss, and Janet Jenkins, 62–97. Minneapolis: Walker Art Center, 1993.

Stokvis, Willemijn. "Constants New Babylon en De Stijl." In *Constant New Babylon: aan ons de vrijheid*, edited by Laura Stamps, 28–37. Veurne: Hannibal, 2016.

Streicher, Hubert. *Die graphischen Gaunerzinken*. Wien: J. Springer, 1928.

Talking Back to the Media – November 29, 1985. TV broadcast. Amsterdam: Shaffy Theater, 1985.

Taylor, T. L. *Play between Worlds: Exploring Online Game Culture*. Cambridge, MA: MIT Press, 2006.

Teasdale, Parry D. *Videofreex: America's First Pirate TV Station & the Catskills Collective That Turned It On*. Hensonville, NY: Black Dome Press, 1999.

Temmink, Theo. "Gangenstelsel gaat leven onder hand videokunstenaars." *De Volkskrant*, May 7, 1983, Dag edition.

Terranova, Tiziana. *Network Culture Politics for the Information Age*. London: Pluto Press, 2004.

Terreehorst, Pauline. "Opkomst en ondergang van videokunst in Nederland." In *Kunst en beleid in Nederland 5*, edited by Fenna van den Burg, Hans van Dulken, Bart van Heerikhuizen, Jan Kassies, Warna Oosterbaan Marinius, and Cas Smithuijsen, 15–65. Amsterdam: Boekmanstichting/Van Gennep, 1991.

"'The Connection' in Amsterdam." *De Telegraaf*. April 21, 1962, Dag edition.

Tiqqun. *Introduction to Civil War*. Translated by Alexander R. Galloway and Jason E. Smith. Los Angeles: Semiotext(e), 2010.

Toepfer, Karl. "From Imitation to Quotation." *Journal of Dramatic Theory and Criticism* 4, no. 2 (Spring 1991): 121–36.

Toffler, Alvin. *The Third Wave*. New York: Bantam Books, 1980.

"TV-piraat zendt harde porno uit." *NRC Handelsblad*. December 14, 1978, Dag edition.

V2_. "Manifesto for Unstable Media," 1987. http://v2.nl/archive/articles/manifesto-for-the-unstable-media/.

———. "V2 Archive: Manifest[o] Exhibition." V2_ Lab for Unstable Media. Accessed June 3, 2018. http://v2.nl/events/manifest-voor-de-instabiele-media/.

"Value of the Guilder / Euro." Institute of Social History. Accessed May 23, 2018. http://www.iisg.nl/hpw/calculate.php.

Vasudevan, Alexander. *Metropolitan Preoccupations: The Spatial Politics of Squatting in Berlin*. Oxford, UK: Wiley Blackwell, 2015.

Velthoven, Willem, and Jans Possel. "Redactioneel." Translated by Fokke Sluiter. *Mediamatic Magazine* 0, no. 0 (December 1985): 3.

Verhagen, Hans. *De gekke wereld van Hoepla: opkomst en ondergang van een televisieprogramma*. Amsterdam: de Bezige Bij, 1968.

Verlaan, Tim. "Stadsgezichten: Mr. Visserplein." *Het Parool*, March 10, 2010. https://www.parool.nl/kunst-en-media/stadsgezichten-mr-visserplein~a283230/.

Vinkenoog, Simon. "Dinsdag 11 April 2006: The Day of the Policy Makers." *Kersvers Archief* (blog), April 11, 2006. http://www.simonvinkenoog.nl/.

———. *Liefde: zeventig dagen op ooghoogte*. Amsterdam: De Bezige Bij, 1967.

Vliet, Tom van. World Wide Video. Interview by Johan Pijnappel, 1993. http://www.wwvf.nl/.

Voorthuijsen, Bert. "Hoofdstad verrast televisiepiraat bracht pornofilm." *De Telegraaf*. December 14, 1978, Dag edition.

Vries, Marina de. "Wat is er nou lekkerder om te scheppen, om een beetje god te zijn." In *Peter L.M. Giele: verzamelde werken*, edited by Harry Heyink and Anna Tilroe, 169–76. Amsterdam: Aksant, 2003.

Vuijsje, Robert. *King Klashorst*. Amsterdam: Vassallucci, 2003.

"W139 – 30 Man Kunst." Accessed October 24, 2017. http://w139.nl/en/article/21658/30-man-kunst/.

Wagner, Anne M. "Performance, Video, and the Rhetoric of Presence." *October* 91 (2000): 59–80.

Wahl, Chris. "Between Art History and Media History: A Brief Introduction to Media Art." In *Preserving and Exhibiting Media Art: Challenges and Perspectives*, edited by Julia Noordegraaf, Cosetta G. Saba, Barbara Le Maître, and Vinzenz Hediger, 25–58. Amsterdam University Press, 2013.

Wark, McKenzie. "The Game of War: Debord as Strategist." *Cabinet*, no. 29 (Spring 2008): 73–75.

Wasielewski, Amanda. "From Rogue Sign to Squatter Symbol." *City* 23, no. 2 (March 4, 2019): 256–67.

———. "Between the Cracks: From Squatting to Tactical Media Art in the Netherlands, 1979-1993. Ph.D., City University of New York, 2019.

———. *Made in Brooklyn Artists, Hipsters, Makers, and Gentrification.* Winchester, UK: Zero Books, 2018.

———. "'We Have Decided Not to Decide': The End of History and the Punk Politics of De Reagering." In *Aftermath: The Fall and the Rise after the Event*, edited by Robert Kusek, Beata Piątek, and Wojciech Szymański, 177–92. Krakow: Jagiellonian University Press, 2019.

Weert, Johannes van de. "Rondos Biography: A Black & White Statement," 2009. http://rondos.nl/rondos_biografie/inhoud/RondosbioA4-EN.pdf.

Whalen-Bridge, John, and Gary Storhoff. *The Emergence of Buddhist American Literature.* Albany: Suny Press, 2010.

Wiener, Norbert. *Cybernetics: Or Control and Communication in the Animal and the Machine.* Cambridge, MA: MIT Press, 1965.

Wigley, Mark. *Constant's New Babylon: The Hyper-Architecture of Desire.* Rotterdam: Witte de With, 1998.

———. "Extreme Hospitality." In *Constant New Babylon: aan ons de vrijheid*, edited by Laura Stamps, 38–49. Veurne: Hannibal, 2016.

"Wim T. Schippers en nieuwe vormen van recreatie 'Mars door Amsterdam' was proeve van adynamische feitenkunst." *Algemeen Handelsblad.* December 7, 1963, Dag edition.

Wingen, Ed. "De maskerade van Maarten Ploeg." *De Telegraaf*, February 15, 1985, sec. Uit de kunst.

Wlislocki, Heinrich von. *Vom wandernden Zigeunervolke: Bilder aus dem Leben der siebenbürger Zigeuner: Geschichtliches, Ethnologisches, Sprache Und Poesie.* Hamburg: Actien-Gesellschaft, 1890.

Wright, Annie. "Modern Myths and Legends." *Talking Back to the Media*, November 1985.

WvS. "Wilden." *Vinyl* 4, no. 7/8 (1984).

Youngblood, Gene. *Expanded Cinema.* New York: Dutton, 1970.

Zippay, Lori. *Artists' Video: An International Guide.* New York: Electronic Arts Intermix, 1991.

Zwart, Hub. "Aquaphobia, Tulipmania, Biophilia: A Moral Geography of the Dutch Landscape." *Environmental Values* 12, no. 1 (2003): 107–28.

Index